T0333665

CITY OF ILLUSIONS

HELEN RODGERS
STEPHEN CAVENDISH

City of Illusions

A History of Granada

HURST & COMPANY, LONDON

First published in the United Kingdom in 2021 by
C. Hurst & Co. (Publishers) Ltd.,
83 Torbay Road, London, NW6 7DT
Printed in the United Kingdom by Bell & Bain Ltd, Glasgow

A Cataloguing-in-Publication data record for this book
is available from the British Library.

ISBN: 9781787385580

This book is printed using paper from registered sustainable
and managed sources.

www.hurstpublishers.com

Quien no ha visto Granada, no ha visto nada.
He who has not seen Granada, has not seen a thing.

Local saying

***

Dale limosna, mujer,
que no hay en la vida nada
como la pena de ser
ciego en Granada.

Give him alms, woman,
because in life there is nothing
like the sorrow of being
blind in Granada.

Francisco de Icaza, Mexican poet
(authors' translation)

CONTENTS

ACKNOWLEDGEMENTS

We should like to express our thanks to the staff at both the Escuela de Estudios Árabes and the Casa de los Tiros newspaper archive for allowing us access to their invaluable collections, and also to all those who work at Granada's wonderful historical sites for providing so much detail during the course of our research, much of which is overlooked in the written sources. Most of all, our gratitude and great admiration go to our neighbours, whose passion for Granada's unique story and determination to maintain its most beautiful traditions have been a true inspiration in bringing this book to life.

A NOTE ON NAMES

A book such as this—written for English-speaking readers, but whose subject matter covers people and places whose names originate in both Arabic and Spanish and have often been changed throughout history—presents a number of challenges in terms of deciding what names to use to make the characters and locations most familiar and accessible for the reader.

In Britain until recent times, the names of Spanish rulers tended to be anglicised in history textbooks; thus the Catholic Monarchs—Isabel and Fernando—have generally been known as Isabella and Ferdinand. Whilst these two names could easily be used in their Spanish form without much confusion, others are more problematic. The Holy Roman Emperor Charles V is known in Spanish history as El Rey Carlos I and also Carlos V, which was a foreign title he acquired three years after becoming Spain's king. Felipe II, as a consort of Mary Tudor, is far better known to English speakers as Philip II, who later dispatched his Armada against Elizabeth I. For ease of reading, therefore, Spanish monarchs are referred to throughout by their anglicised names.

This also allows for consistency when it comes to Arabic. The names in Western sources for the later Nasrids stemmed from the difficulty the Castilians had with Arabic pronunciation.

A NOTE ON NAMES

Boabdil—the last emir of Granada—grew from a mishearing of Abu Abdullah, whilst his father's name in Spanish, Muley Hacén, is a corruption of Maulaya (meaning Lord) Abu-l Hasan. This was not simply ignorance; Arab chroniclers also used their own names for Spanish monarchs, the real ones being equally incomprehensible to their ears. In this book, then, the more famous English renderings of the names of historical Arab figures are used where they exist.

History is nothing if not a journey of change, however, and in recent times there has been a trend in the English-speaking world to using Spanish spellings. It is not uncommon now to see Andalucía in English texts, instead of the anglicised Andalusia, or Córdoba, instead of its traditional spelling in English without the accent. This presents questions over place names that differ more between the two languages, such as Seville and Castile versus Sevilla and Castilla. For consistency, places with Spanish or Arabic names have again been given their anglicised forms where these exist. There are also, of course, nations and borders today that were not around in mediaeval times, so Morocco as it is understood now does not work as well as the Arabic Maghreb, which is used on occasion in this book.

Within Granada itself, places are generally referred to by their Spanish names, even if they date from the Arab period. This is simply to assist the reader in locating these around the city, for whilst sites frequented by tourists may have an official English translation, many do not. The choice is one faced by any author of histories of the non-English-speaking world, and the decision will be different in each individual case. The resolution here was reached by what the authors hope will lead to the ease and enjoyment of the reader.

INTRODUCTION AND EARLY HISTORY

In 1754, an amateur archaeologist named Juan de Flores began digging beneath the streets of Granada's Moorish Albaicín district for signs of the city's early history. Local people were enthralled as, day by day, his excavations unearthed artefacts that pointed to a pre-Islamic, Roman city on the site, including statues, vases, coins, jewellery, and bases of columns—one of which appeared to be from a temple dedicated to Apollo, later consecrated as a church. Granada was jubilant; with Flores's artefacts, it would be able to wash away the shame of its heathen past under the Moors and hold its head high within Catholic Spain as a fundamentally Christian city that pre-dated the arrival of the Muslims. Alas for the local Christians. In 1763 the excavations ended, and a decade later Flores's finds were denounced as elaborate forgeries. For years he and a group of artisans had been fabricating piece after piece of archaeological 'evidence' and burying these in the tunnels beneath the Albaicín, before bringing them to light in front of admiring crowds the next day.[1]

Curiously enough, this was not the first time that local people had attempted to falsify Granada's history for reasons of political expediency. Some 150 years earlier, in the late sixteenth century, the last of the city's Morisco inhabitants—those who had been forcibly converted to Christianity after the Reconquista—had forged and secretly buried a collection of mysterious lead tablets, bound into books and written in a supposedly ancient form of Arabic. These purported that the first Arab to arrive on the Iberian Peninsula had been a first-century saint, St Caecilius, who had been converted to Christianity by Christ himself. This in turn suggested that, rather than being viewed as Muslim invaders, the Moors—the collective term used to describe the Muslims of the Iberian peninsula—should instead be recognised as an integral part of Spain's early Christianity. And, the logic went, if an Arab had originally come to Spain as a Christian, then the looming expulsion of the Moriscos from the Iberian Peninsula—on the suspicion that they remained Muslim at heart—was groundless. A Christian cult emerged in Granada based around these lead books, as well as charred bones believed to be those of the martyred St Caecilius, which culminated in the consecration of the Abbey of the Sacromonte.

Despite the elaborate hoax, the plot to save the Moriscos from exile failed: the year 1609 saw between 200,000 and 300,000 of them forcibly driven out of Spain.[2] Yet for the 'Old' Christians of the city—those who had moved to Granada following the fall of the Muslim emirate in 1492—the cult of the lead books of the Sacromonte lived on. It declined only years later, when, in 1682, the Vatican declared these to be forgeries, leaving the deeply Christian locals frustrated at the lack of proof for a Christian foundation to their city. It was this frustration that was temporarily eased by the theatre of Flores's archaeological digs, only to be dashed once more when his fraud was publicly revealed more than fifteen years later. In the 1770s, Flores was tried and found guilty of falsifying his discoveries. He was sentenced, and his fakes destroyed. The passageways under the Albaicín were sealed, new buildings were erected in the area, and the story of the excavations faded into history. Granada, meanwhile, was about to enter a new era, when first Napoleon's army and later the Romantic artists and writers of the nineteenth century would come to the city—not fascinated by any potential early Christian heritage so yearned for by the city's inhabitants, but instead intoxicated by thoughts of finding and recreating what they imagined was the lost exoticism of Granada of the Moors.

Suddenly, Granada had a new historical face to show to the world. As money from foreign visitors seeking the vestiges of an idyllic, mediaeval, Islamic past poured into the city, Granada gradually set aside its quest to prove its Christian heritage in favour of capitalising on the legacy of the Moors. And, whilst Flores and the Morisco forgers of the lead books had tried to invent a history out of little more than myths and legends, with the visible presence of the Alhambra and other Moorish buildings around the city, providing visitors with an Oriental vision required much less deception than those earlier attempts. Yet, even here, the portrayal was not entirely as it seemed. Indeed, the nineteenth century saw the beginnings of the drive to frame Granada's Moorish past more on contemporary Western preconceptions of the Orient than on the evidence of what the city would truly have been like under the Moors.

In some ways, the trend of representing Granada's past on the basis of preconceptions rather than truth continues today. A prime example of this can be seen within Granada's most famous landmark. The Alhambra was built by the Nasrids in the thirteenth century, but the Moorish palace complex has continued to evolve throughout the ages, up to the present, often based on the restorers' changing perceptions of Oriental history and aesthetics. Today it is often celebrated on tourism websites as a perfectly preserved Moorish fortress, overlooking the fact that what is visible to the modern observer differs in many respects from how the Moors would have viewed their cherished palaces and gardens.[3] However, that is in no way a reason to dismiss the Alhambra as inauthentic. On the contrary, its enduring place at the forefront of conversations between East and West in the fields of art, history, and architecture is what continues to make it such a fascinating monument. It is, of course, also a central aspect of the personality of the city of Granada today. Nevertheless, to understand the Alhambra requires time and reflection, and, unfortunately, so many visitors who pass quickly through the city only really manage to glean a superficial perspective on both the Nasrid Palaces and the city as a whole.

This surface-level appreciation of Granada's history continues across the river Darro in the UNESCO-protected district of the Albaicín. As with the Alhambra, this district is so much more than its frequent depiction as a picture-perfect representation of the city's Moorish past. Tourism websites often claim that the district provides an authentic walking-tour experience around a Moorish quarter frozen in time—this despite a cursory glance at photographic evidence from just a century ago betraying that what exists now differs markedly in parts to its former self. As with the Alhambra, to understand the Albaicín demands more contemplation than mere observation affords: an understanding of how its appearance has changed over hundreds of years of history to reflect the reality of life and mentality of not only its residents but also the leaders of Granada, whose vision of history itself has morphed over time. The reality is an area filled with fascinating treasures of the city's Moorish era and a street plan that in large part still dates back to Nasrid times. But, to fully comprehend these, they must be viewed alongside the changes that have taken place and that continue to be made. Moreover, to visit the Albaicín purely for the remnants of its Islamic past risks overlooking the half millennium of equally fascinating post-Reconquista history that also makes up the picture of a place with many faces and many pasts.

To those passing quickly through Granada, then, it can become nothing more than a city of illusions—a city of Oriental façades that mask its many secrets, and one whose history is hidden behind myths and legends. Modern guidebooks tend to gloss over—or worse, omit—the changes that have, down the centuries, made the city what it is today, in favour of celebrating an Orientalist ideal. For those with the time to delve into Granada's long and complex history, though, what is to be uncovered is fascinating. It is a tale that features the city's changing perceptions of its own history, captivating in itself, and the story of Granada's evolution after 1492 is in many ways as compelling as the folklore that surrounds the rise and fall of the last Muslim kingdom in Western Europe. Granada is one of the most beautiful cities in the world, with buildings dating from every age, set against the magnificent backdrop of the snow-capped Sierra Nevada. Its beauty is such that it famously inspired the Mexican poet Francisco de Icaza to write, 'In life there is nothing like the sorrow of being blind in Granada.' This sentiment applies whether or not one has peeled back the many layers of the city's complex history.

However, to uncover the truth is no easy task. Whilst at times the documentary evidence of the history of Granada and its environs is strong, at others it is scant. For some periods, historians are left with only myth and legend to help piece together the story. Nowhere is this more the case than in trying to get to the truth about one of Granada's greatest mysteries: what existed on the site prior to the eleventh century? This question has taxed the minds of archaeologists, historians, and local people for centuries. Indeed, Juan de Flores was just one of many who have tried to prove their own theories about the city's pre-Islamic past, although most researchers and archaeologists have attempted to use more honest means to do so. The claims about Granada's origins are diverse, with many through the ages proposing various answers to the questions that continue to perplex investigators, all of which makes the study of the city's ancient beginnings among the most intriguing areas of its history to follow, as more and more evidence is revealed from beneath the surface.

Because of the fragmentary nature of the evidence, it is difficult to conclusively establish what Granada was like before it became one of the most important cities in al-Andalus in the eleventh century. The Arabs took a great interest in history and produced some remarkable texts; however, many of these are lost, and those that exist often prove hard to interpret. Then, in the post-Reconquista era, much of the picture of Granada's ancient past was built upon myths, often then taken as fact, with later theories constructed on ideas that had no actual basis in truth.[4] Meanwhile, as in much of the world, interpreting evidence dug up from under the city's streets is also not easy, especially when the texts to support its provenance are few and far between. Still, one thing that is clear from archaeological discoveries is that people were living on the site of modern Granada as early as the Bronze Age. Some of the oldest finds, on display in the city's Archaeological Museum, were unearthed from around today's Gran Vía de Colón; others come from around the University of Granada's Cartuja campus; and many discoveries of an early settlement have been made in the remains of a necropolis located around the Renaissance palace now known as the Mirador de Rolando. It also appears that, like the Berbers of later times, the ancients who lived here saw the strategic advantage of the site that was to become the eleventh-century Alcazaba, in what is now the Albaicín district, where remains including defensive walls have been found of an early settlement known as Iliberri.[5]

This early settlement appears to have existed through to Roman times, when it then became part of the agriculturally rich Roman region of Hispania Baetica, with the countryside around Iliberri prized for its olive oil and its gold mining.[6] The settlement's importance in the region prior to the arrival of the Zirid dynasty would become the subject of one of the city's biggest controversies over the centuries, with Juan de Flores being just one of many in the post-Reconquista era determined to prove a significant Roman past for Granada. Curiously, though, despite his undoubted fraud, evidence now shows that Flores was correct in asserting that such a Roman history did exist, and that he was also accurate in terms of where he undertook his excavations. Indeed, it is now believed that not all of his discoveries were fake—something difficult to prove since, unfortunately, most were destroyed following his trial.[7] Flores's fraudulent digs of the eighteenth century thus, for many centuries, did historians of Granada's pre-Islamic history a great disservice by casting doubt on the Albaicín as the location of an important Roman settlement. In recent times, however, more scientific excavations around Granada have unearthed a significant amount of evidence of Roman life, such as inscriptions, water infrastructure, mosaics, and pottery, many of which can be viewed in the Archaeological Museum. These modern-day excavations have, ironically, demonstrated what Juan de Flores set out to prove: that the site of modern-day Granada was once a major Roman town.[8] And such was its importance that the original pre-Roman name for the settlement Iliberri was expanded at the time into Florentia Iliberritana ('flourishing Iliberri').

Granada's Roman origins have not been the only subject of debate. The city's role within early Christianity in Spain has also been a major point of contention. As was seen with the lead books, the Christians of the post-Reconquista era were desperate to give the city a Christian identity, and some went to great lengths in order to give it this heritage; it was this that led Flores to begin digging, to prove legends long associated with the city in the minds of its Christian inhabitants. One of these was the belief that what became Granada was the location of one of Christianity's earliest Church councils—the Synod of Elvira—held in the early fourth century, its name being a later derivative of the name Iliberri. This synod established some of the foremost canons of Catholicism, including the celibacy requirement for clergy, the condemnation of intermarriage between Christians and Jews, the forbidding of idolatry, and calls for the prohibition of painted images in churches. As an important Roman settlement, it seems reasonable to assume that this synod did, indeed, take place somewhere within what is now the city of Granada. However, as with much of Granada's early history, no concrete archaeological or documentary evidence has yet emerged that can prove exactly where this important meeting took place. And some have argued that the Synod of Elvira could have taken place anywhere in the wider area known by the same name as the city.

Given what is known about Granada's eleventh-century foundation by the Zirid dynasty, what happened here between the end of the Roman era and the time the site was extensively populated again remains one of the many unanswered questions about the city's history. The Romans were supplanted over time by the Visigoths and, in the eighth century, the Arabs conquered the majority of the Iberian Peninsula, which led to the establishment of al-Andalus with its great capital in the city of Cordoba. Arab sources tell us that during the period prior to the eleventh century, there continued to be a small settlement on the Albaicín hill consisting of a fort and a Jewish community. This reference to Jews living in what is now Granada was made by the tenth-century geographer al-Razi, who visited the area and described a Jewish settlement on the site.[9] It was for this reason that, before the arrival of the Zirids, Granada appears to have been known as

Gharnata al-Yahud, or 'Granada of the Jews'. This corresponds with the memoirs of the last king of the Zirid dynasty, who claims that the majority of the early population of eleventh-century Granada was indeed Jewish.[10]

This settlement in those early centuries of Arab rule appears to have been relatively small, although the fort of Granada makes intermittent appearances in Arab histories of the time. For example, the first Umayyad ruler of Cordoba, Abd al-Rahman I, arriving on the Iberian Peninsula after his dramatic escape from Syria, won an important victory against his predecessor, Yusuf, after laying siege to Granada's fort, where Yusuf had taken sanctuary.[11] However, even after this, what would become Granada was to remain only a small hamlet on the top of a hill, while the rest of the region of Elvira began to play a greater role in the affairs of the new Caliphate of Cordoba. During the eighth century, as different Arab and Berber tribes migrated to al-Andalus seeking land, warriors from the former Umayyad capital, Damascus, chose to settle in the region on account of the similarity of its surroundings to their homeland.[12] Within a hundred years a city had formed, known as Madinat Elvira. Situated at the foot of the Sierra Elvira and beside what is now Atarfe, around 10km north-west of the modern-day city of Granada, Madinat Elvira evolved into one of the largest conurbations in al-Andalus, thanks to its excellent position with communication routes allowing trade in food and other goods, both locally produced and imported from places farther afield such as Almeria.[13]

The archaeological remains of Elvira today show it to have been spread across a huge area and largely populated by Muwallads—Iberian converts to Islam—and a substantial community of Christians. It was these people who, in the early decades of the eleventh century, would move up to join the Jewish community on the Albaicín hill to become the first inhabitants of the city of Granada as we know it today. And history has left us with a rare treasure by providing a narrative for this foundation story, albeit one that is none too flattering to the Elvirans: the memoirs of the unfortunate Abdullah ibn Buluggin, last Zirid emir of Granada.

2

THE ZIRID DYNASTY

The people of Elvira lived in a plain, and such was their dislike of one another that each would build by his home a mosque and bath-house to escape any contact with his neighbour. They showed neither obedience nor submission to any ruler. Nevertheless they were most cowardly people and most fearful for their city's safety, being unable to fight anyone, even a fly, without depending on someone else to protect and defend them.[1]

Such is the somewhat less than complimentary verdict on the Elvirans of Abdullah ibn Buluggin, the final Zirid ruler of Granada, writing in the Atlas Mountains of what is now Morocco in the last decade of the eleventh century—some eighty years after the event. We cannot, of course, trust everything written by an emir whose unpopularity reached such heights that his own subjects rose up in revolt, leaving only his beloved mother to support him against the ultra-orthodox Almoravid dynasty who replaced him. Yet, Abdullah's capitulation undoubtedly saved his life and enabled him to leave us something few monarchs have been able to before or since. Living in exile to the south of

Marrakesh, this former king wrote a memoir that provides a great deal of information about eleventh-century al-Andalus, and which, whilst obviously sympathetic to Abdullah's own struggles and the decisions of the Zirid rulers who had preceded him, nonetheless provides a fascinating, largely contemporaneous chronicle of Granada's early history.

According to Abdullah, after a period of violence in the region between 1008 and 1013, during which the once great Caliphate of Cordoba fell into chaos, the allegedly misanthropic Elvirans issued an invitation to the renowned Berber warrior Zawi ibn Ziri to lead and defend them amidst the turmoil, as rival factions fought to carve up al-Andalus between them. The great Zawi, Abdullah tells us, took up the challenge with gusto, though his first act was to suggest the people abandon their city and select a better-defended position to protect their families and possessions. Abdullah describes their assessment of the new site:

> Their eyes lighted on a lovely plain filled with both rivers and trees ... They were quick to perceive that from its central position the mountain on which Granada now stands commanded all the surrounding country ... They were enthralled by the site and ... came to the conclusion that ... an attacking enemy would be able neither to besiege it nor to prevent anyone from leaving or entering ... They therefore began to build there, and ... Elvira then went to rack and ruin.[2]

Although Abdullah had not yet been born when the population of Elvira moved to the high ground on the Albaicín hill, archaeological evidence supports his claims. Thus, in his version of events, began the foundation of the city of Granada, whose status as one of the most important cities in al-Andalus was only to be achieved as the once mighty Caliphate of Cordoba went into decline. Indeed, the founder of Granada, Zawi, had played a major part in the decline of Cordoba, so recently the greatest centre of culture and civilisation on the Iberian Peninsula.[3] For a number of years, this Berber warrior from what is today Algeria was even refused the permission he needed to cross the strait to al-Andalus because of his reputation for being a troublemaker. As events would prove, this had been a wise decision; however, it was reversed by a later ruler, who needed the support of the militarily capable leader. Zawi made his way to Cordoba and, once there, became a prominent leader of the Berber faction vying for power in the city. These Berbers had been brought to al-Andalus, over a number of decades, as mercenaries to form the bulk of the caliph's army and were at that time in conflict with the local Andalusi population, made up of descendants of native Iberians, Arabs, and 'old' Berbers who had collectively become Arabised over the centuries of Muslim rule. Meanwhile, Cordoba's rulers had become weak, and attempts to play one faction off against another were causing major instability.

By 1009, the native Andalusi population were gaining the upper hand in the conflict, and the Berbers fled from Cordoba after rewards were offered for the head of any that remained in the city. In revenge, these North African warriors, with Zawi among their leaders, went on a rampage across the region, causing desperate suffering and hardship. Cordoba remained in chaos, and when the city finally surrendered after three long years, the Berbers entered, looting it and bringing to an end its dominance over al-Andalus. Although Cordoba survived as an important regional centre, it was never again to witness the greatness it had seen in earlier times. However, Cordoba's decline would, conversely, bring about the emergence over the next few decades of other great urban centres in the region including, very soon afterwards, the newly founded Granada. In victory, the Berbers installed their own candidate on the throne in Cordoba, though during the siege their ambitions had begun to change from ruling through a central puppet to actively administrating parts of al-Andalus themselves. Hence the weak, newly installed caliph rewarded with territory those Berber leaders who had supported him, Zawi becoming the governor of Elvira and its environs.

Whilst initially these Berber governors continued to pay homage to the caliph in Cordoba, in time it became clear that there would be no return to a strong, centralised government for al-Andalus. Instead, its separate regions began to form independent jurisdictions, divided up amongst both Berber and Andalusi rulers. Over time, these territories would become known as the 'taifa' states, the name being derived from the Arabic for 'faction'. Divided as they were between different clans, the taifas would come to represent a far weaker system of government for al-Andalus in comparison to the relative stability of the previous few centuries. Larger taifas frequently waged war on their smaller counterparts in attempts to annex them, providing little security for many; bitter rivalries between the leaders of the states also meant that co-operation on issues of importance was rare. This was to have major repercussions over the next hundred years, as Christian forces in the north and east of the Iberian Peninsula began to gather strength.

Although Abdullah claims in his memoir that the people of Elvira invited Zawi to lead and protect them, the intention of his writing is in part to justify his family's history, and therefore his claims cannot simply be taken at face value. Zawi, through his role in the devastation that had been wrought on Cordoba, had a reputation as a warmonger. Nevertheless, there is the possibility of some truth behind Abdullah's claim. After all, in the state of turmoil that followed the fall of Cordoba, every city in al-Andalus required a strong leader to defend it, and moving the population of Elvira to a new settlement on higher ground was a strategic decision of great merit. All the taifas faced the threat of attack from without, or, as happened more frequently, as a result of their own internecine feuding. One of the most significant perils was the hostility of the native population towards the upstart Berbers. This had arisen in the final decades of the Caliphate of Cordoba and was to continue throughout the taifa period. Even before the building work of Granada was completed, the new city found itself under attack by Andalusis aiming to expel the Berbers. However, the new position proved its worth early on, when, according to Abdullah, a thousand Berber defenders defeated an invading Andalusi army four times its strength.

It is a compelling image: a mass of people arriving on the Albaicín hill, eager to build in a short space of time a defensive city in which they could all live and prosper. Of course, the hill was not without a certain amount of infrastructure; as mentioned before, it had been for a number of centuries the site of a predominantly Jewish community and a defensive fort. Archaeological evidence shows that, in addition to this, the original Zirid walls were built on top of earlier ones that had been in use as far back as the pre-Roman tribal communities who had lived on the site. However, it is this period in the second decade of the eleventh century that marks the real birth of the city of Granada as we know it today.[4]

Having established the dynasty that bore his name, Zawi ibn Ziri left Granada in 1019 to fight a campaign in his native North Africa. According to Abdullah, he was later poisoned and never again saw the city he had founded, and, despite his having a number of sons, it was Zawi's nephew Habus who was called upon by the people of Granada to rule them. In Abdullah's estimation, Habus was a just emir, whose popularity ensured that the army grew in strength, attracting enthusiastic volunteers willing to defend the new city. During his reign, Granada became a political force in the region; alongside the extensive building campaign that marked the early Zirid period, an effective administrative system was also developed. And it was under Habus that one of Granada's greatest, yet perhaps unlikeliest, leaders emerged: Samuel ibn Naghrila, a spice merchant in exile from Cordoba, and a Jew.

By all accounts, eleventh-century Granada was a multi-ethnic city. As Berber tribesmen who had only recently arrived from North Africa, the Zirid leaders would have been a minority amongst a population composed of descendants of other North African tribes, Arabs, ethnic Iberian converts to Islam, Christians, Jews, and both white and black slaves.[5] Abdullah tells us that the majority of Granada's early subjects were, in fact, Jews. In addition to the displaced population of Elvira, others of various faiths and ethnicities would also have moved to the new site from the recently sacked Cordoba. Although the Zirids actively recruited into the army from all the different groups in the city and placed the collection of taxes in the hands of the Jewish community, it was virtually unheard of for an adherent of any religion but Islam to be appointed as the right hand of a Muslim ruler. In fact, non-Muslims appear to have been barred from holding such high office. Such obstacles, however, would be overcome by the remarkable Samuel ibn Naghrila.[6]

Samuel emerges in the history of Granada as a spice merchant. Originally from Cordoba, he likely fled that city alongside many other Jews following its sacking and set up his life anew elsewhere in the region, first in Malaga, then moving on to Granada, where his shop was located near to the home of the vizier. An illiterate servant from the palace would pass by his shop and ask for his help in composing letters. The servant had chosen wisely whom to seek assistance from, as Samuel was a highly educated man who was later renowned not only for his political skill but also as a philosopher, poet, grammarian, and mathematician. A Muslim contemporary wrote of him, 'He excelled in learning, endurance, intelligence and wit, charm of character, perseverance, astuteness, cunning, self-control and natural courtesy.'[7] Soon Samuel came to the notice of the vizier himself, who invited this

Jewish shopkeeper to meet him. His impressive ascent of the political ladder thus began; he became a tax collector and after that secretary to the vizier. As time went on, he rose through the administrative ranks and, on the death of Habus, aided the latter's son Badis in securing Granada's throne in 1038. In recognition, Samuel was rewarded with the positions of vizier and leader of the army of Granada, wielding a power second only to that of the emir.

Samuel's rise to the top is often highlighted as a prime example of a kind of sublime tolerance existing in al-Andalus between Jews, Christians, and the Muslim rulers of the time. However, this concept of an ideal, proto-pluralist society is flawed, as is clearly demonstrated by the events that befell the Jews of Granada in the years after Samuel's death. No-one should argue that brief moments of glory over a period of centuries equate to an overarching liberality when all minority groups in al-Andalus were subjected to various levels of persecution at different times. This was hardly a stable environment in which to live for either Jews or Christians, even if it compares well with later experiences of other religious groups in Christian lands. And, in his memoir, Abdullah suggests a different reason for the rise of Samuel ibn Naghrila: the enmity between the Berbers and the Andalusi Arabs, stemming from the earlier conflict over Cordoba, meant that the Zirids preferred to rely on an intelligent Jew rather than a fellow Muslim whose allegiance might be to the Andalusis. By the time of Badis's reign, even other Berbers had become less trustworthy in the eyes of their rulers.

As leader of Granada's army, Samuel spent several months every year on the battlefield, and he recorded his victories in many of his poems. During Habus's reign, and even more so during that of his son Badis, wars and skirmishes frequently flared up amongst the taifas, highlighting the political instability of al-Andalus. The state to cause most concern was Seville, which succeeded in swallowing up many of the smaller surrounding taifas and proved a constant threat to Granada, but there were also internal battles that needed to be fought. The start of Badis's reign was marked by power struggles and regular attempts by one of his cousins to seize control of the city. Fortunately for the king, he was able to rely on his vizier. One story tells of an attempt on Badis's life while he was outside the city walls at his estate called al-Ramla, on the site of today's Plaza de Bibarrambla. In the words of a contemporary, it was Samuel's ability 'to flatter his enemies and remove suspicion from their heart by his fine manners'[8] that enabled him to discover the plot and warn the king, allowing Badis to escape in time and flee back to the citadel.

Yet Samuel was under no illusions about the difficulties that came with serving a king. In one of his poems, he writes:

A monarch will not favor you unless he hopes to be
At ease while you labor and exert yourself in his service.
You are caught in his tongs: With one hand he brings you into
The flames,—while protecting you from the fire which with both
hands he sets against you.[9]

Working under Badis and maintaining his favour would have been no easy task. The king had a reputation for cruelty against those who opposed him; during his reign, for example, he is said to have personally beheaded a renowned astrologer who had escaped from Granada and then later surrendered himself to the king, only to meet his ignominious end at the hands of Badis himself. It has also been suggested that Badis once contemplated the complete annihilation of the Andalusi Arab population of Granada but was prevented from doing so by his vizier.[10] Abdullah, with his memoir, attempts to paint a much kinder picture of his grandfather, noting that the early attacks during Badis's reign had forced him to deal with offenders in a way that would secure the city, and that this sometimes involved diminishing his enemies' status, banishing them, or confiscating their property. Nonetheless, other chroniclers tell a different story. One speaks of a mother who complained to Badis about how her son mistreated her; Badis immediately gave orders for the son to be beheaded, ignoring the pleas of the mother, who had only wanted him reprimanded for his behaviour.[11]

During his reign, Badis was involved in wars in Almeria and Malaga, annexing the latter to the Taifa of Granada in 1056.[12] Meanwhile, within the capital itself, building work continued apace under this third Zirid emir and his able chief minister. Although the city had at first been built as a fortified settlement on the Albaicín hill, later, during the eleventh century, the walls were lengthened to include the level ground at the bottom of the hill, indicating that the population was growing substantially and required an enlargement to the original settlement. The Puerta de Elvira was constructed to act as the main entry point into Granada, and the new city moved closer to the river Darro. The river was culverted during the nineteenth and twentieth centuries in a controversial drive to improve the city's health, and in order to understand much of the Islamic city today, one must be able to imagine it back in place. In Zirid times, the Darro marked a clear boundary along the edge of the settled part of the city and down through the plains. There are archaeological signs that construction of the city's main mosque began during this period on the right bank of the river, on the site of what is now the Church of El Sagrario, next to the cathedral, suggesting that this area of the city was already populated by the late eleventh century. Meanwhile, in today's Realejo district, on the left bank, pottery kilns from the same century have been discovered beneath a sixteenth-century house known as the Casa de los Tiros, which demonstrates that people were also working here as early as the Zirid era.[13]

What is interesting to reflect on today is just how much of Granada was laid out in that first century of its existence. In the thirteenth century, the Nasrids would bring new growth with the building of the Alhambra, and the late nineteenth and entire twentieth centuries saw dramatic changes to the map of Granada's mediaeval past. Yet walking the modern city, following the street plan as it was in the eleventh century, shows just how much of the Granada we see in the twenty-first century was shaped a thousand years ago. Today, the clearest remains of the Zirid city are to be found not on the flatlands but rather within the original Alcazaba—from the fourteenth century known as the Alcazaba Cadima to distinguish it from the later Nasrid Alcazaba. A good place to start on a walking tour is the Mirador de San Cristóbal. From there it is possible to look down on the most well-preserved stretch of the original Zirid walls, which give a clear indication of the defensive purposes of the original city. Heading down from the Mirador, the Carril de la Lona then leads up towards the Zirid city, passing in front of the prominent early gate, the Puerta de Monaita. Continuing up to the top of the hill, it is clear why Zawi's decision to move the population of Elvira had been such a good strategic choice. The former city was located down on the plains at the base of the Sierra Elvira mountain range over to the north-west.

Walking through today's Placeta de San Miguel Bajo, one enters into what would have been the Alcazaba, containing within it the original Zirid Palace, although all remains of the latter are now gone. The Alcazaba walls can be followed around past the later Nasrid palace known as the Dar al-Horra, to the Puerta de las Pesas, and then along past the Chapel of San Cecilio. The Alcazaba's southern walls have largely disappeared, although the occasional, enticing sign of them remains amongst more modern structures. These walls ran more or less along today's Calle San Juan de los Reyes, and, for anyone following this route, a circuit back to the Placeta de San Miguel Bajo will take them past the Church of San José, whose bell tower is an excellent example of a converted Zirid minaret. Walking around the area on which the walled city originally sat, it is difficult to imagine it as it would have looked at the time. Most of the structures are from later eras and, in peak tourist season, large groups of sightseers can make it difficult to envisage the city of a millennium ago. It is also essential, in surveying the site of the former Alcazaba, to try to ignore the dominating presence of the Alhambra on the hill opposite; prior to the thirteenth century, nothing was there but a small fort.

Aside from the remains of the Zirid walls, another example of the early infrastructure of the city can still be seen in its water system. Much is made of the importance of water to peoples whose ancestors came originally from the desert, and though the discovery of Roman-era channels suggests that the Muslims may have built on the remains of already existing water transportation structures in Granada, over the centuries successive generations would certainly demonstrate enormous skill in the field of hydro-logical engineering. Indeed, by the time of the Nasrids in the thirteenth and fourteenth centuries, this had risen to something of an art form. Meanwhile, as this infrastructure was being con-structed, a system was devised to pull water up directly from the river Darro just below the original walls. It consisted of a walled corridor running down today's Calle Bañuelo, and it allowed people to access the river without fear of attack and to bring water back up inside the city's defensive walls. Today the remains of one of the most important pieces of Zirid infrastructure in Granada can still be seen: the extant half of a sluice gate, known in Arab times as the Bab al-Difaf, which could be opened and closed to control the flow of the river.

Before long, Granada's water supply infrastructure became more sophisticated. Throughout the Albaicín, a network of *aljibes*—Moorish cisterns—can still be seen. These were gener-ally located next to mosques to enable worshippers to perform their ritual ablutions before prayer. Water was channelled into the city to these cisterns from sources higher up in the mountains beyond; in the case of the Albaicín, this supply originated at the Fuente de Aynadamar, a spring some 10km outside the city that can still be visited today. Water was channelled along manmade canals known as *acequias*, and as these reached populated areas of the city, branches ran off underground to feed each of the numerous *aljibes*. Over time, several *acequias* serving other parts of the city were created, running down from different water sources, such as the Acequia Gorda on the right bank of the river Genil. Drinking water would have been distributed by water sellers, who were a feature of Granada—indeed across much of Spain—until well into the nineteenth century.

Alongside its growing infrastructure, eleventh-century Granada also began to turn into something of a vibrant city of culture, helped in no small part by the status of the poet Samuel ibn Naghrila as the right-hand man of the emir. Samuel can be viewed as bringing to this rough, new city founded by warriors some of the great intellectual spirit that had flourished in Cordoba for so many centuries. And in the cultural mix of Zirid Granada, as in other taifa-period cities such as Seville, a long-standing Andalusi poetical tradition inspired a lively musical tradition. Musicians performed poetry to rhythmic dance melodies played on Arabic instruments such as the drum and oud. A new and scandalous form of poetry was created, known as *muwashshah*,[14] which began to challenge traditional styles fixed in classical Arabic by including a final line in the vernacular language, a derivative of Latin that remained as a spoken language in the region after the Arab invasions.[15] These poems frequently included the female voice and sang openly about love and the delights of wine and intoxication. Such was the mixing of cultures in the taifa cities that this newly developed form of Arabic poetry also inspired a similar form in Hebrew, with Samuel using his skill and fluency in Arabic literary expression to enhance Hebrew poetry by incorporating this new style into the canon.

Samuel ibn Naghrila died in 1056, leaving behind a substantial city with a strong administrative system. He was replaced as vizier by his son Joseph, to whom he had addressed an earlier poem, expressing both his respect for the wisdom of the Arabs and his desire to pass this wisdom on to his son:

> Joseph, take this book that I have selected for you from the choice works in the language of the Arabs.
> ... I cease not from teaching you though death's mouth is opened all about me,
> In order that wisdom may come upon you,—for it is dearer to me than discovering my foes defeated.
> ... Know that the man of understanding is like a tree of sweet fruit whose leaves are healing remedies,
> While the fool is like the tree of the forest whose limbs and branches will be consumed by fire in the end.[16]

Yet, whilst Samuel may have had a lot of faith in his son, this confidence is not reflected in the memoir of Abdullah. Whereas he is generally respectful towards Samuel, his animosity towards Joseph is clear. He frequently refers to the new vizier as 'the swine' and portrays him as scheming and preoccupied with increasing his own power and wealth whilst turning Badis against his other advisors.

One of the major reasons for Abdullah's animosity towards Joseph was the allegation that he had poisoned Abdullah's own father—Badis's son Saif al-Dawla. The story as told by Abdullah is that Saif al-Dawla was a universally popular man, in contrast to his violent father. Joseph, it is alleged, ingratiated himself with Saif al-Dawla and manipulated a deal to bring the income of nearby Guadix into the hands of both himself and the heir to the throne. However, in doing so he alienated other advisors at court. These, in turn, conspired to turn Saif al-Dawla against

Joseph and, when they succeeded, persuaded him that it was in his interests for Joseph to die. It seems, though, that Saif al-Dawla was too open about his intention to kill Joseph, and, Abdullah states, the latter was still too powerful to be easily outmanoeuvred. Joseph invited Saif al-Dawla to his house one evening to partake in some drinks, but at the end of the evening as he left the house, the prince fell down in the street in agony, vomiting violently. After two days of terrible suffering, the heir to the throne died.

The charges Abdullah makes against Joseph do not end with allegations of poisoning. It is said that the vizier managed to persuade Badis that others were responsible for the killing of his son, and these were then put to death. Abdullah recalls that, by this time, his elderly grandfather had lost the desire to rule and placed the running of the state entirely in Joseph's hands, allowing him to dominate the court. Again, rumours soon began to circulate of Joseph's involvement in other intrigues, murders, and plots to manipulate the royal succession for his own ends. One of these plots would finally bring about Joseph's downfall, after ten years at the emir's side. Abdullah relates how Joseph conspired to enable the ruler of Almeria, Ibn Sumadih, to enter Granada and take its throne. The conspiracy involved having all the nobles and slaves whose influence he feared posted away from Granada under the pretext that they were needed to co-ordinate a defence in outlying areas of the realm. Then Joseph wrote to Ibn Sumadih telling him that all people of merit had left the city and it was now an easy target. Badis, meanwhile, had declined into old age more content with wine than with ruling, and was almost certainly unaware of the plot against him and his dynasty.

Unbeknownst to Joseph, however, Ibn Sumadih had a change of heart and backed out of the plan, perhaps baulking at the thought of conquering somewhere as well-defended as Granada. Oblivious to the fact that his treasonous scheme was unravelling, on 30 December 1066, Joseph went out for a night of drinking with some of Badis's slaves. During the evening, he informed some of his companions about his plot—that the king of Almeria would be arriving imminently and would shower them with favours. Unfortunately for Joseph, he also seems to have been ignorant of the great enmity those slaves, like many in Granada, felt towards him. One, in a bout of drunkenness and having alleged that Joseph might actually have poisoned Badis, is said to have run away from the group shouting that the emir had been betrayed by his vizier and that the enemy was about to enter the city.

Abdullah, who was by that time eleven years old, recalls how the whole city erupted in anger and poured out onto the streets. Joseph managed to get to the safety of the palace and talked Badis into appearing before the crowd to prove he was still alive. But by this point, the anger was out of control. The crowd broke into the palace and hunted down the hated vizier. It is alleged that Joseph met a brutal end, crucified by the crowd on one of the gates of the city. But worse was to come, because Joseph's death prompted the mob to seek vengeance on the rest of the city's Jews. Abdullah's account suggests a spontaneous outbreak of violence; however, according to other accounts, the mob had been waiting impatiently for some time for an opportunity to take their revenge on the hated vizier and, in turn, on the entire Jewish community of Granada, who they claimed had become arrogant and haughty towards Muslims because of their influence at court. It is also said that an inflammatory poem written by a jurist and poet named Abu Ishaq had been circulating round the city for some time, calling for Badis to rid Granada of the Jews. Whatever the cause for the rancour, the repercussions of Joseph's actions were to be felt by all of Granada's Jewish inhabitants, for whose blood the emboldened crowds were now baying.

The massacre of Granada's Jews in 1066 is the Muslim city's most infamous act of mass slaughter. Stories told about it today often describe the complete destruction of the city's Jewish community, although this must be an exaggeration. The family of the renowned Hebrew poet Moses ibn Ezra was certainly still living in Granada at the time of the Almoravid invasions in 1090, from which he fled to the northern Christian kingdoms. And a Jewish community continued to be present in the city throughout the Almoravid period, with their eventual expulsion from the city or forced conversions taking place in the 1160s under the Almohads. Nevertheless, the brutal murder of a large proportion of Granada's Jews in 1066 ended a period of relative tolerance, where an intelligent, cultured Jew could lead a city as the right-hand man of a Muslim king.

Abdullah acceded as emir in 1073 at the age of eighteen, on the death of his grandfather Badis. His memoir, in addition to providing tremendous detail about the founding dynasty of Granada, is particularly telling about the problems caused by the constant conflict among the taifas, and how this infighting allowed their Christian neighbours to the north to gain momentum in their bid to conquer all the Muslim lands of the Iberian Peninsula. One of the first stories Abdullah relates of his rule is how Alfonso VI of Leon and Castile sent an emissary to Granada to extort money from the new king. Abdullah refused to pay the tribute, believing that, as Granada lay safely beyond the Taifa of Toledo, it would therefore be buffered against Christian attack. Moreover, naive about the extent of disunity amongst his fellow Muslims, Abdullah mistakenly trusted that the taifas would protect one another rather than ally with the Christians and in so doing weaken Muslim rule. In this he made a dangerous miscalculation.

The vizier of the Taifa of Seville, so frequently an enemy of Granada, would soon clearly prove the new king's folly. On hearing of Abdullah's refusal to pay the tribute, Seville's vizier contacted Alfonso's envoy and offered the Christians a large sum of money and a share in the spoils if they aided Seville in an invasion of Granada. Alfonso, not one to miss the opportunity of sowing discord amongst the Muslim states, accepted the deal, and an army of Christian mercenaries united with the Muslim forces of Seville to begin a campaign of harassment against Granada, the severity of which prompted Abdullah to admit that he 'regretted not having concluded a treaty with [Alfonso] in the first place as he had asked.'[17] The siege of the city was only lifted when Seville's army was needed elsewhere. From this experience, Abdullah gained a bitterness towards the other taifa rulers and an awareness that he had to strengthen Granada's own defences.

As the vizier of Seville continued to pursue Alfonso's assistance in capturing Granada, Abdullah was advised to seek an accord with the Castilian king. His account of his meeting with the Christian ruler might suggest to the modern reader the ominous undertone of a mafia shakedown: 'He received me with cheerful countenance and kindly manner and promised to protect me as he would his own territory.'[18] With negotiations underway, Alfonso swiftly got the measure of his counterpart and the amount he could inveigle from him in tribute, waxing lyrical about Abdullah's intelligence. In the words of Abdullah, Alfonso ended the negotiations by saying:

> in honeyed tones: 'Ibn 'Ammar [the vizier of Seville] was hoping I would betray you, but God forbid that people should say that a man as great as I among Christians came to you, equally as great among your own kind, and then betrayed you! You need have no fears. I ask you for nothing but the tribute and that you send it me promptly every year.'[19]

With the continued threat from neighbouring Seville, Abdullah had no choice but to comply with Alfonso's demands. However, the tributes—known as *parias*—brought their own problems. The high taxes needed to finance their payment were bitterly resented by Abdullah's people, and ultimately it was this fiscal burden, alongside the interminable discord among the rival rulers of the taifas, that would bring about the downfall of the Zirids.

The third quarter of the eleventh century saw the Christian menace to al-Andalus greatly amplified, culminating in the fall of the strategically significant Taifa of Toledo to Alfonso VI in 1085. In a move that was to have dramatic consequences for all the rest of the taifas, al-Mu'tamid, emir of Seville, turned to the Berbers across the sea for assistance. Answering the call in 1086, a force of Almoravid tribesmen—Berbers who had recently conquered vast swathes of north-west Africa—crossed the strait to aid the taifas in combatting the Christians. Abdullah joined the ruler of Seville in making a treaty with the Almoravid leader, Yusuf ibn Tashfin, by which they agreed to join together to fight the Christians but gained assurances that the Almoravids would not involve themselves in the taifas' internal struggles. At first, all appeared to go well with this new alliance; the Muslims gained early success in battle, and Yusuf's subsequent return to North Africa appeared amicable.

But even with the military victories, the problem of the taxes was not resolved. With the Almoravid departure, an emissary of the Castilian king came to Granada bent on the continued extraction of the *parias*. Again, the high taxes levied to pay these tributes led to the growing unpopularity of all of the taifa rulers among their own subjects, who struggled under the yoke of such a financial burden. Worse still, Abdullah was beginning to suspect that the previously accommodating Almoravids were perhaps not the brothers in arms they had at first appeared to be. If paying tribute to a Christian king had not been enough, Abdullah now found himself the subject of coercion from another direction—an Almoravid general, left behind to support the defences of the taifa states, was also beginning to extort him for money.[20] Thus Abdullah's situation continued to spiral downwards. On top of this, he suspected his own advisors of turning against him and allying with the Almoravids.

Trapped between the debt of gold that he had to pay to the Christians and that demanded by the Almoravids, Abdullah began to worry that he was losing his grip on Granada. Aware of the attraction of the Almoravids' widely proclaimed policies of minimal taxes, in panic he garrisoned his fortresses and stock-piled provisions. He oscillates in his memoir between claims that he was aiding the Almoravids in their jihad and that he was bolstering his city against the Christians. What is clear, though, is that he was deeply troubled by the prospect of the Almoravids taking his kingdom, and by the hold they now had over him: 'Whenever the Amir of the Muslims [Yusuf ibn Tashfin] calls on me to provide an army or money ... I must lose no time in com-plying with his demands. To do otherwise would give him a case against me and do me harm.'[21] And his fears of Yusuf grew stronger still when he received communication from the emir absent of all former cordiality. Yusuf warned Abdullah:

> I well know your conniving ways and mendacious utterances. I shall soon know just how highly your subjects regard you and your trans-actions in view of your allegation that you have served their interests. Do not pin your hopes on the long term. The near future is what matters to you.[22]

Abdullah was becoming frantic, aware that friends and allies were scarce and convinced that his courtiers had turned, allying themselves with the Almoravids and poisoning Yusuf against him. His memoir becomes full of tales of ministers and nobles leaving his court to ingratiate themselves with the Almoravids. At the same time, other taifa rulers remained deeply suspicious of one another and were unable to unite against either the Christians or the looming threat posed by the Almoravids.

By June 1090, Abdullah would have been fully aware that the greatest danger to his throne came from the Almoravids, as

Yusuf gathered his armies at Ceuta on the coast of North Africa. In an effort to persuade the emir of his friendship and support, Abdullah sent two envoys to swear that Granada would join the Almoravids in their jihad against the Christians. Once again, however, he was to find himself betrayed, as those same envoys, on seeing the strength of the Almoravid forces, pledged their allegiance to Yusuf and informed him that the people of Granada would welcome an Almoravid invasion and the replacement of Abdullah as their king.[23]

Yusuf's armies set out across the strait. In a now predictable show of disunity amongst the taifas, al-Muʿtamid met with the Berber leader to accuse Abdullah of intrigue with the Christians, almost certainly to turn Yusuf's attentions towards Granada instead of towards his own kingdom of Seville. Abdullah sent more envoys to plead his innocence to Yusuf, but to no avail. The Almoravid leader imprisoned the envoys and had their escort beaten, before sending them back to Granada in a terrible state. Meanwhile, Yusuf sent messages to all of Abdullah's northern border fortresses, warning of terrible repercussions if they refused to surrender. As each capitulated with barely a fight, Abdullah realised his position had become untenable, and it would now be beyond his power to maintain control of the city of Granada itself: 'Never had I witnessed days and nights more distressing to my heart and more calamitous to my soul than that period of my life.'[24]

While Abdullah sat panicking in his palace, Yusuf's army continued to go from strength to strength. As he took control of the fortifications north of the city, he began to send men ahead to lay siege to the capital, although he clearly felt in no need to rush. Just as four centuries later the Catholic Monarchs Isabella and Ferdinand would be prepared to bide their time through a lengthy siege until Granada surrendered, Yusuf was disposed to wait it out for a weak ruler to capitulate in order to take the city of Granada intact. Indeed, such was Yusuf's appreciation of Abdullah's psychological state and minimal chances of fighting off the Almoravid forces, he even sent requests into the city for food and fodder. The terrified Abdullah complied as he struggled to find the best solution to his predicament, one potentially being the safe passage Yusuf had offered him in exchange for handing over the city.

Weighing up the various outcomes, Abdullah consulted those who had remained in Granada and recognised that none of them any longer supported him as ruler. The Berbers of the city had already pledged allegiance to Yusuf in exchange for retaining their positions once the Almoravids had control. Berber troops based in the Alcazaba moved their families and possessions down into the lower part of the city in anticipation of Yusuf's arrival. The merchants and the commoners also backed the Almoravids, eager for an end to the crippling taxation they had suffered under Abdullah. Even the women and eunuchs went over to the enemy, Abdullah notes, the latter receiving promises of rich estates from Yusuf if they sided with him. Aware that the city now supported Yusuf, Abdullah watched his people gradually abandon him, and finally he too resolved to submit to the invader, valuing his own life above being ruler of an empty city. Having determined to go out and meet Yusuf, he described feeling, 'as though I was being driven to the jaws of death, not knowing my fate.'[25]

Throwing himself on the mercy of Yusuf and the Almoravids, Abdullah was subjected to the indignity of being searched and the humiliation of threats to his life until such time as his captors were satisfied that he had surrendered all his treasures to them. Abdullah was left friendless, with only his beloved mother by his side. Yusuf himself appears to have felt completely unthreatened by Abdullah, and perhaps feeling a sense either of lingering friendship or of pity towards the deposed king, he did not kill him, but instead honoured his word and exiled Abdullah to the

Atlas Mountains in what is now Morocco. It is thanks to this that we have such an important and detailed source on the early history of Granada in the memoir Abdullah subsequently wrote in retirement.

Historians, whilst acknowledging the huge importance of the information that Abdullah's memoir provides us about the history of the taifas, can often be dismissive of the author's motivations for writing it. Although to a certain extent it is true that Abdullah is seeking to justify his actions and defend his dynasty's reputation, there is something rather moving about the account. At times it has a certain honesty that emanates from a man who has suffered total failure yet been given the chance at the end of his life to reflect and pass on his wisdom to future generations. He laments how he was let down by friends and allies who had prospered under the Zirid dynasty. After all, he had shown them a respect and tolerance that his grandfather Badis never had. He offers this advice on the lessons learned about the type of person that makes a good friend:

> Your best friend is he who will share your suffering and who has suffered the same trials and tribulations. It is of no consequence that he may not be related to you. Depend only on this type of person. Do not complain about your troubles to someone who has not suffered the same, for he will either pay no attention to what you say ... or he will take the opposite point of view ... this is human nature. Do not listen to someone who, by his words, seeks to show that he believes you, for truth comes hard to people; falsehood comes more readily and is easier to bear.[26]

A much wiser Abdullah spent the remaining years of his life in Africa. Meanwhile, no longer in danger but having lost its independence, Granada now found itself under the rule of a very different dynasty: the veiled Almoravid warriors.

3

THE ALMORAVIDS AND THE ALMOHADS

To imagine Granada under the Almoravids, it is necessary to evoke the same Zirid city, with its walled Alcazaba high up on the Albaicín hill and its growing commercial district on the flatlands below, but with a dramatically changed atmosphere. At least at first, it may be presumed that something darker and more austere pervaded. The city once dominated by the poetry and scholarly inquiry of intellectuals such as Samuel ibn Naghrila became a place where a stringent interpretation of Islam was imposed on the population, enforced by veiled warriors who loomed large on horseback.

The Almoravids were a confederation of tribes originating in present-day Mauritania.[1] Until the middle of the eleventh century, just a few decades before they came to rule al-Andalus, they had been a hardy desert people known for shunning luxury and possessing the characteristics associated with those accustomed to living in harsh conditions. They became strict adherents of Islamic law and, in their original conquests across northwest Africa, were noted for imposing bans on music and wine and for destroying any places associated with these. Largely illiterate and fiercely devoted to their own interpretation of their religion, as they left their desert surroundings and battled their way into more urban areas, they were seen to have little tolerance for people of other faiths. They discarded their nomadic lives on founding their capital, Marrakesh, and their military successes made them attractive potential allies for the taifa emirs of al-Andalus.

At the forefront of the Almoravid conquest of the Maghreb had been Yusuf ibn Tashfin, whose reputation by 1085, when the taifa kings requested he join their fight against the Christians, was that of a strong military figure whose courage and judgement were feared and admired in equal measure. Not only did he have the sharp intelligence of a great leader of men, but he was also deeply committed to his faith; despite his conquests and the vast wealth these had brought him, he continued to live the life of an ascetic, dressing in coarse woollen clothing and existing on the diet of a man of the desert.[2] He was an old man, nearing eighty, when he began his first forays into al-Andalus to help his fellow Muslims fight the infidels, but it appears that during those early battles he suffered disillusionment with the taifa kings' constant internecine squabbling. On returning to al-Andalus in 1090, it was with a new ambition. This time he arrived armed with religious backing in the form of a fatwa for an invasion of the taifas themselves. Issued by the leaders of the Maliki school of thought to which the Almoravids subscribed, the fatwa supported Yusuf's war of conquest on the basis that not only had the taifas succumbed to worldliness, but they could no longer be considered true Muslims after submitting to the payment of tributes to the Christians. With this conviction, Yusuf launched his campaign with the siege of Granada, forcing the abdication of Abdullah.

The fall of Granada was just the start for the Almoravid leader, and his ambition was aided by the disunity amongst the taifa states. Their infighting had been at such a level that even at the point that Granada fell, the other taifa emirs refused to join forces, seemingly oblivious to Yusuf's threat to their own realms. Astute military leader that he was, Yusuf took advantage of this discord, biding his time and not allowing the other emirs to see the extent of his ambition over the whole of al-Andalus. In proposing to seize Granada, for example, he initially promised that, having prevailed, he would hand it over to al-Mu'tamid, the emir of Seville. Yusuf claimed only to be acting to prevent Granada from falling into Christian hands and at first gave no inkling of a desire for conquest. This was a shrewd strategy to manipulate the taifa rulers, whose covetousness made them more willing to annex their neighbours than to stand united with them against a common enemy. Abdullah expresses in his memoir his frustration at this greed as well as his anger at the other taifa rulers for not coming to the aid of Granada, instead letting it fall to the Almoravids. He sent word to each warning them, 'To this end you will also come. Today it is my turn but tomorrow it will be yours.'[3]

Abdullah's cautions went unheeded. Indeed, al-Mu'tamid journeyed to Granada to congratulate Yusuf on his victory, little realising the next stages of his plan. But it was not long before al-Mu'tamid and his contemporaries learned the folly of their imprudence. After the fall of Granada, Yusuf continued his campaign against the other taifas, including Seville, which fell in 1091, its emir being sent to join Abdullah in exile. Just a year later, Yusuf controlled almost all of al-Andalus and, after centuries of self-rule either under the Caliphate of Cordoba or as independent taifas, the majority of Muslim Iberia found itself subject to the jurisdiction of a foreign sovereign whose capital lay across the sea in Marrakesh.

Although Granada acted as a regional seat of power during the Almoravid period, a provincial capital in some respects, al-Andalus became culturally rather barren after so long a period of vibrancy. Whilst poetry, architecture, and other intellectual pursuits would flourish to a certain degree in Marrakesh, particularly following Yusuf's death, the cities of the former taifa states were marginalised, at the periphery of this new empire. Gone from Granada was the scholarly spirit of the eleventh century, and many of the leading thinkers of Muslim Iberia moved to Fez or the Almoravid capital itself to escape the cerebral stagnation of their native lands. As the cities of the Maghreb blossomed, al-Andalus withered in a cultural decline hastened by the burnings of books written by philosophers opposed to the Maliki interpretation of Islam.

The impact on intellectual life was felt particularly acutely by the Jewish community, whose culture had so flourished under Samuel ibn Naghrila. Among those who fled the city in the early years of Almoravid rule was Moses ibn Ezra, considered one of al-Andalus's greatest Hebrew poets. There is some suggestion that Ibn Ezra fled Granada after his unrequited love for one of his nieces provoked the ire of his brothers as well as his own heartache. More likely, however, is that he left the city due to the severity of the new regime. His description of Granada from exile in a letter to a friend is of 'a city of spirit and splendour ... upon which the chastising hand of God is still stretched out.'[4] Ibn Ezra had been deeply involved in the great musical and poetic life of Zirid Granada, and his later poetry suggests he suffered terribly at having been forced to leave Granada for what he perceived to be the cultural dearth of the Christian north. Reflecting on the day he left his city, he writes:

> That rash and bitter day of departure
>   left me drunk with the wine of desire.
> Desolate now, I dwell among mules,
>   where no one sees to the needs of my soul.
>
> I call to the left—there is no answer,
>   then turn to the right and find—only strangers.[5]

Whilst many among Granada's Jews departed in those early days of Almoravid rule, the local Jewish community would continue to exist in the city until the next set of invaders came along, albeit facing constant intolerance at the hands of their new overlords. However, the city's Jews were not alone in facing intolerance. Perhaps greater still was the oppression felt by Granada's Mozarabs—Christians living under Muslim rule. Whilst much has been written about the Jews of Granada, very little information is available about the number of Christian inhabitants at that time, or about the conditions under which they lived. From archaeological evidence it is clear that, in the early eleventh century, the city of Elvira had had a significant Christian contingent,[6] and it can be assumed that they, along with the rest of the population, had moved up to the new settlement of Granada under Zirid rule. How they were treated at the end of the Zirid period, as the northern Christian kingdoms began to assert their dominance, is unclear, but it appears that with the coming of the Almoravids, a period of persecution against them began. Arab sources record, for instance, that Yusuf ordered the destruction of a church widely renowned for its beauty, located close to the Puerta de Elvira.[7]

For the half century that the Almoravids ruled al-Andalus, it remained a distant province of their empire. When Yusuf died, he was succeeded by his son Ali, who visited the territory on just four occasions during a reign that lasted almost forty years. In his stead, Ali entrusted the region to his brother Tamim, who garrisoned his troops in fortresses around the region, including in the Alcazaba of Granada. Historical records from the period are scant, and life in the city can mainly be interpreted only through evidence that survives from other parts of al-Andalus.[8] Events recorded in Cordoba, for example, suggest that the Almoravid rulers of a city were generally small in number and lived within the palace compound. When rebellions took place it was necessary, therefore, for reinforcements to be sent over from North Africa.

It is hard not to imagine a fearful Granada during this period. The Almoravids relied on religious scholars to impose their strict interpretation of Islamic law on their subjects, and the cities of al-Andalus were patrolled by warriors with fully veiled faces. These coverings originally stemmed from the necessity to keep the sand and wind out of faces in desert conditions. In the cities of al-Andalus, however, they proved a symbol of intimidating power. Such was the impact of these horsemen that brigands and mercenaries also took to hiding their faces to instil fear in the local population, to the point where—in Seville at least—a code was issued that forbade any man not a member of the Almoravid militia from veiling himself.[9] Yet, setting aside their exacting school of jurisprudence and the measures taken to enforce adherence to this, the Almoravids nevertheless gained a certain acceptance at the outset thanks to their insistence on keeping taxes to a minimum—in stark contrast to the ruinous burden imposed on the people under the taifa system. The new rulers were also accepted because, after years of uncertainty, they brought stability and with that relative prosperity. Since they controlled vast swathes of north-west Africa, the Almoravids oversaw valuable routes for trade, including in gold, and this brought economic benefits to their subjects across the empire.

Notwithstanding this early prosperity, the era of greater financial security ushered in by the Almoravids was not to last for long. The Christian kingdoms continued their campaign of attack on Muslim cities along the northern frontier of al-Andalus; the most famous of the battles from this time that we continue to hear about today were those fought around Zaragoza and Valencia between the Almoravids and Rodrigo Díaz de Vivar, better known as El Cid. In addition, having originally pledged to keep taxes low, the Almoravids, like the Zirids before them, soon found themselves needing to increase these in order to pay for their defences against the Christian onslaught. This spelt the beginning of the Almoravids' decline in popularity, even amongst the majority Muslim population. But their reputation as strong rulers protecting al-Andalus took a further hit when, in 1118, Zaragoza fell to King Alfonso I of Aragon.

Perhaps it was this event, alongside the continual harassment under the Almoravids, that led Granada's Christians to take measures in 1125 to try to end their persecution. According to an Arab historian writing around two and a half centuries after the events, Granada's Mozarabs sent messages to Alfonso—known to history as 'The Battler'—to tempt him to journey down and liberate their city, claiming 12,000 of their co-religionists would be there to support him. The chronicler tells how the Christians extolled the great beauty of Granada in order to 'rouse his ambition and stir up his greed',[10] enticing him with a description of, 'Granada and its advantages over other regions, its abundance of wheat, barley and flax; its wealth in terms of silk, vineyards, olive oil and wide variety of fruits; its many springs and rivers; the invincibility of its alcazaba and the disposition of its subjects.'[11] The description appears to have worked, because soon Alfonso, possibly inspired by the growing legend of the exploits of El Cid, was at the head of 4,000 troops and making his way down into Almoravid territory, attacking towns and cities en route to the distant city of Granada, Mozarabs swelling the ranks of his army as they fled their homes in Muslim-controlled areas.

As Alfonso's army drew closer to Granada, the plot hatched by the Christian residents came to light. The chronicler tells us how the leaders of the city tried to arrest the Christians but were incapable of doing so, and as Alfonso reached the Vega, the Mozarabs began to pour out of the city to join him at his camp. Meanwhile, the governor of the region, Tamim, had received reinforcements from North Africa, and a defensive ring had been formed around the city, Muslim troops facing out towards the Vega where Alfonso and his greatly enlarged force had become a threatening presence. The city was tense; the people congregated to utter a 'prayer of fear'. In the end it was the weather that would thwart Alfonso's initial attempt to capture Granada: rain and ice prevented him from launching an attack. For ten days, Alfonso's camp remained tantalisingly close to their goal before finally withdrawing to try their luck with other settlements in the region.

After a number of confrontations with Almoravid troops, the Christians' route took them south, where the chronicler records perhaps the most audacious act of Alfonso's incredible, fifteen-month journey through Muslim territory: symbolically going fishing in the sea off the coast near Malaga. Then, returning once more to the outskirts of Granada, Alfonso set up camp in the region around today's Dilar, leading again to a number of confrontations between Muslims and Christians. But the city's defences were too strong for Alfonso's forces. Meanwhile, after so long in the field, his soldiers were beginning to fall ill. Realising the Christian conquest of Granada was out of reach, and probably also acknowledging that his journey had in itself done much to demonstrate the increasing threat of the Christian kingdoms to the north, Alfonso began the long journey back to Zaragoza. Whilst the Christians had not taken a single walled city during their campaign, they had caused great devastation to the countryside, and they returned home carrying large quantities of looted goods.

These events effectively wiped out the Christian population of al-Andalus and brought to an end a society that had been shared by all three Abrahamic faiths since the Muslim conquests of the eighth century. As Alfonso had made his way through the region, many Christians, including those of Granada, had left their cities to join his troops. With his retreat they left behind their homeland and accompanied him into Christian territory in the north. Viewed now as traitors by the Almoravids, those Christians left behind were deported to North Africa, many dying along the way. From that point until the Reconquista there is no mention of a permanent Christian community in Granada, only prisoners of war, traders, or visitors.

Almoravid control of al-Andalus lasted for a mere half century. During this period their Christian neighbours continued to gather strength, and even after Alfonso's retreat with his Christian supporters in tow, fighting persisted elsewhere between the Almoravids and the Aragonese. Amongst the meagre sources about the city of Granada during this period is a gruesome story from 1130, wherein we are told that one of the great heroes of the Crusades, Gaston de Béarn, was killed by Muslim forces at Valencia and his body sent to Granada. There, his head was cut off and paraded through the streets of the city.[12] Yet these shows of victory were becoming fewer in number by the middle of the twelfth century, and the more the Almoravids had to fight the Christians, the more money they needed to do so. As taxes continued to be raised across al-Andalus, the Almoravids had to renege on their original promise not to bring back the onerous levies seen in the taifa period, which of course made them unpopular among the local people. The end of the veiled dynasty was to come, however, not through a popular revolt by their Iberian vassals, but as Almoravid lands across the sea in the Maghreb began to fall to a rival tribe, the Almohads.

Like the Almoravids, the Almohads were Berbers, but unlike the veiled, nomadic desert dwellers, the Almohads were mountain folk. They had established a state in the High Atlas in 1120, where they adhered to what they considered a much purer interpretation of Islam than even that of the Almoravids. Although, to the modern Western reader, both groups might appear to have practised a very puritanical form of the religion, the Almohads excoriated the Almoravids, charging them as being riddled with corruption and lax in their approach to the tenets of the faith. It is possible that following the death of Yusuf ibn Tashfin, the original asceticism that had characterised the early days of Almoravid rule had been diluted, as often happens as dynasties progress. The Almohads were distinctive in their strict interpretation of the Islamic doctrine of *tawhid*, the unity of God, and followed the lead of Ibn Tumart, who had become infamous for his debates with, and attacks on, the Almoravids and their understanding of Islam. In 1121 he 'revealed himself' as the Mahdi, a Messianic guide through the end times, giving divine weight to his crusade against the supposedly heretical Almoravid state. For twenty years, these mountain tribesmen became a growing problem for the Almoravids, and in 1147, in their most crucial victory, the Almohads swept down from the mountains and conquered Marrakesh, where their leader Abd al-Mu'min declared himself caliph in the capital of their fallen enemies.

Pushed out of their African lands, the Almoravids now found themselves the rulers only of what had once been the fringes of their empire, al-Andalus, and here the Christians had for years been unrelenting in their attacks on the northern borders. As the Almohads took control of the Maghreb, Alfonso VII of Leon and Castile was quick to exploit the situation, temporarily seizing the seaport of Almeria from the Almoravids in 1147 and, in the process, launching raids in the direction of nearby Granada. As it became clear that the Almoravids were losing control, many cities in al-Andalus turned briefly into new taifas, seeking the protection of local strongmen rather than of the Almoravid rulers who had lost all favour. Al-Andalus was once again thrown into chaos, and the Almohads were quick to take advantage, launching their own invasions from across the sea. Despite their resistance, Cordoba and Seville rapidly fell to these new Berber invaders in the late 1140s.

THE ALMORAVIDS AND THE ALMOHADS

The defence of Granada lasted for some years, longer than that of many other cities in the region, before it finally succumbed in the mid-1150s, whereupon Caliph Abd al-Mu'min appointed his son Uthman governor of the city.[13] Now the majority of al-Andalus was under Almohad control. As a sign of these rulers' lack of toleration for other faiths, Granada's Jews were forced to convert to Islam; those who could leave, fled. This included Judah ben Saul ibn Tibbon, a poet, translator, and philosopher, whose statue stands today at the entrance to the Realejo district. However, whilst Granada adjusted to life under the Almohads, other parts of al-Andalus continued to resist, most importantly the area around Murcia that remained in the hands of a local taifa leader—Ibn Mardanish. The boundaries of his territory lay in close proximity to the city of Granada, making him a serious threat to the Almohads there and a remaining hope for their opponents to throw off the new rulers.

Given their intolerance towards non-Muslims, the Almohads were considered, at first, to be even more fanatical than the Almoravids. However, even in those early years in Granada, one story of love and poetry shows them to have been far from immune to the beauty of the arts, and this story is centred around one of al-Andalus's most famous female poets—Hafsa bint al-Haj al-Rakuniyya.[14] Hafsa had been born into a wealthy Berber family in Granada, and as the Almohads fought for control of the city, she was embarking on an intense love affair with another local poet, Abu Ja'far. The two lovers would exchange passionate poems to express their feelings. In one of these, a clearly smitten Abu Ja'far recalls a night-time tryst in gardens beside the river Genil and imagines how the wonders of nature around them must have been celebrating the intensity of their passion:

> The meadow quivered with delight
> Beholding such a joyous sight,

The interclasp of bodies white,
And breasts that touched, and lips that met.

Hafsa, though, teasingly brushes off his romantic notions and argues that, far from being happy for them, nature only looks with jealousy on love such as theirs:

I scarce suppose that yonder sky
Displayed its wealth of stars on high
For any reason, but to spy
On our romance with jealous eyes.[15]

Unfortunately, as is often the case, life was to imitate art, and jealousy would indeed intervene in their love—not that of nature, however, but rather that of Abu Ja'far, for soon a third party interrupted the flames of their romance. After the fall of the city, Abu Ja'far was appointed secretary to the new governor, Uthman, and it appears that over time Hafsa's beauty and intelligence came to bewitch the governor too. Moreover, poems suggest that Hafsa may not have been immune to Uthman's advances, provoking a fit of jealous rage in Abu Ja'far.

Such was the intensity of Abu Ja'far's resentment that out of spite he joined the most dramatic of any rebellion against the Almohads, which began in Granada in 1162. This event was chronicled by the caliph's treasurer, Ibn Sahib al-Sala, whose account sides squarely with the Almohads.[16] He blames the outbreak of this rebellion on Granada's recently converted Jewish community, who, he reports, took advantage of Uthman's temporary absence from the city and opened a gate in the Albaicín to the forces of Ibn Hamushk, father-in-law to the Murcian leader Ibn Mardanish. As Ibn Sahib al-Sala tells it:

The treacherous Ibn Hamushk ... gathered the infidel around him and they broke the lock and the gate. [They entered] screaming out for comrades. And when the people of the city heard the battle cries and the fighting, those in authority, committed to their faith, sought shelter by escaping to the Alcazaba.[17]

THE ALMORAVIDS AND THE ALMOHADS

As Almohad supporters piled into the Alcazaba on the Albaicín hill, Ibn Hamushk led his troops through the city and across the river Darro to the Sabika hill—the site of today's Alhambra—where he pitched camp and began to rain down rocks on the enemy on the opposite bank. Outraged at this rebellion against his masters, Ibn Sahib al-Sala relates stories of these forces torturing their captives and scorning God's creation with their mockery of their prisoners. Meanwhile, with the city now under his control, Ibn Hamushk sent word to Murcia urging Ibn Mardanish to join him with reinforcements. The Murcian leader presently arrived at the head of a large force, replete with a cavalry of 8,000 Christian mercenaries under the command, the chronicler disdainfully notes, of a man he calls 'the bald one', grandson of one of the legendary companions of El Cid.

On hearing of the invasion, Uthman returned with all haste from North Africa, where he had been visiting his father the caliph, reinforcing his army along the way with troops based in Seville. Seeing their approach, Ibn Mardanish led his forces down into the Vega, where he demonstrated the severity of Murcia's threat to Granada. The Almohads were routed, many dying on the field. Ibn Sahib al-Sala describes it as the gravest of calamities. Uthman and the survivors were forced to flee to Malaga, where Uthman appealed for help from his father. Angered at this challenge to his growing empire, Caliph Abd al-Mu'min responded by sending 20,000 men across to al-Andalus, promising them great rewards from God for their fight against the infidel. They arrived in Granada to find Ibn Hamushk's army dominating the city from their camp on the Sabika hill, whilst Ibn Mardanish's forces, including his Christian mercenaries, held the top of the opposing Albaicín hill, looking down over the Alcazaba, where an Almohad garrison was holding out against the invaders.

With enemy forces dominating both of Granada's main hilltops, it would take something special for the Almohads to win the day. And this is exactly what occurred. In the dead of night, the Almohad forces silently climbed the rocky tracks up to the top of the Sabika hill by moonlight. Their approach would have been from the side that today is the Realejo district—an area at that point still largely undeveloped. Then, at first light, they launched a surprise attack on Ibn Hamushk's men. The chronicler paints a gruesome picture of events, describing how the Almohads 'attacked them in their beds, unravelling their intestines with their swords and their spears', the enemy unable to reach their horses to counterattack. He describes how 'the air became dark and full of dust, with no sounds to be heard apart from the deathly blows of swords, the cries of battle, and the chopping of skulls.'[18] To make matters worse for Ibn Hamushk's men, it appears many became confused, believing that they could escape over to where their allies, Ibn Mardanish's troops, were stationed on the opposite hill. Unaware of the sheer drop between the two hills, many fell down into the river Darro far below, Ibn Sahib al-Sala noting with glee how 'their bodies became dismembered on the river's edges as they met their deaths on that happy morning.'[19]

Ibn Sahib al-Sala portrays a cowardly Ibn Mardanish watching the destruction of his allies across the narrow valley from his camp in the Albaicín, and claims that he fled, abandoning his own men and his Christian 'friends' to their fate. Meanwhile the Almohads, now fully back in control of the city, were jubilant, and the caliph personally rewarded those who had courageously held out in the Alcazaba with food and weapons. At the same time, severe reprisals were meted out against the Jews for their support for Ibn Mardanish. Many were killed, and those who were not were forced to advertise themselves as being converted Muslims, rather than 'true' Muslims, by wearing distinctive clothing and praying separately from other Muslims at a mosque for the converted, which stood on the site of today's Church of

San Juan de los Reyes. The city once known as 'Granada of the Jews' was now without a Jewish community, though unlike the Christians, Jews would return to the city as a settled group during the Nasrid period. Meanwhile, the poet Abu Ja'far, whose jealousy of Uthman's advances towards his lover Hafsa had prompted his part in the rebellion, was executed. Hafsa herself, it appears, left behind her life of poetry for one of teaching and ended her days educating the caliph's daughters in Marrakesh.

With the invasion of Ibn Mardanish's troops behind them, the danger for the Almohad dynasty receded. The severed head of the defeated Christian commander, 'the bald one', had been sent to Cordoba as a warning to other cities in the region not to rebel as Granada had. The stability that followed these events, then, allowed for greater urban development across al-Andalus, and in Granada this meant an expansion from its original Zirid nucleus.[20] Already by the end of the eleventh century, the city had spread down from the Albaicín hill onto the plains around the river Darro. In the twelfth century, under both the Almoravids and the Almohads, this area seems to have become a much more formally integrated part of the city. For example, beyond the wall that stretched along today's Calle San Juan de los Reyes, the neighbourhood known today in Spanish as the Barrio de Axares was further developed. This area differed rather from the typical Moorish layout of irregular, winding thoroughfares; instead, roads ran straight and in parallel down from the walls to the river. The easiest way to see this pattern today is to walk towards the Paseo de los Tristes and take any of the streets on the left after the Church of San Pedro y San Pablo.

Further into the centre of modern-day Granada, the walls of the lower part of the city were completed, and building continued on the main mosque begun by the Zirids, where the Almoravids extended and embellished the original structure with marble columns brought from Cordoba.[21] An Egyptian apothecary visiting the city in the fifteenth century would describe the great beauty of these columns, but he was most surprised by what he saw on the outside of the mosque: crowning the main minaret, instead of the usual Islamic crescent moon motif, stood a rooster with its wings spread, which locals claimed was a talisman for the city and prevented strong winds that could lead to the destruction of Granada's beautiful architecture. This most important of buildings in mediaeval Granada was at the heart of its commercial district and remained standing until the early eighteenth century, despite being turned into a church soon after the Reconquista.

Also in the twelfth century, construction of the city spread further over onto the left bank of the river Darro into what is now the Realejo district.[22] Whilst the manufacture of ceramics had taken place in this area since Zirid times, during this century the potteries moved further away from the river to around today's Calle Solares. Meanwhile, on the site of the former kilns a mosque and Arab baths were built, the remains of which still exist beneath the current Colegio de las Mercedarias. This area of the city, to the south of the Darro, was also to become the location for other industries, such as the tanneries in the area around the later Corral del Carbón, and the brick-makers' district around the Bab al-Tawwabin. And, in parts of this area, the thirteenth century also witnessed the laying out of *huertas*, or city gardens and agricultural spaces, making use of the Acequia Gorda constructed during Zirid times to channel water to irrigate the land. One residential building that survives from this period in the Realejo district, although much altered over time, is the Casa de los Girones.

The lack of strong historical evidence for the appearance of Granada under either the Almoravids or the Almohads makes it difficult to definitively declare which parts of the city stem from which period. Furthermore, buildings from early Nasrid times could easily have been started earlier, under the Almohads. One recent exciting find from the Almohad period, however, was unearthed during underground construction work on Granada's metro system. In what is now the Alcázar Genil metro station on the Camino de Ronda, passengers find themselves surrounded by the remains of a large, early-thirteenth-century water tank that is believed to have been used for mock naval battles staged for the entertainment of the city's rulers.[23] The Alcázar Genil itself was, in Muslim times, a palace situated beyond the city walls amidst gardens and agricultural land. Remodelled and much used by the later Nasrid dynasty, one intricately decorated section of the original building remains, on the left bank of the Genil, hidden amidst modern housing developments.

By the early thirteenth century, then, Granada was a substantial city of essentially two parts: a densely populated area with a growing commercial district, from the original Alcazaba on the Albaicín hill running down to the flatlands on the right bank of the Darro; and other parts of the city, including the left bank of the Darro, inhabited in part by artisans and increasingly characterised by urban gardens. Yet, as with other cities across al-Andalus, Granada was about to be thrown into turmoil by the swift downfall of yet another dynasty.

The encounter in 1212 known in the West as the Battle of Las Navas de Tolosa was a major turning point in the fortunes of al-Andalus. The Almohads, led by their caliph, were dealt a crushing defeat by the combined Christian forces of Castile, Aragon, and Navarre, who, according to the story, were led by a shepherd across the Despeñaperros Pass, to the north of Jaen, to launch a surprise attack on the Almohads' mountain camp. The caliph fled home to Marrakesh in defeat and died a short time later, leaving behind a succession crisis in the Maghreb and causing the once tightly knit Almohad dynasty to begin to unravel. As those Berber warriors concentrated their defences on their North African territories, on the Iberian Peninsula the cities of al-Andalus were left to fend for themselves against the threatening presence of the northern Christian kingdoms. Over the next few years, these cities were to lose faith in the remaining Almohads, rising up instead in favour of local leaders, effectively bringing about a third taifa period, with different regions again ruled by different leaders. The most notable of the warlords to emerge at this time was Ibn Hud of Murcia, who was, for a time, to win control over much of al-Andalus, including, at times, Granada.

Ibn Hud's task of holding Muslim lands together was far from easy. Although for some time the northern kingdoms of Leon and Castile failed to capitalise on the spectacular victory at Las Navas de Tolosa, caught up in problems between themselves and therefore unable to launch a further united assault against al-Andalus, raids on Muslim territory continued. Granada itself directly experienced the fear and turmoil of Christian attack when, in June 1225, Ferdinand III of Castile penetrated deep into Muslim territory and, in the process of taking nearby Loja, ravaged the Vega surrounding the city.[24] But it would be in 1230 that the Christian threat would truly loom large again, when Ferdinand finally reunited the crowns of Leon and Castile, a year later adding Galicia to his kingdom. These northern kingdoms, now united under one king, seized the advantage and forayed ever deeper into Muslim territory. As had happened under previous taifa rulers, taxes had to be raised as Ibn Hud, like kings before him, agreed to pay the Christians *parias*. Once again, these taxes were resented, and as a consequence Ibn Hud's leadership skills began to be questioned.

Worse, however, was that despite Ibn Hud's deals with the king of Castile, Christian attacks continued, and these attacks were at their worst on the northern borders of al-Andalus. It is therefore no surprise that the main rival to Ibn Hud would emerge in this region. Muhammad Yusuf ibn Nasr ibn al-Ahmar was a farmer in the town of Arjona to the north of Jaen, a region bordering Castile. Born at the end of the twelfth century, like many in his town he became well-versed in fighting the Christians, not only defending al-Andalus, but also taking part in cross-border raids into enemy territory. At first, it appears, he was an ally of Ibn Hud in the battles against the Christians; however, as Ibn Hud's ability to protect Muslim lands fell into serious doubt, here was a rival with a healthy reputation for defending the Moors against their infidel assailants. Indeed, such were Ibn al-Ahmar's military successes on the northern borders that in 1232, his native town of Arjona declared him king.[25]

Thus in the small town of Arjona began the Nasrid dynasty, soon to have a profound impact on the city of Granada. Yet Ibn al-Ahmar's ascendancy was not immediate; Ibn Hud remained strong, but with the Murcian leader's popularity starting to decrease, a number of cities began to look elsewhere for leaders to protect them. This allowed Ibn al-Ahmar to seize control of a number of cities across al-Andalus, including briefly Cordoba and Seville. It appears, though, that Ibn al-Ahmar's inexperience of non-military leadership did not go down well in the city of Cordoba, where the people considered him to be a harsh ruler, and he was soon kicked out of the city to be replaced once again by Ibn Hud—an act that would have consequences later for the former capital of al-Andalus. Meanwhile, Ibn al-Ahmar withdrew to a small territory comprising parts of Jaen and the city of Guadix, watching for further opportunities to defeat his Muslim rival.

Once again in the history of al-Andalus, fighting between taifa kings would strengthen Christian forces. The Christian territories were united; the Muslim territories were in disarray. And the rivalry between Ibn al-Ahmar and Ibn Hud was stronger than their desire to stand together against the Christians.

Indeed, like taifa kings before them, both were willing to ally themselves individually with the Christians to achieve power over a rival. This can be seen most dramatically in 1236 when, in a bid to weaken his opponent, Ibn al-Ahmar refused to come to the aid of Ibn Hud as he tried to defend Cordoba against Ferdinand III. In not intervening, perhaps due in part also to the fact that Cordoba's citizens had turned against him just a few years earlier, Ibn al-Ahmar watched from the side-lines as the end came to more than 500 years of Islamic rule in the once glorious Umayyad capital city of al-Andalus. Yet, through his inaction, he was able to elicit a truce with Ferdinand that would allow him to consolidate his own territories and strengthen his hand against Ibn Hud.

It would be the sudden, brutal death of Ibn Hud, however, that would bring about the final victory of Ibn al-Ahmar. According to Ibn Idhari, a historian writing a century after the events, the Murcian leader was murdered in Almeria by one of his men, who had turned against him over a shared attraction towards a Christian slave girl. As Ibn Hud was directed by his rival to the baths where he was told he would find the girl, he was leapt upon by four men and drowned.[26] This dramatic turn of events in early 1238 made it clear to the Moors who had the upper hand in the battle for al-Andalus. The leaders of Malaga and Granada soon pledged their allegiance to Ibn al-Ahmar; Almeria would follow shortly afterwards. With support for Ibn al-Ahmar from these three cities, and amidst all the turmoil with other parts of al-Andalus continuing to fall to the Christians, paradoxically, and in a way no-one would have dared to predict, Granada was about to enter its golden age.

4

THE NASRIDS

FOUNDATION OF A DYNASTY

In 1371, a century and a half after the fall of the Almohads, with the Nasrid dynasty at its height, a distinguished traveller furtively boarded a boat on the coast south of Granada and sailed across to North Africa. This was no ordinary man and no ordinary crossing. The traveller was Ibn al-Khatib, friend, advisor, and chief vizier of Muhammad V of Granada. This great politician, who had presided over the administration of Granada and whose poetry adorned the walls of the magnificent Nasrid Palaces of the Alhambra, appears to have been fleeing for his life. At the rival Marinid court in Fez he sought and was granted asylum, whilst back in Granada he was tried *in absentia* for heresy and treason, the many enemies he had made over the years relishing the opportunity to bring the great man down. For a time, Ibn al-Khatib was given refuge by the Marinids and spent his days adding to his already prolific writing on the history of the city of Granada. However, his luck was not to last. In 1374, this celebrated man of culture met a brutal end; after being tried again in Fez, he was strangled in his prison cell. The final treachery was committed at the behest of Ibn al-Khatib's former pupil and protégé Ibn Zamrak, whose poems are inscribed alongside those of his deposed master on the walls of the Alhambra. In a final indignity, the day after Ibn al-Khatib's burial, his body was exhumed, burned, and tossed into a ditch.

It is impossible to understand the Nasrid dynasty of Granada without knowing the story of Ibn al-Khatib. His many histories of the city provide us with much of the knowledge we have of Granada up until the second half of the fourteenth century, and he oversaw its administration during its greatest era. Yet this writer, poet, and statesman of such standing in the final kingdom of al-Andalus is barely known to students of Western history. Just over a century after his death, the society he left such an indelible impression upon had ceased to exist. The Nasrids' northern enemies, the kingdoms of Castile and Aragon, had united and concluded their conquest of the Muslim lands of al-Andalus. And for many centuries outside of the Arab world, Ibn al-Khatib's legacy would fade into obscurity.

In contrast to Ibn al-Khatib, Ibn Khaldun, his contemporary and another Arab intellectual, was to enjoy a renown for his work that continues to this day. Considered by many to be the father of sociology, Ibn Khaldun was both a friend and, on occasion, an intellectual rival of Ibn al-Khatib, and he too spent time at the Nasrid court in Granada. After Ibn al-Khatib's death, Ibn Khaldun was to live with Berber tribes in the North African desert, analysing how dynasties rise and then fall, his theories going on to inspire many a great thinker from both East and West. He suggested dynasties tend to be founded by hardy stalwarts, capable of graft and enduring hardship, then lead on to a middle period marked by intense productivity, culture, and enlightenment. Finally, the dynasty declines through decadence and decay, allowing new hardy stalwarts to overthrow one dynasty and begin another. This trajectory could well describe the rise and fall of the

Nasrid dynasty that Ibn Khaldun was, for a short time, to serve. The early period of the Nasrids was marked by a monarch establishing a state surrounded by enemies, and over time, under successive rulers, Granada became a centre of artistic pursuit and intellectual inquiry. But by the fifteenth century, decline had set in, its former scholarship and opulence succumbing to bitter infighting which would allow its eventual conquest by the united Christian kingdoms of Castile and Aragon.

The founder of the Nasrids, Ibn al-Ahmar, who would reign as Muhammad I, in many ways fit the criteria for a founder of a dynasty as attested by Ibn Khaldun: hardy and willing to sacrifice in order to build a legacy. Ibn al-Khatib writes approvingly of this new monarch for refusing to adopt the opulent trappings of kings, noting that Ibn al-Ahmar was a simple man and a down-to-earth ascetic who scorned greatness, wore rough clothes, and even mended his own sandals.[1] Indeed, even at the moment of his greatest triumph—on his arrival in the city of Granada in the spring of 1238 as its newly proclaimed king—Ibn al-Ahmar was wearing the unadorned clothes of a man more used to battle than pomp and ceremony. In his humble garb, he entered the city as the sun began to set and made his way up to the Albaicín hill, where he was welcomed at the mosque and ushered by the sheikhs of the city to the front to symbolically lead the Friday prayers.[2]

Ibn al-Ahmar installed himself in the Zirid palace within the Alcazaba, a building, sadly, no longer in existence. Having learned from his failed experiences of ruling Cordoba, which had led to his expulsion from the city, in Granada he began to turn himself into an effective and popular king. Twice a week he would give an audience, during which his subjects could come to inform him of injustices and present petitions; thereafter he would ensure that his ministers and advisors acted on what he had heard. He also proved to be a skilful propagandist, placing himself squarely in the tradition of being a righteous leader in the religious sense as well. Arab chroniclers of the Nasrids charted his family's (questionable) descent from the companions of the Prophet Muhammad. He used the religious calendar to his advantage by shrewdly aligning his major achievements with sacred days of the Islamic year. Moreover, he adopted the Arabic motto *wa-la ghalib 'illa Allah* (there is no victor except God), and this would later be inscribed on the walls throughout the Alhambra's palaces.

This is because it was under Ibn al-Ahmar that work began on the foundations of what would become the architectural jewel in the city's crown.[3] An Arab chronicler describes how Ibn al-Ahmar began construction of the Alhambra in the first year of his rule and the speed at which its foundations were laid:

> Ibn al-Ahmar rode out of Granada to the place of the Alhambra, where he cast his eye across the area and marked the foundations of the fort ... The year had not yet ended before the castle had its lofty defensive constructions, and he had brought it water from the river, by constructing for it a dam and an *acequia*.[4]

The pace of this construction was impressive, especially considering how vast a feat of engineering was required to build the Acequia Real—the canal that transported water down from the head of the river Darro to feed and irrigate the Alhambra complex—without which the fortress-city could not have existed as it did. The Sabika hill seems an obvious choice for a military structure given its position high above the surrounding area. Indeed, a fortress had existed on the site even prior to Zirid times. In his memoir, Abdullah ibn Buluggin mentions this fortress and also suggests that Joseph ibn Naghrila, the Jewish vizier he so loathed, had built a palace there to hide and watch his intrigues play out on the Albaicín hill opposite.[5] Later, Abdullah mentions a treasure trove discovered on the hill when the city's fortifications were being strengthened in anticipation of a

Christian or Almoravid invasion. However, it was not until the time of Ibn al-Ahmar that a way was found to supply the hill with the water necessary for a major fortress.

Looking up at the Alhambra, it is not hard to see why Ibn al-Ahmar chose the spot for his seat of power. The building still dominates the city, looking down on everything that surrounds it, a perfect place for a dynasty that would find itself so frequently under attack, both from enemies without and, with increasing frequency, from adversaries within. The first part of the Alhambra to be built and inhabited was the citadel at the western end of the hill. The towers of Ibn al-Ahmar's keep were built to be taller and narrower than any Granada had seen before, thus serving to further amplify the commanding aspect of the building high above the rest of the city.[6] Inside what would become known as the 'new' Alcazaba—to distinguish it from the 'old' Alcazaba in the Albaicín—houses were erected to garrison troops. Although today only the foundations of these barracks can be seen, in Nasrid times this would have been a noisy and densely populated area, with the first Nasrid ruler himself living amongst his men.

The Alhambra in Nasrid times would have impressed the inhabitants as much as it does modern-day visitors to the city, although its appearance would have been somewhat different. As Ibn al-Khatib describes: 'It crowned [the Sabika hill] with its white battlements, its lofty towers, and its inaccessible forts, which dazzle the eyes and overwhelm the faculties of reason.'[7] This reference to white battlements highlights the fact that under the Nasrids, much of the red stone was rendered with lime.[8] The cliffs below would also have appeared very different to the way they do now, as the woods as we see them today were not planted until after the Reconquista.[9]

Having established his fortress in Granada, and with Almeria, Malaga, and Jaen comprising the other main cities of his kingdom,

Ibn al-Ahmar became the most powerful Muslim leader remaining in the face of the Christian threat. However, even then, stability for Granada was not yet on the cards; in fact, far from it. Other areas of al-Andalus that remained under Moorish control, for example Murcia, were still being subjected to repeated attacks by Christian forces, and it was therefore essential for Ibn al-Ahmar to find a way to survive the continued onslaught. Paradoxically, this survival was to come through an attack that took place in 1245, when Ferdinand III laid siege to Jaen, then still a part of Ibn al-Ahmar's territory. Unable to resupply the inhabitants despite heroic efforts, by 1246 Granada's Moors conceded defeat and agreed to come to terms with the Christians. It must have been a painful task for Ibn al-Ahmar to visit the Castilian king. The *First General Chronicle of Spain*, compiled a generation later, describes the scene:

> The king of Granada along with his Moors ... seeing no other route so beneficial to be able to establish their honour and their dignity and in order to free his Moors and his land from destruction ... came to put himself directly in the power of the King Don Fernando and at his mercy, and he kissed the hand and became a vassal in this way.[10]

Whilst this capitulation to the king of Castile may, at first, have seemed a humiliation for Ibn al-Ahmar, as it turned out it was a highly astute move. Although in giving up Jaen to keep his hold on Granada Ibn al-Ahmar rendered his tiny emirate officially a vassal of Castile, the Nasrid dynasty was able to consolidate its position from that point forward with clear boundaries for the kingdom.[11] There were, however, obligations the Moors of Granada had to fulfil for their Christian overlords. Just as his predecessors had done before him, Ibn al-Ahmar agreed to the payment of *parias*. He was also required, when asked, to send troops to assist the Castilians in battle. None of the conditions could have been more painful than the last. In 1248, Granada was compelled to send men to support Ferdinand's attack on

Seville, which culminated in the loss of another of al-Andalus's great Moorish cities to the Christians.

By the 1250s, almost all of the territory of the once mighty Caliphate of al-Andalus had been reduced to a mere coastal strip stretching from Gibraltar in the west, through the mountains and up to just past Almeria in the east, with the city of Granada strategically located at its centre and in a key defensive position. The Castilian advance halted at this point owing to a desire on the part of the new king of Castile, Alfonso X, to focus on conquest in North Africa, in which he believed the emir of Granada, as his vassal, could help. Alfonso's wide-ranging ambitions, which also included a relentless campaign to be named Holy Roman Emperor, assisted Ibn al-Ahmar greatly in giving him time to settle his kingdom. In many ways, it would be the relationship between these two complex monarchs that would set the framework for future relationships between the rulers of Granada and of Castile.

Alfonso has been given the historical epithet of 'the Wise' for his poetry and astrology, as well as for his patronage of intellectuals at his cosmopolitan court, where Christian, Jewish, and Muslim ideas intermingled, producing important works of high culture.[12] Yet Alfonso was not always so wise when it came to his dealings with others, and perhaps here the label of astute leader would be better applied to Ibn al-Ahmar. Under Castile's new king, Granada's emir continued to play the role of obedient vassal. Yet it is clear from subsequent events that he was always determined to release Granada from its vassal status. Ibn al-Ahmar's ability to read his counterpart well meant that he never lost awareness of Alfonso's deep desire to capture the last outpost of al-Andalus, despite the seemingly cordial relationship, at first, between the two kings. An Arab chronicler records how Ibn al-Ahmar would meet with Alfonso every year on the outskirts of Seville, to deliver gifts and discuss affairs of mutual interest.[13]

However, Ibn al-Ahmar was not always obedient to Alfonso's demands for aid in his military endeavours, something that angered the Castilian king. In one of their subsequent annual visits to Seville, Granada's entourage found themselves fenced into their accommodation by the Christians, an incident that would become the spur for Ibn al-Ahmar to openly rebel.[14]

This rebellion began in 1264, when Ibn al-Ahmar roused the Muslims living in recently conquered areas of al-Andalus along the borders of his realm to rise up against their new Christian rulers and to recognise him as king. This mass rebellion became known as the 'Revolt of the Mudéjars', Mudéjars being the term used for Muslims living under Christian rule.[15] And for a while this rebellion was a major threat to the new Castilian territories, with towns such as Jerez, so recently brought under Christian rule, now recaptured by their Muslim inhabitants. The revolt lasted for almost two years and saw mercenaries from North Africa brought over to support their fellow Muslims. These fighters, known as the Volunteers of the Faith, went on to form an essential element of Nasrid Granada's army for the next century. Their origins were in the tribal areas of Morocco, and although they were garrisoned in various towns around the kingdom, they would make a lasting impression on the capital, with suggestions that the name of their tribe—the Zenata—was given to the area of Zenete, just below the old Alcazaba.[16]

Despite the intervention of these mercenaries, the Revolt of the Mudéjars ultimately failed. This was largely due to the overwhelming power imbalance in favour of Castile. Christian forces counterattacked, and as the rebellious towns were pacified, the Mudéjars were expelled from their homes, which produced a wave of refugees who poured into the city of Granada. Meanwhile, Ibn al-Ahmar's involvement in inciting the Mudéjars' revolt gave Alfonso all the excuse he needed to recommence hostilities with the emirate. To aid in this, he began to seek potential allies inside Granada itself who would be ready to turn against Ibn al-Ahmar. This did not prove too difficult for Alfonso; he soon discovered the willingness of a disgruntled branch of the Nasrid ruling class based in Malaga, the Banu Ashqilula, to side against their ruler.

Close relatives of Ibn al-Ahmar, the Banu Ashqilula had been important allies during the emir's battles against his rival Ibn Hud in the years prior to the establishment of the Nasrid Kingdom of Granada. However, they had become disillusioned with him during the Mudéjar revolt—so much so that they were now prepared to side with the Castilians against him. Yet, once again in the ongoing rivalry between Alfonso and Ibn al-Ahmar, Granada's emir would find the opportunity to act likewise and meddle in Castile's internal affairs. In the late 1260s, a group of disgruntled nobles at Alfonso's court—including the king's own brother Felipe—approached Ibn al-Ahmar to ask for his support in a dispute that was taking place between the Castilian lords and their king. In exchange for their backing against the Banu Ashqilula, Ibn al-Ahmar pledged them his support, and in 1272 these rebel noblemen sought sanctuary in Granada, where they were housed in palaces around the Vega.

In January 1273, Ibn al-Ahmar died after falling from his horse.[17] The founder of the Nasrids left behind a kingdom that had risen from the ashes as the rest of al-Andalus fell. Yet he also bequeathed to his heir unresolved problems surrounding the kingdom's relationship with Castile, in addition to the continued internal threat to his dynasty from the rebel clan in Malaga. However, Ibn al-Ahmar was fortunate in being able to leave his throne to an experienced successor—the thirty-eight-year-old Muhammad II, who had long been at his father's side both in battle and in politics. This experience was crucial as Muhammad now had to address his father's unfinished business: to resolve the dispute with Alfonso concerning the Castilian nobles living in exile in Granada, as well as the conflict with the Banu Ashqilula, still allied with his enemy. It was to tackle these two issues that, early in his reign, Muhammad visited Alfonso at the latter's court in Seville, having gained guarantees that the rebel Castilian nobles who accompanied him would be welcomed with honour. All appeared to go well at first; Alfonso agreed to end his support for the rebels in Malaga in exchange for a tribute, which Muhammad duly paid. Unfortunately, as Granada's new monarch was to learn, Alfonso was not a man to be trusted. He reneged on the deal, taking the money and continuing to back the Banu Ashqilula.

Hoodwinked by the king of Castile, Muhammad needed a new strategy to help protect his kingdom and turned to the Marinids of Morocco for help, even though the previous two centuries had well demonstrated the risk inherent in this strategy. When the eleventh-century taifas had sought support from the Almoravids, the North Africans had soon turned their mission from reinforcement to conquest, and the current rulers across the strait were no less covetous of the remnants of al-Andalus. This resulted in what became a highly complex war over many decades between the Nasrids, the Banu Ashqilula, the Marinids, and the Castilians to gain control over the Strait of Gibraltar, which saw frequent incursions by the Moroccans into southern Castile, and by the Castilians into North Africa. This ongoing conflict would involve frequent changes of alliance, which included, on a number of occasions, the North African Muslims allying with the Christian kingdoms against Granada. However, Muhammad II's military abilities acquired under his father's training were to serve him well, and despite the constant fighting along the coast, he was eventually able to defeat the Banu Ashqilula and win back Malaga. There he placed a loyal member of his family in the position of governor of this port city so important to his kingdom. To cement the family ties,

Muhammad wed his accomplished daughter, Fatima, to the new governor, and within a generation this marriage would produce a new branch of highly cultured Nasrid kings.

By the middle of Muhammad II's reign, then, the Kingdom of Granada had more or less taken on the shape it was to retain until the resumption of the Reconquista under Isabella and Ferdinand in the fifteenth century. Malaga and Almeria were the only other major Andalusi cities left in Muslim territory, and the city of Granada had been established as the capital. Yet the wars between the Marinids, the Castilians, and the Nasrids continued along the Strait of Gibraltar for many years, with battles occasionally taking place inland closer to the city of Granada itself. This meant that the capital's defences had to be strengthened. Key amongst these was a large fortress built around the Gate of the Brick-Makers—Bab al-Tawwabin in Arabic—which would be later known in Spanish as the Castle of Bibataubín. This was constructed to guard the entrance to the city from the direction of the Vega, close to the bridge across the Genil constructed in Zirid times. Sadly, whilst the much-restored bridge continues to be used, the castle was pulled down in the modern era and replaced by an eighteenth-century Baroque building.[18]

The early Nasrids' most important defensive structure, though, was the Alhambra, sitting high atop the Sabika hill. Whilst Ibn al-Ahmar had left behind the beginnings of a mighty military installation, his son Muhammad II would bring another strength to its construction, thanks to something for which the Nasrid dynasty would become renowned: a keen interest in scholarly pursuits and support for intellectual inquiry. Muhammad II was known for his passion for knowledge—Ibn al-Khatib writes admiringly of his poetical abilities—and it was this intellectual side to the emir that led to his sobriquet of *al-faqih*, meaning expert in jurisprudence. Whilst he continued to develop the defensive aspects of the Alhambra, Muhammad's intellectual interests also led him to construct the first of several royal residences within the complex, including the beginnings of the royal pleasure gardens at what would become known as the Generalife. Sadly, the palaces constructed under Muhammad II no longer exist, and neither does another feature of the Alhambra that appeared in Muhammad's reign—the royal cemetery. This was largely destroyed after the Reconquista; however, some of the stone epitaphs, including Muhammad's own, are preserved today in the Alhambra Museum.

By the beginning of the fourteenth century, with its royals, its soldiers, and the growing community of artisans who had moved into the complex to service it, the Alhambra had almost taken on the form of a rival city to the over-populated Albaicín across the river. The overpopulation had been fuelled by the massive influx of refugees from other cities across al-Andalus now fallen under Christian control, and this led to an expansion beyond the traditional boundaries of the city marked by its eleventh-century walls. There is a legend that the name of the Albaicín is derived from the Arabic *al-bayazeen*, meaning the people of Baeza, and that it became so named after the arrival of Muslims fleeing from that city, which lies a few hours north of Granada in today's Jaen province.[19] Estimating populations of these periods without census data is problematic, but it does seem that the emirate as a whole became relatively densely inhabited, numbering perhaps around 300,000 people.[20] Whilst numbers for the city itself are not known, as the capital and largest city, Granada can safely be assumed to have been particularly crowded.

Yet, despite the strain it must surely have caused at first, the arrival of such numbers of fellow Moors seeking the sanctuary of Muslim rule probably helped Granada's survival in the long run. Whereas the former Muslim cities of al-Andalus, such as Seville, became severely depopulated after their fall to the Christians, Granada almost certainly benefitted from waves of labourers, craftsmen, and merchants alike all pouring in. Unlike the Christian territories to the north that were becoming increasingly reliant on the wool trade, Granada's economy appears to have grown more substantial and enjoyed greater diversity, with silk, sugar cane, and dried fruit exports being key sources of income. Granada had its place in international trade; merchants from Genoa played a significant role in the local marketplace throughout the existence of the Emirate of Granada, ensuring Granada's goods were distributed along European trade routes, and naturally Granada had its markets in the North African kingdoms too.

Meanwhile, with a growing economy, early Nasrid Granada experienced the start of a construction boom that was not just there to serve defensive purposes. Alongside the Alhambra, other major building projects were undertaken by the early Nasrids; new palaces popped up around the city, while existing ones were significantly extended and embellished. Many of these buildings, surrounded by gardens and fountains, could be used as a means of pleasurable escape by the royals, at the same time ensuring they were never too far from the centre of government to prevent a swift return if necessary. For example, the Alcázar Genil, first built by the Almohads, was further developed by the Nasrids and used for leisure outside the city. Within the walls, though away from the densely populated parts of the city, the building known today as the Cuarto Real de Santo Domingo was also created as a recreational space. Unfortunately, as with the Alcázar Genil, all that remains of this palace today is one recently restored, beautifully decorated tower.

Yet, as Granada experienced its growth spurt, the first inkling appeared of the animus that would eventually spell the downfall of the Nasrids: deadly divisions within the ruling family itself. In his immense series of biographies of the people of Granada, *al-Ihata*, Ibn al-Khatib suggests that Muhammad II's life was brought to a premature end when in 1302 he ate a poisoned cake sent from the palace of his son and heir.[21] The vizier gives further evidence to suggest that this prince, now Muhammad III, a man afflicted by an eye disease, was inclined towards cruelty, offering a story about his treatment of his father's former guards. The new emir imprisoned these loyal retainers in the dungeons of the Alhambra, forbidding those in charge of their incarceration from giving them food. The guards were forced to hear their prisoners calling out in pain from hunger, and over time the inmates resorted to eating the corpses of their companions as one after another succumbed to starvation. Moved by pity, one of the guards tossed the remaining prisoners a lump of bread, prompting Muhammad to order that that guard's throat be slit above the entrance to the dungeons so his blood would rain down onto the unfortunate captives below.[22]

As with many of Granada's kings, this gruesome tale illustrates but one side of Muhammad III, because alongside his alleged cruelty he had a deep love of poetry. Indeed, Ibn al-Khatib tells us, the problems with his eyes came about as a result of his passion for reading, which he often indulged late into the night by candlelight. It was this poetic and artistic side to the king that led to new contributions to the Alhambra complex that placed an even greater emphasis on art and beauty. One of the earliest of the celebrated Nasrid Palaces of the Alhambra still in existence today was built during Muhammad III's reign: the picturesque Palacio del Partal, sitting at the head of a large rectangular pool and emulating in many ways earlier palaces from around the Muslim world. And it must have been Muhammad's passion for poetry that led compositions to be incorporated into the interior walls of the Royal Palaces, because it was during his reign that one of the first great poet-viziers of the Alhambra, Ibn al-Jayyab—a predecessor of and teacher to Ibn al-Khatib—began his ascent of the political ladder. During this reign, too, the Alhambra was to become much more of a large settlement in itself. The main mosque was built on the site of what is now the Church of Santa María de la Alhambra; its baths for performing ritual ablutions can still be visited today. Meanwhile, a road was built linking the newly erected Puerta del Vino with the large area of the complex allocated for non-military residents. Artisans and shopkeepers lived and worked at the most easterly end of the complex, which now lies almost completely in ruins and where visitors to the site today enter from the ticket office on their way to visiting the Nasrid Palaces.

Whilst the building of the renowned Alhambra palaces took off under Muhammad III's reign, this period was also to see another recurrent theme of the Nasrid era emerge, namely the precarious position of its viziers. With the emir's eye disease becoming progressively more debilitating, more and more power was placed in the hands of his vizier—Ibn al-Hakim. And like all men in power, Ibn al-Hakim was not without his rivals ready to bring him down. As the vizier oversaw the continual battles between Granada and its various enemies, those waiting in the wings were quick to find fault. This, coupled with Muhammad's reputed cruelty, appears to have been the spur for rebellion, when in 1309 the emir's half-brother, Nasr, led a coup against him. The people of Granada were encouraged to storm the Alhambra, where they looted and pillaged the properties of Ibn al-Hakim before lynching the minister himself. Muhammad's fate was less bloody; he was forced to abdicate and was sent into exile in Almuñecar.

Nasr seized a country at war with each of its enemies—Castile, Aragon, and the Marinids of North Africa—and his reign would be marked by frequent battles along the coast. Ultimately this would see Nasr signing treaties with the Castilians, which, along with the fact that his mother had been a Christian slave, would rouse the hostility of his subjects and cause a decline in his popularity. Worse still, in terms of his reputation, was his attachment to his Christian-born minister, who would grace the court dressed in Castilian attire. But it wasn't just his perceived closeness to the Christians that stirred the suspicions of those around him at court. Like his poetry-obsessed brother before him, Nasr was passionate about intellectual enquiry. His particular obsession was with astronomy, and, as Ibn al-Khatib tells us, his skills were such that he created his own charts and tables of the stars, as well as making incredible apparatus for his hobby with his own hands.[23] However, this passion was rumoured to be drawing the emir away from affairs of state. Such became his unpopularity that a group of courtiers attempted to restore the sickly Muhammad III to the throne, bringing him back to court from his coastal exile. However, Nasr was not to be outmanoeuvred. Muhammad was soon found dead in his home, drowned in a water tank at the behest of the king. But even with one sibling out of the way, Nasr's rivals to the throne remained. And this time it would be a sister who caused him trouble.

Fatima bint al-Ahmar had married the governor of Malaga after the defeat of the Banu Ashqilula to secure the relationship between the capital and the emirate's most important port. Fatima, like her brother Muhammad III and her half-brother Nasr, was renowned for her thirst for knowledge.[24] It would now be her family who would play the decisive role in the downfall of Nasr. Like many a princess before and after, her father had used her to strengthen alliances in his kingdom, but like many highly educated women at the time, unable to take the highest office herself, she played a key role behind the scenes. She is believed to have encouraged first her husband and then her son to lay siege to Granada to depose its unpopular king following Nasr's murder of Muhammad. The initial attempts to take Granada by her husband were unsuccessful. Although Nasr suffered defeat on the field of battle in front of the city walls, his horse becoming bogged down in the mud, the emir managed to sprint back to the city and close the gates on his attackers.

Yet it was clear to the Malaga branch of the Nasrids that Granada was ripe for rebellion, the next attempts on the capital being made by Fatima's son Ismail. This time, the people of the city rose up to show their support for this challenger to the throne. Ibn al-Khatib relates how the common people of the Albaicín, tired of Nasr's rule, climbed to the top of the city's minarets, the roofs of their houses, and the hills and urged Ismail on, soon storming down to the Puerta de Elvira, where they smashed the locks to allow him to enter their city.[25] Ismail lodged himself in the old Alcazaba in the Albaicín, with Nasr holed up in the Alhambra on the opposite hill. It soon became apparent that despite the strong defences surrounding him, the emir no longer had the support of the people. The standoff came to an end with Nasr accepting exile in Guadix, leaving Ismail to take the throne in February 1314. Nasr would remain for the rest of his life a thorn in Ismail's side, continually intriguing with the Castilians against the new emir's rule.

Despite Nasr's persistent meddling, Ismail's reign was to mark the beginnings of that middle dynastic period proposed by the historian Ibn Khaldun, when greater emphasis is given to culture and refinement, and this would be particularly demonstrated through the additions made to the Alhambra during his rule.[26] These included improvements to its fortifications: to the Alcazaba were added the Torre de las Armas and within that the Puerta de las Armas, the gate that became the principal entrance to the citadel for anyone approaching from the city. The path up would have passed through the district now known as La Churra, then home to the Volunteers of the Faith. In addition, following on from the work begun by earlier kings, Ismail greatly transformed the Generalife, very much turning it into a separate leisure area across from the Alhambra. Its palace was remodelled with courtyards and water features, and prominence was given to Ibn al-Jayyab's poetry on the walls, much of which eulogises the link between the beauty of the buildings and the majesty of the king:

Palace of marvellous perfection and beauty,
In which the sultan's majesty shines.
Clear are his qualities, radiant his light,
The clouds stream away before his plenteous generosity.
An inventive hand stitched on its walls
Embroidery like the flowers in the garden.[27]

Ismail's reign was not only one of increasing culture. He also proved himself on the battlefield by dealing one of the most famous military defeats to the Christians of the Nasrid era. Known in Spanish history as *La desastre de la Vega de Granada*, Ismail's stunning victory took place near Pinos Puente in June 1319 and, as the name suggests, was a shameful defeat for the Castilians. Both the regents of Alfonso XI of Castile—his uncle Don Pedro and his great-uncle Don Juan—were killed in combat, and the Nasrids took full advantage of this defeat by signing favourable treaties with their northern enemies.

Despite the emir's successes, however, as was becoming commonplace among Granada's emirs, Ismail's reign was cut short when he was murdered, in this case by his cousin in what appears to have been a rivalry over a slave girl. The bloody assassination took place in 1325 right in the heart of the Royal Palaces of the Alhambra. Accompanied by a group of his friends, the cousin approached the emir seemingly to give him a customary embrace, but as he did so he pulled out a dagger concealed within his clothes and stabbed him three times, one thrust cutting the artery above the king's collarbone. As Ismail fell to the floor screaming in pain, his vizier ran in but was overpowered by the companions of the assassin. As more guards arrived, the rebels were forced to flee the Alhambra, but it appears the city acted with haste to prevent their escape. The roads were blocked off and the assassins were murdered by the people of the city, their bodies hung up around the walls.

Ismail would soon die of his injuries, his throne inherited by his ten-year-old son, Muhammad IV, who would also meet his death at the hands of assassins just eight years later. Granada, then, was developing a pattern of both monarchs and viziers meeting violent ends, and this bloody saga would continue through much of the rest of the Nasrid period. Nevertheless, in spite of this, following the murder of Muhammad IV the crown passed to his brother Yusuf, and it would be under his rule, and later under Yusuf's son Muhammad V, that Granada truly reached the heights of its splendour.

5

THE NASRIDS

SPLENDOUR AND DECLINE

The reigns of Yusuf I and, later, his son Muhammad V mark the high point of the Nasrid dynasty; the magnificent buildings that date from this period are a testament to the extent to which art and architecture flourished under these two rulers. Ibn al-Khatib was to serve both, starting with Yusuf, about whom he writes with great admiration:

[The sultan] was of a fair and luminous beauty, with a fine figure, beautifully proportioned, with sparkling eyes, long black hair, and an attractive thick beard.

He continues with a description of Yusuf's intelligence and sense of culture:

His speech was sweet and pleasant to hear ... he was of great intelligence, showing great dignity and a keenness of thought ... he excelled in many of the practical arts, was inclined towards peace ... was passionate about architecture, clothes, and collecting jewels and other treasures.[1]

Such a love of art and culture, said to have been instilled in him by his grandmother Fatima bint al-Ahmar, was to have a profound impact on the city of Granada, and as it prospered under both Yusuf and Muhammad, there was a great flowering of literature within the Alhambra. Three viziers under these two monarchs would be immortalised as poets, their verses forever etched into the very walls of the palaces in which they served. These poet-viziers were Ibn al-Jayyab, Ibn al-Khatib, and Ibn Zamrak.

This trio of statesmen-poets thrived during the construction boom that took place under Yusuf and his son that saw some of the Alhambra's finest buildings erected. Among the most magnificent of these from Yusuf's reign are the Puerta de la Justicia and the majestic Torre de Comares, festooned with the poems of both Ibn al-Jayyab and Ibn al-Khatib.[2] The former had already achieved the distinction of having his verses adorn the palaces of earlier monarchs within the Alhambra complex, and it would be his protégé, Ibn al-Khatib, who would take the blending of politics, writing, and art to a new level. This future historian of Granada came to Ibn al-Jayyab's attention as a young boy when his father was working at the court. He received a wide-ranging education from some of the western Islamic world's foremost scholars, studying subjects including law, language, literature, medicine, and philosophy; and it was under the watchful eye of Ibn al-Jayyab himself that Ibn al-Khatib was schooled in and developed his love for poetry. It is clear that Ibn al-Khatib was held in high esteem by both the emir and his vizier, for whilst the walls of the earlier buildings of Yusuf's reign display the work of Ibn al-Jayyab, as time moved on, Ibn al-Khatib's poetry also began to be added.[3]

It was not just inside the Alhambra complex that Yusuf would make his mark. Beyond the citadel, the visionary emir was also responsible for the founding of one of Granada's most prestigious institutions: the Madraza. Built in 1349 right in the heart of the commercial district, next to the main mosque, the Madraza became a major institution of learning, teaching theology, philosophy, language, and literature, and also provided accommodation for its students. It attracted to Granada teachers of the calibre that had been involved in the education of Ibn al-Khatib, though it was not only its pre-eminent scholars that brought the Madraza fame; the beauty of the building itself drew people from far and wide. Ibn al-Khatib describes the institution as 'unique in terms of its splendour and elegance'.[4] Unfortunately, little of that celebrated charm remains today. The building was given a Baroque makeover during the eighteenth century that has made it now virtually impossible to imagine the beauty of the original Nasrid building, apart from that of one restored room that can be visited inside.

The outer walls of the city that still overlook their surroundings from the very top of the Albaicín hill were also constructed during Yusuf's reign, after Granada had far outgrown its original Zirid defences. The Puerta de Elvira was completely reconstructed, with the original Zirid gate replaced by a larger and better-defended entrance to the city. It became more of a fortress than can be seen from the shell of a gateway that remains today.[5] The city faced the constant threat of attack from Christian forces and these improved defences were essential, particularly the new walls needed to contain the vastly increased population—the result of waves of immigration from other parts of al-Andalus that had fallen to Christian conquest throughout the thirteenth century. Today, walking up the steep path from one of the few remaining gates in the fourteenth-century walls, the Puerta de Fajalauza, to one of the city's most impressive viewing points, the Mirador de San Miguel Alto, it is easy to look over at the original Zirid walls and appreciate the extent of Granada's expansion in Nasrid times. The highest point of the Nasrid walls today is marked by a chapel known as the Hermitage of San Miguel Alto, but it was originally home to a defensive structure known as the Borg al-Zeitun, the tower of the olive tree.

Whilst Granada experienced a building boom during the four-teenth century, and magnificent additions were made to the city, there was also a dark aspect to this period. As it had across the rest of Europe, North Africa, and large parts of Asia, the Black Death struck the city in 1348. Although it appears to have been less devastating in Granada than elsewhere across Europe, it had a direct impact on the administration at the Alhambra when, in January 1349, Ibn al-Jayyab contracted the disease and died. This had a profound effect on Ibn al-Khatib, who always praised his mentor highly, and he later put his medical training to use by writing a treatise based on his observations of the disease.[6] Yet, even after the death of his teacher, Ibn al-Khatib continued his ascent, becoming increasingly valued by both the emir and another highly esteemed vizier, Ridwan, for his celebrated pen-manship, put to use in drawing up some of the court's most important correspondence.

Despite the effects of the bubonic plague, Yusuf I's reign was on the whole a glorious one for Granada. The city's splendour at this time is chronicled by the famous North African traveller Ibn Battuta, who arrived in al-Andalus following years of adventures that had taken him across the Middle East, India, China, and even to the Maldives. He describes Granada as 'the Metropolis of Andalusia and the bride of its cities' and claims that its environs were without equal anywhere in the world:[7] high praise from so prolific a traveller. His admiration for Granada stemmed primar-ily from its 'orchards, gardens, flowery meads, noble buildings and vineyards'.[8] He gives particular mention to the Fuente de Aynadamar—the source of the water supply to the Albaicín, located in the hills behind the city—which he claims to have been unparalleled in its beauty. Unfortunately, it seems he was unable to meet Yusuf, who was suffering from an illness during Ibn Battuta's time in Granada, which would explain why the great traveller did not visit and subsequently detail the wonders of the Alhambra.

It was not only foreign visitors who were enchanted by Granada; its residents themselves also appreciated the beauty of their surroundings. Ibn al-Khatib paints a glowing picture of the standard of living of Granada at the time, describing its abundant productivity, which allowed even the poor to eat well as the surrounding countryside kept the markets stocked throughout the year. He provides physical descriptions of the people themselves, including of their clothes and how these were made. He also talks of the celebrations that took place each year, the people in their finery, the rich heavily adorned with precious stones, all going out into the Vega during the vine harvest to celebrate with their families and their servants.[9]

But the instability within the ruling family cast an ever-present shadow over the Nasrids, even during Granada's golden age in the mid-fourteenth century. Yusuf's reign ended abruptly in 1354 while he was attending the mosque on the festival of Eid al-Fitr. Ibn al-Khatib relates with horror the fate of such an esteemed monarch: it seems a man suddenly threw himself upon Yusuf as he prayed, stabbing him with a dagger. Immediately the emir was surrounded by his entourage, who carried him back over the heads of the crowd to his palace, where he died shortly afterwards. His loyal subjects took vengeance on the murderer, it is said, tearing him apart and throwing him onto a fire. Aside from the suggestion that the killer was insane, no explanation has been offered as to why this popular ruler was murdered.

The question of who would succeed Yusuf led, over the next few years, to another internal struggle for the throne. Yusuf had had two wives, Buthayna and Mariam, both born as slaves. Mariam is reputed to have been the more scheming of the two and wished her eldest son, Ismail, to become king. However, on the sudden death of Yusuf, the vizier Ridwan chose the fourteen-year-old Muhammad, son of Buthayna, who became Muhammad V. Mariam and her children were banished to one of the towers of the Alhambra to live in a gilded prison, where, it would later be learned, they plotted with the husband of Mariam's daughter, a man named Abu Abdullah, to overthrow Muhammad. Meanwhile, the new king surrounded himself with close advisors, including Ridwan and Ibn al-Khatib.

The reign of Muhammad V marked the zenith of the Nasrid era, despite being split into two discrete periods. This occurred because in August 1359, as Ibn al-Khatib describes it, a hundred men under the leadership of Abu Abdullah scaled the walls of the Alhambra in the dead of night. Their climb was aided by some scaffolding protruding from a half-constructed building, and when they reached the top of the walls, they were easily able to silence the guards. As they entered the complex, pandemonium ensued. Amidst the shouting and scuffling, the attackers broke into the home of Ridwan and stabbed him to death in full view of his family before ransacking his house. Mariam and her family, meanwhile, were released from their prison tower. Ismail, Muhammad's half-brother, was mounted on a horse by the rebels and, to cheers and the beating of drums, proclaimed Ismail II. However, there was a complication: Muhammad was not inside the Alhambra that night. Instead, he was across in the Generalife and, alerted to the coup in progress by the commotion coming from the Alhambra, he escaped on horseback, galloping across the hills to nearby Guadix, where he was able to take stock of the situation.

For a while there was a standoff: Ismail reigned in Granada while Muhammad remained a threatening presence in Guadix. Yet Muhammad had little hope of reclaiming his kingdom, until a childhood friend rescued him in his hour of need. As a boy during his father's reign, Muhammad had become close to a young exile from North Africa living in Granada. That childhood bond was to become invaluable with Muhammad now in exile himself, all the more so since his friend had risen to become the

Marinid sultan, Abu Salim. Hearing of Muhammad's misfortune, the sultan sent word to Guadix that his old friend would be welcome at his court in Fez. Thus, on 4 November 1359, the deposed monarch set sail, taking with him some of his supporters, including Ibn al-Khatib and the vizier's young protégé, an aspiring poet and politician named Ibn Zamrak.

Ibn al-Khatib made an immediate impression on the Marinid court, reciting a great ode to Abu Salim. It was at this point that Ibn Khaldun, the great historian and thinker considered by many to be the father of sociology, first met Ibn al-Khatib, and he later recalled how the ode brought tears to the eyes of those who heard it.[10] The friendship between the pair that developed from that point was such as would be expected between two intellectuals of great character and ambition in similar fields. At times their relationship was one of rapport and admiration, yet at others it showed signs of envy and rivalry. Nonetheless, in their writing both displayed the highest regard for one another. Indeed, it was Ibn Khaldun who, in less happy times to come, would plead with Granada's king to spare the life of his friend.

Back in Granada, it was not long before the palace coup was revealed for what it really was: a plot by the unscrupulous Abu Abdullah to seize the throne for himself. In the summer of 1360, Ismail and his brother Qays were murdered at the Alhambra and Abu Abdullah declared himself emir, to rule as Muhammad VI. Known to the Castilians as El Rey Bermejo, in reference to his red beard, he was considered a coarse man with little sense of dignity. He also lacked the political talent of his exiled rival. Despite a change of ruler in Fez, the deposed Muhammad V continued to receive the favours of the Marinids, who helped him return across the strait and set up a base at Ronda from which to attack Granada and attempt to recover his throne. Abu Abdullah, meanwhile, had ceased paying the traditional *parias* to Castile and instead allied himself with Aragon, an act which guaranteed the enmity of King Peter 'the Cruel' of Castile.

Peter was much criticised by his enemies at the time for his great interest in and affinity for the Moors, an admiration most visible architecturally in his monumental contribution to Seville, the Alcázar. This fourteenth-century palace, built on the site of an earlier Islamic building, was constructed with the assistance of builders and architects from the Alhambra, sent by Peter's ally Muhammad V before he was deposed. These skilled men enabled Peter to produce a palace straight out of the Orient, replete with Arabic inscriptions mimicking those of the Nasrid Palaces in Granada. And this Christian palace, built in large part by Muslims, was to have its own influence in return on the Alhambra by way of the Christian techniques learned by the Muslim builders during their time in Seville. This is because it was Peter's support for Muhammad V against Abu Abdullah that would allow the restoration to the throne of the man who would become one of the Alhambra's greatest architectural patrons.

When Muhammad V returned to the Iberian Peninsula, therefore, he had the support not only of the Marinid sultan, but also of the king of Castile. In search of allies, the usurper Muhammad VI paid a visit to the Castilian court in Seville and, ignorant of Peter's support for Muhammad V, plied the king with jewels and demonstrations of his loyalty. Peter played the part of an interested potential ally to begin with and honoured his visiting guests with a feast. But as they sat down to eat, they were suddenly leapt upon by the palace guard, arrested, and stripped of all their possessions. Two days later, dressed in scarlet and riding an ass, the pretender Muhammad VI was led out onto a field, where he is said to have been killed at the hands of the king of Castile himself. As a mark of friendship, Peter sent the head of El Rey Bermejo, along with those of thirty-seven of his supporters, to Muhammad V.[11] With the death of his rival in that spring of 1362, Muhammad V rode back into the city of Granada and reclaimed his throne, later returning to Peter some Castilian prisoners captured in earlier battles as a mark of his gratitude.

The restored Muhammad V would go on to rule for another thirty years, and these were in general peaceful and prosperous for Granada. For much of the period, Castile was embroiled in either civil war or conflicts with other Christian kingdoms, and Muhammad was able to take advantage of these to ward off attacks on his realm. Also presiding over the early years of this period was the emir's right hand, the formidable Ibn al-Khatib. From subsequent events we can draw conclusions about the type of power held by this vizier, because he clearly made numerous enemies throughout the kingdom who bided their time for a chance to bring about his downfall. Indeed, in his writing Ibn al-Khatib himself describes the immense wealth he accumulated over his years in power at the Alhambra, which would surely have roused the envy of his rivals. Yet Muhammad, early on after his return to Granada, must have felt a great sense of gratitude towards Ibn al-Khatib for the assistance he had given him during his exile. Therefore, he was at first deaf to any complaints that might have been made about his vizier.[12]

Ibn al-Khatib's importance in helping us to gain an understanding of Granada and its history cannot be overstated. Without his written records, we would know far less about the Nasrid dynasty or the city's past in general than we do today. Despite holding the most important position under the king and being actively involved in all aspects of Granada's affairs, he was a prolific writer and left behind an immense collection on topics as wide-ranging as politics, mysticism, philosophy, medicine, mathematics, and poetry. But of greatest importance to those interested in Granada were his histories. These great works provide both physical descriptions of the city and extensive biographies of its most notable inhabitants from the time of its foundation to the author's own contemporaries. He consulted manuscripts at home and in the Maghreb, and recorded oral testimonies, making use of many sources no longer available to modern historians. Yet with few translations of his works into English, made problematic both by his complex written style and the sheer volume, this incredibly significant writer of the Islamic world is largely ignored in the English-speaking world today. One writer who does receive recognition in the modern world, however, is Ibn al-Khatib's friend and rival Ibn Khaldun. During the early period of Muhammad V's restoration, Ibn Khaldun came for an extended stay at the Nasrid court. Naturally, he was welcomed by both Muhammad and Ibn al-Khatib for the services he had rendered them during their time in exile, and such was the respect and admiration felt for him by the emir that he was appointed ambassador to the court of Peter in Seville and dispatched with gifts for the Castilian king. The journey would doubtless have been an emotional one for Ibn Khaldun, who was a descendent of the Moors of Seville who had left for North Africa after the fall of that city to the Christians. And he so impressed Peter that after his arrival, the king offered him some of the Khaldun family's confiscated ancestral property if he agreed to stay. This he refused, instead returning to Granada, where he was showered with favours by Muhammad.

A time of great intellectual debate between Ibn al-Khatib and Ibn Khaldun, this was also the era when some of the most beautiful features of the Alhambra were installed. Indeed, Ibn al-Khatib provides today's restorers of the Alhambra with a detailed text about the palaces through his record of a great feast that was held in December 1362, both to celebrate the return of Muhammad V to his throne and to show off the newly constructed Mexuar to the great and the good of Granada and beyond.[13] This festival was held as a *mawlid*—a celebration of the Prophet Muhammad's birthday—and is said to have lasted for twelve hours, marked by the striking of a magnificent clock at every hour. It consisted of banquets, music, and dance performances by the kingdom's professional musicians, poetry recitals by its greatest poets, including Ibn al-Khatib himself, and religious observances to mark the occasion. All this was set against the backdrop of a luxuriously festooned marquee on the site of the yet-to-be-built Patio de los Leones. So splendorous was the event that Ibn al-Khatib claims:

> The chroniclers, the veteran travellers and the men of government, who regularly attend such festivals, acknowledged as one voice that this feast, both for its setting and for its banquets, its music and its clock, had been an event without precedent, which would never be repeated or outdone.[14]

Despite this period of art and intellectual enquiry, Ibn Khaldun's stay in Granada was not to last for long. Over time, it seems, he began to suspect that the emir and his vizier were becoming cool towards him, perhaps due to Ibn al-Khatib's sense of rivalry, and he was given permission to return to North Africa in 1364.[15] Of course, it should not be ruled out that Ibn Khaldun perhaps deserved his poor treatment, since his life was so often marked by his own grandiosity and his turning against friends when it was expedient to do so.[16] However, he and Ibn al-Khatib continued to correspond after the former had re-established himself in North Africa, and over the next few years, as the vizier's power at the Alhambra went from strength to strength, it would be to Ibn Khaldun that he would write to complain of the oppressive weight of the duties he held and to tell of his weariness of the never-ending power plays of life at court.

It was this deeply competitive nature of court life that would, within a few years, cause a dramatic reversal in the fortunes of Ibn al-Khatib. Despite his writing—and most likely because of some of it—Ibn al-Khatib, like many men in power, made enemies, and these wanted nothing more than to orchestrate his fall from grace. In a sympathetic seventeenth-century biography by the Algerian historian al-Maqqari, it is said that the horror of the fall of this celebrated vizier came from the fact that it was the very men whom he himself had promoted—his own friends and associates—who sought his demise. Among these was the *qadi*, or sharia judge, of Granada, al-Nubahi. For ten years Ibn al-Khatib and al-Nubahi had managed Granada's affairs on behalf of the king in relative harmony, but at some point, this relationship broke down. Another, more infamous, enemy was Ibn al-Khatib's student and protégé, Ibn Zamrak, who had accompanied Muhammad and his mentor into exile in Fez and appears to have come from a poor family, receiving his education and position at the Nasrid court only through the grace of his benefactor. Ibn al-Khatib's writings show his great fondness and admiration for his own teacher—his predecessor Ibn al-Jayyab—and perhaps this inspired him to show the same fatherly affection to his student. Ibn Zamrak's love of poetry made him the perfect pupil for Ibn al-Khatib, who corrected him in his poetic technique and pushed him in his gifts, and as Ibn Zamrak advanced in his art, the two would dedicate their poems to one another.

What was it that convinced al-Nubahi and Ibn Zamrak to turn on Ibn al-Khatib? Certainly, he himself claims not to have known about their duplicity until it was too late. Yet, in December 1371, Ibn al-Khatib excused himself from the court at the Alhambra and went off to make inspections of outlying areas of the kingdom. For reasons that have never been satisfactorily explained, on reaching the coast he boarded a boat to Ceuta. He may have been intending, as he claimed, to perform the pilgrimage to Mecca; others claim that he left Granada to escape the weighty burden of life at court and to pursue his literary interests instead. Whatever his reasons, it seems his enemies back in Granada seized the opportunity to capitalise on his absence and alleged the powerful vizier had committed various offences. Afraid to return, Ibn al-Khatib requested the protection of the Marinids, and this was granted.

With Ibn al-Khatib now living under the safe refuge of an overseas monarch, his former colleague al-Nubahi wasted no time in bringing a case against the vizier that would hold wherever he sought refuge in the Islamic world: an accusation of heresy. Al-Nubahi pored over Ibn al-Khatib's works for signs of apostasy, settling on a text whose title translates into English as *The Garden of the Knowledge of Sublime Love*. This book espoused Sufi philosophy and at the time of its publication appears to have created no consternation among the religious scholars of Granada. Sufism, a mystical form of Islam, seems to have developed quite a following in Granada under the Nasrids and was generally tolerated. When Ibn Battuta visited the city during Yusuf's reign, he was shown around by some Sufis, who had come to the city from as far afield as Samarkand, in present-day Uzbekistan, and Tabriz, in modern Iran.[17] A key feature of the city at this time was its numerous *morabitos*—small buildings where holy men lived that later became their tombs and were centres of worship for the local population. An example still in existence in Granada is the Hermitage of San Sebastián, close to the Palacio de Congresos, which prior to its conversion into a chapel had been a *morabito*. It appears, therefore, that there was nothing out of the ordinary in Granada in following a mystical interpretation of Islam.

However, for al-Nubahi, Ibn al-Khatib's book provided the requisite, albeit questionable, evidence of the vizier's supposed heterodoxy, and he wrote to his onetime friend and ally listing the charges being drawn up against him. These additionally included an over-subjectivity in some of his biographies, disloyalty to the king, and the derivation of personal benefit from the position he held at court. The letter ended with a yet more poisonous postscript, wherein Ibn al-Khatib's family were assailed, aspersions cast on his noble status, and the exiled vizier himself labelled as an intruder into politics.[18] Incensed with rage, Ibn al-Khatib fought back with his greatest weapon, his pen, and wrote his own scathing biography of al-Nubahi, mocking his physical appearance, scorning his relatives, and questioning his fitness to be a judge. Meanwhile, a trial was held in Granada, which found the exiled former vizier guilty *in absentia* of the crime of heresy, and his books were condemned to be burned.

If the situation were not bad enough, whilst for years Ibn al-Khatib had been able to rely on his friendship with Muhammad V, who had refused to hear a bad word against his faithful courtier, now all of a sudden the emir had become his most powerful enemy. Convinced that Ibn al-Khatib would betray state secrets to the Marinids, even suspecting him of plotting to aid them in an invasion of the Nasrid kingdom, Muhammad embarked on a course to win over the sultan, sending emissaries and precious gifts in a desperate attempt to persuade him to extradite Ibn al-Khatib. Al-Nubahi himself was dispatched to Fez to plead for the former vizier to be returned to face trial in Granada, but the sultan remained unmoved and continued to back his guest. For a while, then, Ibn al-Khatib was able to live in exile in Fez and continue his writing. However, even there he was not without his enemies, who patiently awaited a time when he would be without his powerful protector.

That time arose when the Marinid sultan died. Seizing the opportunity, Granada's king threw himself into the battle that took place for the succession, promising help to one of the pretenders in exchange for the life of his former friend and minister. When this pretender achieved his aims, becoming the new sultan in 1374, he was obligated to Muhammad and acquiesced to his demands. Ibn al-Khatib now found himself on trial in Fez, facing charges submitted to those present by his former student and protégé, Ibn Zamrak, recently arrived from Granada. The charges for heresy in his writings were serious enough to warrant the death sentence. Ibn al-Khatib, once the right-hand man of Granada's emir, was now left to face trial and even torture alone.

Nevertheless, one long-lasting friendship still remained for the former vizier of Granada, even in those dark days. His long-time intellectual sparring partner Ibn Khaldun pleaded with Muhammad V to spare his friend's life. Unfortunately, these entreaties fell on deaf ears. Yet even then, hope remained for the former vizier: those overseeing the trial struggled to reach a unanimous verdict on the case, and Ibn al-Khatib was sent back to his cell without a death sentence yet declared. Perhaps it was this uncertainty about his fate that led Ibn al-Khatib's enemies to take matters into their own hands, determined as they were that the former vizier must not be allowed to escape under any circumstances. Sometime in the night, the door to Ibn al-Khatib's cell was forced open, assassins entered, and he was strangled to death in his bed. He was given a funeral the following day, but the hatred of the vizier's enemies was such that two days later, his body was found to have been taken from its tomb, burned, and tossed into a ditch.

Outraged at the fate of a man of such high standing and intellect, Ibn Khaldun described Ibn al-Khatib's death as that of a martyr and included a long poem about him in his writings, ending with the following impassioned warning to those who had sought his downfall:

So say to the enemies, 'Ibn al-Khatib is gone, passed away;
But who is there who won't die?'
And to those who rejoice about this,
Tell them, 'Only those who will never die can be happy today.'[19]

Muhammad V was to reign for another seventeen years after the death of Ibn al-Khatib, supported by his new vizier, the treacherous Ibn Zamrak, who also supplanted his former mentor as the poet whose work would henceforth adorn the new additions to the Alhambra. This period continued to be one of great building projects, including the celebrated Patio de los Leones, with Ibn Zamrak's verses decorating the famous fountain at its centre. Another of Muhammad V's constructions, also decorated with Ibn Zamrak's poetry, was a great recreational palace on the hill above the Alhambra, known in Spanish as the Palacio de los Alijares.[20] The ruins, now hidden away deep inside a cemetery, belie its former magnificence; it was said to have been a building of great beauty and fragility. Sadly, it was unable to withstand the effects of a tremendous earthquake that struck the city within only half a century of its construction, and it was never rebuilt.

Meanwhile, by the fourteenth century, Granada had built up a thriving economy.[21] In particular the kingdom had earned a reputation as one of the great European centres of silk production. Often overseen by Genoese traders living in Granada, who had negotiated preferential trading rights in the kingdom, the export of the precious fabric took it—by way of other Iberian cities such as Valencia—across Italy and as far afield as Paris and Flanders.[22] Whilst silk manufacture was widespread across the kingdom, with key production areas in the Alpujarra and the Valle de Lecrín, within the city of Granada itself the main centre for trade was the Alcaicería—the silk market—a covered building, in its heyday containing at least 200 shops. Here, in the busy commercial centre of the city, silk produced in the countryside would be valued, tax would be added, and then merchants such as the Genoese would buy it in bulk to ship to their markets across Europe. The Alcaicería was preserved much as it had been since Nasrid times right up until 1843, when it was completely destroyed by a huge fire; it was later rebuilt as a pastiche on a far smaller scale, today playing host largely to tourist shops.

The silk market sat at the heart of the Nasrid commercial district, where the main commercial street was Calle Zacatín.[23] Around the site of Granada's main mosque there was also a spice bazaar, as well as temporary stalls set up by traders coming into the city to sell their produce. These traders would stay at an inn for travelling merchants known in Arabic as a *funduq*. An excellently restored example of one of these inns is the Corral del Carbón, which prior to the covering of the river Darro was on its left bank and connected to the silk market and Calle Zacatín by a bridge. This was certainly not the only inn in the city, and it is likely that different ones were frequented by traders of different products, the Corral del Carbón being a place for trading wheat, whilst another on Calle Zacatín specialised in a variety of general food products, from olive oil and honey to dried fruits and nuts. The Genoese had their own separate *funduq*, situated on today's Calle Cárcel Baja, which was, of course, also close to the central point of the commercial district, the main mosque.

Along with the silk business, these Genoese traders were also involved in the promotion of ceramics from Granada, as these too turned into an important export.[24] Granada's potters improved on earlier techniques from the Arab world for decorating their wares, using geometric and vegetal patterns, generally in blue or green on a white glazed background. The complicated techniques required to produce this type of ceramics meant that those made in Granada could be sold across Europe as a luxury item. Today a wide variety of examples of Nasrid ceramics can be seen in the Alhambra Museum, whilst in the upper Albaicín, workshops producing *fajalauza*, a ceramics tradition dating from the Christian era but with clear roots back in the Nasrid period, can be visited today.

With a strong economy and the construction of some of the city's most beautiful buildings, Granada under Muhammad V reached the pinnacle of its achievements, and when the emir died in 1391, unlike many of his predecessors and most of those who came after, he did so peacefully of natural causes. Unfortunately, the period of relative stability was not to last into the next reign. Muhammad was succeeded by his son, Yusuf II, whose one-year reign is most remarkable for the violent fate met by his chief advisor: suspecting the vizier, Khalid, of attempting to poison him, Yusuf ordered that he be tied up and hacked to death in front of him. It was also during this reign that the reckoning began for the perfidious poet Ibn Zamrak. For many, including Ibn al-Khatib's seventeenth-century biographer, al-Maqqari, the brutal murder of Ibn Zamrak reeked of divine retribution for his treatment of his guide and teacher. First, under Yusuf, he was imprisoned, and then, under the next ruler, Yusuf's son Muhammad VII, he was stabbed to death in his home, so the story goes, his sons butchered along with him and his wives watching helplessly, unable to prevent the massacre.

Muhammad VII was succeeded in 1408 by his brother Yusuf III, who had until then been imprisoned in the castle at Salobreña for sixteen years to prevent him from challenging his brother's place on the throne. His reign saw the last of the great Nasrid additions to the Alhambra, with Yusuf himself, along with his vizier, composing new poetry for the walls of the palaces. It was also to be the final reign of the Nasrid era to enjoy any sense of stability. The fifteenth century, the last of the dynasty, would be marred by a series of weak and incompetent rulers, internal struggles for power within the Alhambra, and the growing efforts of the kings of Castile to meddle in these power plays, all of which eventually allowed the Christians to relaunch their crusade to conquer the Emirate of Granada.

The early fifteenth century should have been a time for Granada to consolidate its position.[25] After the fall of Antequera to Castile under Yusuf III, its northern neighbours were too busy fighting amongst themselves to continue with the Reconquista— the on-and-off struggle by the Christian kingdoms of Iberia to claim lands occupied by Muslims since the eighth century. Yet despite the lack of an outside threat, Granada also became a scene of terrible internal strife between factions fighting for political influence. The most famous of these contingents was the clan known as the Banu Sarraj, more familiar to visitors to the

Alhambra today by the Hispanicised name Abencerrajes. Unfortunately, whilst evidence of events from an internal perspective is fairly good in the fourteenth century, historians are mainly left relying on Castilian sources for details of what took place in Granada by the 1400s, and much of this material is distorted, often romanticised. Later these tales of the Moors were turned into stories and art, and they remain the basis for the 'history' that proliferates—often officially—today.

In terms of the Abencerrajes, so romanticised did this family later become by way of European storytellers that it is difficult to sift out truth from fiction.[26] It appears that they were a clan of kingmakers whose power evolved in the early 1400s and whose decisions saw the rise and fall of a number of monarchs during the last seventy years of the emirate. Indeed, the fifteenth century is complex for historians to follow owing to the abundance of scheming and duplicity among the different factions at court, as well as between individual members of the Nasrid family vying for the throne. Many of Granada's rulers would reign, be deposed, and later return to the throne, depending on the support they had from the powerful factions at court. Muhammad IX, for example, appears to have reigned on four separate occasions. And the people of Granada were not averse to taking sides in the many disputes between the rival powerbrokers at the Alhambra. In 1427, Granada's citizens rose up in revolt against Muhammad IX over their concerns about higher taxes levied to pay *parias* to the king of Castile. The Abencerrajes subsequently fell out of favour, and another faction, the Banu Bannigas, known later in Castilian as the Venegas family, came to prominence.

These rival factions would, at times, use appeals to the Christian kingdoms to aid them in their struggles for power, and this fundamentally weakened Granada, as it empowered the kings of Castile to toy within its political sphere. And it would be such an appeal to the Christians that brought about one of the most famous acts of interference in Granada's affairs by the Castilians. In 1431, John II brought troops into the Emirate of Granada in order to support the claims to the throne of the man who would, for only a matter of months, reign as Yusuf IV. This was achieved through victory at the Battle of La Higueruela, which took place within sight of the city around the remains of the former settlement of Elvira, next to modern-day Atarfe, and was later immortalised in a series of frescoes adorning the walls of Philip II's monastery-palace outside Madrid, El Escorial. These subsequent depictions, copied from a sketch made closer to the time, give one of the earliest visual impressions of the city of Granada with its walls, palaces, and gates.[27]

Such was the victory for John II and his allies at La Higueruela that there was tremendous fear the Castilians would continue their success by taking the city itself. However, Mother Nature intervened on this occasion, although in a manner that must have terrified everyone in the city, and indeed across much of the Iberian Peninsula. Shortly after the Castilians achieved their victory, a powerful earthquake shook the region. This was to be one of a series of earthquakes to strike over the next few years, one result of which was the destruction of Muhammad V's Palacio de los Alijares, although this was not the only royal palace to be affected. The serious damage to the Alhambra complex that Isabella and Ferdinand were to find after conquering Granada sixty years later was a direct consequence of these earthquakes and of the lack of available resources at the time to carry out repairs.[28] Yet the most concerning harm done to the city's infrastructure was the destruction of large sections of its walls. This laid the city open to attack, but in part thanks to the earthquake and also because of Castile's own internal problems, John withdrew his army after La Higueruela, leaving the Moorish capital to survive for another six decades.

The details of Granada's history during the early to mid-fifteenth century become more definite as the emirate approaches its demise, although many of the writers from the time are Christian, inevitably bringing biases to the story. One important source is the memoir written by Hernando de Baeza—a Castilian translator working for the Nasrids in the years prior to Granada's fall to the Christians; a man who would become a close friend of Boabdil, Granada's final king; and someone who lived for a short time inside the kingdom itself.[29] His account of the final decades of the Emirate of Granada begins with the successful attempts to gain the throne of the Emir Sa'd. Sa'd appears to have gained his throne through his willingness to ally himself with the Castilians and, because of this, was said to be deeply unpopular with his subjects. He was also reputed to be a violent king, in much the same way as his son, Muley Hacén, would later become. Indeed, an act of violence perpetrated by both father and son was what actually led to this branch of the Nasrids achieving the throne. Baeza relates how the young Muley Hacén set up an ambush on a road into the city, where he captured an earlier, now deposed, king, who was a rival to the throne. This man was taken to the Alhambra, where Sa'd ordered that his throat be slit and his two very young children suffocated. This murder was the origin of the supposedly indelible bloodstain on the marble floor of a room next to the Patio de los Leones, although later romantic tales, some of which continue to be told today, claim that the red mark stems from the massacre of the Abencerrajes—something that Baeza tells us actually took place in the next reign.[30]

As Baeza recounts it, Sa'd was an unpopular ruler, and the people of Granada soon decided to call on his son, Muley Hacén, to rule instead. Muley Hacén, showing no loyalty to his father, imprisoned Sa'd in that oft-used Nasrid royal prison, the castle of Salobreña, where he died shortly afterwards. According to Baeza, the early years of Muley Hacén's reign were promising, one of his early acts being to marry the daughter of an earlier king, possibly the one that had been murdered on the orders of

Sa'd. This woman is known in Western history by the name of Aisha, although her true name was almost certainly Fatima,[31] and this marriage appears for many years to have healed divisions in the kingdom between rival factions at court. Indeed, as Baeza tells us, their first twenty years of matrimony were peaceful, producing two sons and a daughter. Yet the relationship between Muley Hacén and Aisha was to become the cause of great division in the city, and it would ultimately play a key role in Granada's downfall.

As the Nasrid kingdom moved into its final decades, it is not only Baeza's account of events that helps us to understand what took place there. There is also an Arabic account by an anonymous author, which is probably the memoir of a soldier from Granada written years afterwards from his exile in North Africa. This is one of the only sources to tell us the history of the fall of the Nasrids from an Arab perspective.[32] Highly unsympathetic to Muley Hacén, the record begins in 1478 with the emir holding a magnificent military parade at the Alhambra, attended by people from across the kingdom. These festivities had been going on for a number of days when suddenly, on the final day, the heavens opened; thunder and lightning brought chaos to the city, as the rains came down in torrents like never seen before in living memory. Such was the strength of the storm that flooding and mudslides brought down buildings and bridges along the river Darro, and large swathes of the city were devastated. Baeza also recounts this story, adding that the most serious damage occurred after an uprooted tree blocked the passage of the river beneath one of the bridges. The most important economic centres in the city, Calle Zacatín and the silk market, were inundated. Muley Hacén was said to be so shocked by these events that he had a nervous breakdown and from that point forward went into a decline, becoming a loathsome man whose final years were marked by high living and immersing himself in the pleasures of his harem. This tempest and the appearance of a comet in the sky around the same time were taken by some in Granada as terrible omens for the future. Sadly, their worst fears would shortly be realised.

6

THE RECONQUISTA

On 2 January 1492, the last emir of Granada, known in Western history as Boabdil, rode out from the Alhambra for the last time. In order to avoid the crowds of the city, he and his entourage descended the steep slopes of the area that is today the Barranco del Abogado and passed alongside the river Genil to a spot beyond the walls where now lies an open space in front of the Palacio de Congresos. There waiting for him were Isabella and Ferdinand, the rulers of the recently united kingdoms of Castile and Aragon, who would the following year be given the dispensation 'Most Catholic Monarchs' by Pope Alexander VI. The royal couple were attended by a retinue of knights and courtiers, who had been living with them at a military encampment just outside the city for most of the previous year. The siege of Granada had finally come to an end. As Boabdil began to alight from his horse in order to bow to the victors, Isabella and Ferdinand bid him to remain—an acknowledgement of a fellow king. There, on that winter's day, the keys to the kingdom were ceremonially handed over to the Christian conquerors.

Whilst the fifteenth century had been characterised by great instability amongst the ruling classes of Granada, the same political disarray within the Christian kingdoms to the north had meant that for many years, no real impetus had existed for launching a full-scale attack on the Muslim lands. Border skirmishes had been common, yet no Christian army had ever been strong enough to make a serious attempt at reinitiating the Reconquista. In 1469, however, the marriage of Isabella, half-sister of King Henry IV of Castile, to Ferdinand, heir to the throne of Aragon, set a course for the eventual unification of the two Christian kingdoms and a renewal of meaningful hostilities against the Emirate of Granada. The match did not bring immediate resolution to the political instability, however, since Henry had a daughter, Joanna. When the king died, Castile descended into civil war between the supporters of Joanna's claim and the faction that backed Isabella and challenged the legitimacy of Joanna's birth. The struggle lasted for five years but, when it ended in 1479, with the victory of Isabella and her husband—who had succeeded his father as Ferdinand II of Aragon earlier that year—the union of the two powerful Iberian realms posed the ultimate threat to the comparatively tiny Emirate of Granada.

In fact, Granada presented the newly victorious monarchs with an opportunity to unite their kingdoms in spirit by way of an age-old appeal. Calls for a new crusade against the Moors had been voiced by popes since the fall of Constantinople in 1453; that event had unleashed a new enthusiasm for holy war and prompted Henry IV to resume the Reconquista just two years later. The recommencing of hostilities, however, generally resulted in little more than the burning of fields and crops around the borders, and whilst this had caused hardship to the people of Granada, it was far from an invasion. This all changed in the 1480s, when crusading zeal provided the ideal means for Isabella and Ferdinand to bring together their peoples of Castile and Aragon after the years of civil strife. It was a perfect opportunity for them to earn their spurs as noble defenders of Christendom in the vein of their predecessors and, in so doing, to cement themselves in the image of earlier Iberian warrior kings.

There was, then, a certain inevitability about the coming conflict.[1] Nevertheless, many tales of the Granada wars lay the blame for the initial attacks squarely at the feet of the Catholic Monarchs' opposite number, Muley Hacén. Perhaps his descent into drinking and womanising following the disastrous floods at the end of his military parade also led to a parallel decline in his skills of diplomacy. The Castilian chronicler Hernando del Pulgar records that Muley Hacén provoked the ire of Isabella and Ferdinand by refusing to pay the *parias*, telling Castilian ambassadors in a fit of bellicosity that 'The kings of Granada who used to pay the tribute were dead, and ... the places in Granada where the coins had been struck to pay these *parias* were now forging lance-heads instead.'[2] But it was his attack, in 1481, on the settlement of Zahara—a border town seized from Granada by the Christians seventy years earlier—that provided the excuse Isabella and Ferdinand needed to retaliate against the Moors. Rumours circulated in Christian territories of brutal treatment meted out to the Christians of Zahara by the Muslim invaders. For Muley Hacén, the attack on Zahara might have been seen as just another tit-for-tat cross-border expedition of the type that had gone on for centuries, rather than a strategic blunder leading to serious and avoidable repercussions. But the motivation for carrying it out notwithstanding, he misjudged the enthusiasm of the Christians to reinitiate the Reconquista. Castilians and Aragonese alike flocked to join the attack on the 'infidel', and with them came mercenaries and other volunteers from across Christendom to take part in the new crusade.

The first town to be attacked by the Christian forces was Alhama, to the south-west of the city of Granada. Alhama was of great strategic importance, as it lay between Granada and Malaga and was therefore vital to the capital's communication with the sea. The brutal fighting there went on for days, Muley Hacén himself riding to its defence after the Christians invaded and threw the bodies of many of the defenders over the walls to be consumed by dogs. Despite his attempts to save the town, a more romantic legend speaks of how Muley Hacén, on receiving the news of Alhama's fall, ran through the streets of Granada in despair, crying, 'Ay de mi Alhama!' This story was turned into a popular poem, translated into English centuries later by Lord Byron,[3] and while there is certainly more make-believe than truth to this legend, as with many of the romantic ballads that portray Christian and Moor pitted against one another, it cannot be doubted that the capital was thrown into turmoil as the surrounding towns began to face attack. Moreover, the victory of the Christians at Alhama was almost certainly aided by the disquiet within the ruling family at the Alhambra.

To determine an accurate picture of what really happened in the city of Granada during the Reconquista is no easy task; legend and folklore abounded after the fall of the Nasrids in 1492. History, as the adage goes, is written by the victors, and later writers certainly romanticised the Moors to such an extent that many of the tales told of this period and even before may be no more than the product of Christian revisionism or Orientalist fantasy. As an example, there was a general tendency to portray the Nasrids as excessively sensual. Hieronymus Münzer, a German visitor to the Alhambra in 1494, describes a marble basin where he claims women and concubines would have washed naked, observed from behind a *mashrabiya* by the king, who would throw a piece of fruit to the woman who pleased him most as a sign that he would receive her that evening.[4] However, it is not only Christian sources that suggest this problem of sensuality. The anonymously written Arabic chronicle of the final years of the Nasrids also portrays Muley Hacén as deeply engrossed in the pleasures of the flesh, rather than concerned with the pressing needs of his kingdom.[5]

Indeed, both sources from within Granada in the 1480s lay the blame for the initial turmoil at the feet of an increasingly lustful and erratic Muley Hacén,[6] his greatest folly, according to the two writers, being his lack of fidelity to his wife Aisha. As Baeza tells it, Muley Hacén became infatuated with a Christian captive called Isabel de Solís, who had been abducted in a cross-border raid when she was just twelve years old and given to the king's daughter as a slave. The story has it that Muley Hacén had different women from the harem brought to him each evening and over time became taken with this particular girl. Yet one evening, as she returned from the king's chamber, the other female servants leapt upon her and beat her within an inch of her life. On hearing of the attack on his favourite, the king flew into a rage, believing Aisha was responsible for the situation. As a sign both of his anger at his wife and of his infatuation for the girl, he began to shower the Christian with jewels and clothes, the likes of which, Baeza says, had never been worn by a queen of Granada. And he would soon take things much further: the Christian converted to Islam and changed her name to Zoraya in order to marry him. It was, of course, not unusual for a Muslim monarch to have more than one wife, nor, indeed, for a king of Granada to marry a Christian slave. Nevertheless, Islamic tradition expects rules of respect for different wives to be maintained, and all of these were broken by Muley Hacén, with terrible consequences.

Aisha was the daughter of a previous monarch and a woman of immense power, whose marriage to Muley Hacén had brought together a number of feuding factions at a time when the emirate had been in a terribly weak state. Both tradition and political nous therefore demanded she be treated with the utmost respect. Unfortunately, Muley Hacén seems to have gone out of his way to slight Aisha in every way possible. At one of the annual feasts, he placed Zoraya at his side instead of Aisha and ordered the people of Granada to pay homage to her in place of his first wife. Few things could have been more insulting to Aisha and her allies, and thus, from the late 1470s, the Alhambra was a scene of great tension. Aisha and her children were living in rooms off the Patio de los Leones, whilst Muley Hacén and Zoraya resided in the Palacio de Comares with their own two sons. And it was at this point, according to Baeza, that one of the most infamous incidents in the history of the Alhambra occurred, and one that would inspire romantic tales and art for centuries to come: the slaughter of the Abencerrajes.

So many of the stories of Granada during those years derive from later, romantic images of the last of the Moors written by Christian storytellers. The Abencerrajes are at the forefront of these vignettes, portrayed through the ages as noble warriors, almost in the Christian tradition, yet Muslim. It has become difficult to separate fact from fiction in terms of the role they played in the ever-present feuding between the various branches of the royal family.[7] The famous act of mass murder within the walls of the Royal Palaces is steeped in myth, with sources differing in terms of which king was responsible. Baeza's account that Muley Hacén was the architect seems, in many respects, a reasonable suggestion, given what the sources claim of the emir's increasing madness and lust for violence. Legend has it that he invited thirty-six members of the clan to a banquet in a hall beside the Patio de los Leones, and there they were leapt upon by palace guards, their throats were slit, and—in a conflation of these events and Muley Hacén's earlier role in the murder of a king—their blood left an indelible stain on the marble floor.

It was in this atmosphere, with a king obsessed with womanising and willing to put a number of his own best warriors to the sword, that the early Reconquista battles took place. Misgivings amongst Granada's nobility about the effectiveness of such a ruler led them to seek a new and potentially more effective leader to counter the growing threat, and they turned to Aisha and her sons in their desire to remove Muley Hacén from the throne. This was no simple feat, as Aisha and her children were effectively imprisoned in the Alhambra. However, a copperware seller was co-opted into smuggling letters to Aisha from her allies as he went about his business in the Nasrid Palaces, and through these a plot was hatched to enable the escape of her two sons, Boabdil and Yusuf. This plan was put into action one evening: a group of horsemen gathered close to the Generalife, two of their comrades silently creeping beneath the windows of the palace. When the previously arranged signal came from below, Boabdil let down out of the window a thin cord, which he had hidden in his hands. His co-conspirators tied a strong rope to the cord, which Boabdil then pulled back up and fixed to a marble column. Both Boabdil and his brother Yusuf then lowered themselves down the walls to waiting horses. With all haste, the pair of princes escaped to the east of the kingdom, where Boabdil was welcomed by supporters in Guadix, whilst Yusuf continued on eastward to Almeria to act as local ruler on behalf of his brother.

For six months there was a standoff; the people of Guadix recognised Boabdil as king, but his father, Muley Hacén, continued to rule most of the emirate from the Alhambra. Soon, however, the people of the city of Granada also rose up in favour of Boabdil, forcing Muley Hacén and his brother al-Zaghal to flee the city in 1482. Boabdil, now King Muhammad XII,[8] seized the Alhambra, and with it the majority of the emirate. Muley Hacén, supported by his brother, became, as so many deposed Nasrid kings of the previous century had, a rival ruler in the south of the emirate around the Alpujarra and Malaga, leaving the country in a state of civil war. In theory, this situation was a political gift for the Castilians. However, even as the infighting amongst the Nasrids raged on, the war against the Christian invaders continued too, and not all of the battles in the early 1480s went against the Muslims. Firstly, the Christians suffered a terrible defeat when they tried to take the town of Loja. Later, a victory led by al-Zaghal in the hills close to Malaga brought hope to the emirate that the momentum hitherto enjoyed by the Christians could be arrested or even reversed.

With al-Zaghal's impressive victory in the south, Boabdil, reigning from the Alhambra, was desirous of demonstrating his own prowess against the old enemy. Against the advice of many of his advisors, he decided to launch an attack into Christian territory in an attempt to take the city of Lucena. This was to prove a decisive moment in the war: on 21 April 1483, Boabdil himself was captured, an event during which King Ferdinand demonstrated just the kind of cunning that shows why he became the inspiration for Machiavelli's *Prince*. Aware of the infighting among the Nasrids, Ferdinand realised that releasing his prisoner back to Granada would mean that the Moors would continue fighting on two fronts: externally, against the Christians, and also internally, against each other in the ongoing civil war, which would be beneficial to the Christians. Therefore, Ferdinand offered Boabdil his freedom in exchange for a promise to wage war against his father and remain a vassal of Castile. Perhaps, in fairness to Boabdil, he saw little to distinguish this accord from the many treaties of the past made between the rulers of Granada and the Christians wherein the Moors retained their kingdom in exchange for a tribute.

Ferdinand's decision was extremely astute. As Boabdil languished in a Castilian castle, Muley Hacén had been quick to take advantage of his son's captivity and had returned to the Alhambra to assert his rule over the whole emirate. With the city of Granada now back in Muley Hacén's hands, fatwas were issued against Boabdil for the deal he had struck with the infidel. The people were forced to decide which ruler to support. Some saw hope that Boabdil's close relations with the Christians would mean he could negotiate terms for them to be left in peace, yet by this point a large number felt that fighting on was the only option for the survival of the Muslim state. Having lost his support amongst many in the capital, Boabdil returned to the emirate and set himself up once again in Guadix in opposition to his father. And if two rival kings dividing the country were not enough, another pretender was now to throw his hat into the ring in the person of Muley Hacén's brother al-Zaghal.

Al-Zaghal had rebelled against Muley Hacén before, in the 1470s, but peace had been restored, and in the early years of the war against the Christians, the two brothers had been allies against Boabdil. Now, with al-Zaghal's military victories in the battles around Malaga behind him, his ambitions for the throne were also aided greatly by the fact that Muley Hacén was increasingly suffering from an illness that caused him to have fits and become incapacitated, something the anonymous Arabic source suggests was divine punishment for the evil life he had lived.[9] Unfortunately, like his brother, al-Zaghal was also compulsively violent towards any who stood in his way. Removing all possibility of a reconciliation that could have reunited the family against the external threat, this brutal proclivity was soon to bring great tragedy for Boabdil and Aisha: the murder of Boabdil's younger brother, Yusuf.

With Muley Hacén debilitated by his illness, al-Zaghal had taken over military operations against Boabdil, and he began by laying siege to Almeria, where Yusuf was ruling on behalf of his brother and where Aisha had sought shelter. As Almeria fell into al-Zaghal's hands, Muley Hacén sent to the city a signed death warrant for those who opposed his reign. It is said that the king had been persuaded by Zoraya to include his son Yusuf's name in this list, since the queen believed that would allow her own sons by Muley Hacén to inherit the kingdom. Baeza narrates a moving account of Yusuf's demise, with the young prince questioning his executioner about whether the orders had truly come from his own father and then, on hearing that they had, performing the ritual ablutions with great dignity and calmly accepting his fate of being beheaded. The murder of the young prince on the orders of al-Zaghal and Muley Hacén made the rift in the family permanent and ensured they would never be forgiven by either Aisha or Boabdil.

With Almeria now in al-Zaghal's hands, Muley Hacén continued to reign from the Alhambra, but his illness was growing worse. Just six months after Yusuf's tragic execution, the emir was to demonstrate quite clearly his increasing insanity. Seemingly having forgotten the orders he had sent for his son to be killed, Muley Hacén began to express a desire for Yusuf to visit him, much to the consternation of his servants, who were only too aware of the fate of the young prince. It was some time before one dared to break the news to him of how his son had been killed on the orders that he himself had sent to Almeria. Baeza recounts how Muley Hacén, suddenly understanding what had occurred, broke down in abject grief, beating the walls violently in anger and pain and screaming, 'Never has such evil been seen, nor an uncle beheading a nephew ... couldn't he have seen that I ordered it out of anger and not for it to be carried out?'[10] Within days, an already very ill Muley Hacén went blind.

With Muley Hacén incapacitated and Boabdil still unpopular because of his pact with the Christians, in 1485 al-Zaghal overthrew his brother, and the people of Granada now found themselves living under another ruler at the Alhambra. Muley Hacén was sent to the castle of Salobreña—the same prison castle where he himself had sent his father, Saʿd, just two decades earlier—and died soon after. Legend has it that he was buried on the highest peak of the Sierra Nevada, which today bears his name: Mulhacén. Baeza, however, claims his body was brought back to the city and was buried at the Alhambra alongside his ancestors. Meanwhile, al-Zaghal is said to have kept Zoraya at the Alhambra, claiming he would marry her if she revealed the location of treasures hidden in the complex by her deceased husband.

The infighting between the remaining branches of the Nasrid royal family was incessant, and in 1486, major strife erupted in the capital itself as Boabdil returned to the Albaicín to face his uncle across the river Darro at the Alhambra. After years of terrible hardship, the residents of the Albaicín were in desperate need of a leader who could alleviate their hunger and provide them with some hope of security. With the backing Boabdil had obtained from Isabella and Ferdinand, leaving the city to get food without facing attack looked likely to be easier for his supporters, as the Christian forces would withhold from attacking their allies.[11] Some of the residents of the Albaicín had been in correspondence with Boabdil and had urged him to return to the city with promises of their obedience and recognition of him as their king. Baeza relates how Boabdil's night-time journey across the hills from the east was one of great daring and his meeting with his supporters outside the city one of great warmth and kindness, in acknowledgement of the risk that they were taking by assisting his cause. These supporters then helped Boabdil to secretly enter the district. This is traditionally held to have been by way of the Puerta de Fajalauza; from there he was taken to a house where a crowd had gathered, who unanimously proclaimed him king. Then, aware of the danger that faced them from the enemy over at the Alhambra, Boabdil's supporters closed the gates to the area and built barricades to protect themselves.

For many months civil war was fought right in the city itself. From the Alhambra, al-Zaghal used artillery that could and should have been used to protect Granada from Christians rather than to bombard Boabdil's supporters in the Albaicín. Such was the hatred between uncle and nephew that for all this time, neither was willing to negotiate, despite the external threat from the Christians, and this situation played entirely into the hands of Ferdinand and Isabella. Granada was in chaos, and there was no sign that the city would be able to put up a united front against the Christians even if the internal struggles abated. It would be Boabdil who, eventually, accepted that this was doing no-one any good. Through the probable mediation of religious leaders, al-Zaghal and Boabdil struck a deal whereby the latter would leave the city, and, as had become so common over the past century, the emirate would be divided up once again between two kings. This arrangement was no solid front to present against the invaders, and it also implies that Boabdil had reneged on his pledge to Ferdinand to continue fighting against his relatives.

The settlement between the two emirs was to be short-lived. Boabdil was captured by Christian troops again later that year at the fall of Loja, but once more he declared his vassalage to Isabella and Ferdinand, and he was freed to return to Granada. Boabdil's willingness to ally himself with the Catholic Monarchs in the mistaken belief that he would retain his crown under their protection played a key part in the end of Moorish rule over Granada, while contributing to his reputation for being a weak monarch and responsible for the downfall of the Muslim state. This assessment of Boabdil has never been entirely fair. The Nasrid Emirate of Granada had largely survived, even in its early years under Ibn al-Ahmar, through the reigning monarch's ability to deal with his Christian counterparts. Boabdil was, in so many ways, following the example of some of his most admired ancestors. But times had changed. In the past, his predecessors had been able to play a clever game of manipulation in using the rivalry between the northern Christian kingdoms to their own advantage. Now, that rivalry had largely ended, with Castile and Aragon united through the marriage of Isabella and Ferdinand.

Once again Ferdinand's decision to release Boabdil as an ally was tactically astute. As the Christians made their next line of attack on the coastal region around the strategic port city of Malaga, al-Zaghal was forced to defend what had long been an area that had provided him with support. This meant leaving the Alhambra, but before doing so, he received the solemn promise of the people of Granada gathered at the Alhambra's mosque that they would not support any attempt by Boabdil to retake the throne in his absence. No sooner had al-Zaghal left the city, though, than Boabdil's supporters rose up to declare him king. Baeza relates how one sixty-year-old man, a vendor of women's bathing products described as having a neck covered in spots, climbed to the top of one of the city's towers and began to call out in favour of Boabdil, soon being joined by others from more towers around Granada, allowing Boabdil to return to the Alhambra with the support of the city behind him.

The defence of Malaga, which was taking place as Boabdil regained the capital, was one of great hardship, but also of great heroism. Ultimately, however, the Moors were defeated, and the vast majority of the city's inhabitants were sold into slavery as a punishment for holding out against the Christian forces. The significance of the loss of the strategically important Malaga to the rest of the emirate cannot be overstated. As the embarkation point for Granada's exports, in particular silk, the port was essential for the economy, and without it, Granada also lost its main communications with potential allies in Muslim North Africa. The fall of Malaga therefore made the subsequent fall of Granada itself from that point virtually inevitable.

Yet even now, unity between Muslim forces could not be found, as the battle between the two emirs continued, each with his own method for bringing an end to the Christian attacks. Boabdil continued to rely on his alliance with Isabella and Ferdinand, to whom he sent word that he would be willing to hand over the city of Granada in exchange for being created a Castilian noble with jurisdiction over Guadix and Baza. Al-Zaghal, in contrast, fought on undeterred, and the battlefront moved to the east of the province, where the Christians looked to secure Guadix and Baza to exchange with their ally Boabdil for the capital. Baza was captured in 1489, and in a clear example of how the internecine strife proved as fatal for the Emirate of Granada as was the Christians' decision to attack, al-Zaghal surrendered the towns of the east to the Christians rather than to his despised nephew, renouncing his claim to the throne in the process. Al-Zaghal's fate, we are told, was exile to North Africa, where he was blinded in punishment for his role in the downfall of Granada. He ended his days a beggar, with a sign hung around his neck saying, 'This is the unfortunate King of the Andalusis.'[12]

With al-Zaghal's capitulation, it should have been a straightforward task for the Catholic Monarchs to return to Boabdil and take the city of Granada based on his promise. Yet, in the time it had taken for them to occupy the east of the emirate, it appears their ally had had a change of heart. Instead of surrendering Granada as agreed, Boabdil chose to renege on his word and fight for the last remaining major settlement of the Moorish kingdom. Two of Ferdinand's officers, Gonzalo Fernández de Córdoba—later immortalised as El Gran Capitán—and Martín de Alarcón, were allowed into the city to negotiate with Boabdil. The Boabdil they addressed, however, was not the pliant one the Christians had been used to. Indeed, he was much changed, now willing to defy the invaders and defend his city.

Much has been made of Boabdil's seeming inconsistencies in terms of defending Granada. Yet, in many ways, he was unfortunate in being the wrong type of monarch living at the wrong moment in history.[13] Unlike the incompetent and self-centred prince that legend and stories after the event have painted him as, willing to do anything to save his own skin and that of his family at the expense of his people, contemporary sources by contrast portray a man who was dignified, respectful, and not at all lacking in courage, who treated people in a far better manner than his violent and erratic father and uncle ever had. Indeed, Hernando de Baeza, who had got to know Boabdil well in his position as the emir's Castilian translator, speaks very highly of him, saying that if he had been a Christian, he would have been among the best there had ever been:[14] high praise in sixteenth-century terms. In fact, sources from the time seem quite clear that the blame for the downfall of Granada lay ultimately with the folly and erratic behaviour of Muley Hacén, rather than with his son who was left to pick up the pieces. Even so, it would fall to Boabdil to gain the infamy of being the last emir of Granada, responsible for handing the city over to the Catholic Monarchs. Perhaps Washington Irving, writing over 300 years later, gets closer to the truth about Boabdil, saying, 'Never ... was name more foully and unjustly slandered,'[15] and claiming that the last king of Granada was:

> of a mild and amiable character. He in the first instance won the hearts of the people by his affable and gracious manners ... He was personally brave, but he wanted moral courage, and in times of difficulty and perplexity was wavering and irresolute. This feebleness of spirit hastened his downfall, while it deprived him of that heroic grace which would have given a grandeur and dignity to his fate.[16]

It is very possible that Boabdil had always been playing a duplicitous game with the Christians, emulating the first of the Nasrids, Ibn al-Ahmar, who always appeared the obedient vassal until the time came to show his true colours. But in the two and a half centuries that had passed since that first Nasrid king, the Christian kings had grown stronger, and Boabdil's tactical alliances with them quite clearly failed. By 1490, the city of Granada found itself alone. However, Boabdil may well have been moved by the intense atmosphere to make a last stand; as the rest of the emirate disintegrated, the capital had been flooded with those forced off the land, willing to fight, possibly to the death, for their religion, their way of life, and the homeland that had been theirs and their ancestors' for eight centuries.

Little happened initially in terms of military action; Ferdinand continued his scorched-earth campaign across the Vega, bringing hardship to Granada, but as yet there was no siege. That would truly begin only in April 1491, when the Christians erected an encampment on the site that would become the town of Santa Fe, to the west of the city of Granada. As threatening as this must have been to the city, the campaign had—as was common at the time—been a seasonal affair, and the defenders prepared to see out the siege until the Christians withdrew for the winter. In the early days, in July 1491, hope must have arisen for the people of Granada when fire broke out in the Christian camp. An accident with a candle caused Isabella's tent to go up in flames, putting her life in real danger. Although the queen herself managed to escape, the blaze tore through the camp, wreaking havoc. Guards were posted to the access route from Granada to prevent any attack from the Moors looking to capitalise.[17] In the event, the fire proved only a temporary setback, and instead of retreating, the Christians rebuilt the camp in stone. It is said that the construction of a bricks-and-mortar settlement at Santa Fe took just eighty days, and it would surely have demonstrated to the defenders of Granada that Isabella and Ferdinand were going nowhere.

Meanwhile, for the Christian soldiers in the camp, there was an air of adventure harking back to the romantic tales of crusades past, with warriors hoping to prove themselves on the battlefield. One of the most famous stories of bravado, occurring just prior to the construction of the camp at Santa Fe, was that of Hernán Pérez del Pulgar, who, along with his squires, in the early hours of 18 December 1490 secretly entered the besieged city by creeping along the bed of the river Darro and, without being discovered, pinned a parchment bearing the words '*Ave Maria*' to the door of the main mosque with his dagger. His audacity would be acknowledged in the years following the Reconquista by the renaming of the main mosque as the Church of María de la O, in recognition of the Catholic festival celebrated on the date he undertook his adventure, and also by his later being given burial in a tomb in this temporary cathedral of Granada.

There was, however, nothing romantic about conditions for the people in Granada during the siege.[18] As time wore on, they began to suffer a severe shortage of food. Many of the battles fought around the city were so the Moors could secure supply routes for food to get in; some of the most desperate fighting was around the village of Alfacar, owing to its strategic importance in terms of supplies. These battles in the hills and across the Vega, so crucial to the survival of the city, led to casualties on both sides but had the greatest impact on the Moors, who had no way to replenish their numbers. They were also painfully aware that requests for reinforcements from their fellow Muslims in North Africa continued to go unanswered. No allies were coming to their aid; they would make their last stand alone.

The onset of winter in 1491 saw the worst of the food shortages as heavy snows in the mountains cut off routes into the city and markets began to empty of produce. Suffering from hunger, their morale low, citizens both high- and low-born approached Boabdil to plead for a negotiated surrender, aware that victory was now impossible and that honourable capitulation offered a higher likelihood of their being allowed to remain in the city than defeat in a last-ditch battle would. In fact, the Christians, through the royal secretary, Hernando de Zafra, had already been working to bribe some of Granada's nobility to hand over the city peacefully even prior to this moment of crisis, which meant that talks between the two sides had, in effect, already begun. Now, however, with the people facing starvation, there was widespread support for negotiation and open dialogue with the enemy.

His people now clamouring for an end to their suffering, the emir invited Zafra and Gonzalo Fernández de Córdoba to visit him in secret at the Alhambra. There, negotiations began for the handover of Granada. These talks were not immediately straightforward; Baeza relates a number of obstacles that had to be overcome, including the fate of the *elches*—Christian captives who had converted to Islam, often to marry a Muslim—as well as Boabdil's determination not to face humiliation in any formal ceremony with the conquering Christians, for which he obtained assurances that he would retain his dignity and be greeted by Isabella and Ferdinand as an equal. By the end of November, a treaty had more or less been agreed. On paper at least, this looked promising for the inhabitants of the city. Little about their lives as Iberian Muslims would have to change apart from their allegiance to new monarchs. The Christians had even conceded that the *elches* would not be forced to revert to Christianity under the new regime. As a seal of commitment to the treaty, 500 men from Granada were sent as hostages to the camp at Santa Fe as a guarantee that the handover of the city would, indeed, take place.

On New Year's Day 1492, officials and a group of soldiers from the Christian camp entered the Alhambra in secret, setting themselves up at key points around the walls. The formal handover of Granada took place a day later, on 2 January, as Boabdil rode out to meet Isabella and Ferdinand in the allotted place by the river Genil. A copy of a romanticised composition of the scene painted some 400 years after the event by Francisco Pradilla y Ortiz now hangs in Granada's Royal Chapel—the Capilla Real. It portrays the Catholic Monarchs perched majestically on their horses, at the head of a crowd of Christian onlookers and greeting Boabdil on his smaller, black mount with a congregation of Moors at his back. One observer of these momentous events was an Italian adventurer from Genoa named Christopher Columbus, a frequent presence at the camp of Santa Fe as he sought funding from the Castilians for an expedition to explore a westward sea passage to India. Thus, the moment of the passing of one realm was observed by the great 'discoverer' of what was to be Spain's next area of conquest. Columbus noted in the journal of his first voyage:

> on the second day of the month of January ... I saw the royal banners of your Highnesses placed on the towers of [the Alhambra], which is the fortress of that city, and I saw the Moorish King come forth from the gates of the city and kiss the royal hands of your Highnesses.[19]

Meanwhile, Cardinal Mendoza, a key ally of Isabella and Ferdinand, rode into the city with the Castilian troops, passed through the Alhambra's Puerta de los Siete Suelos, and raised a crucifix and the royal standard above the Torre de la Vela. It must have been a subdued Granada that bore witness from across the river Darro in the Albaicín as these symbols of Christianity and foreign sovereignty were held aloft to mark the end of eight centuries of Muslim rule in al-Andalus. For Granada's citizens, there would surely have been a great deal of trepidation about what the future would hold.

Horrified at the downfall of their city, a number chose to leave. Among those to depart were Boabdil and his immediate family, who, under the terms of the surrender, had been given an estate in the Alpujarra region to the south. As he left Granada behind, Boabdil is famously said to have looked back on the beauty of the city and wept. According to the popular legend, his mother, Aisha, reproached him: 'Cry like a woman for what you weren't able to defend like a man!'[20] The purported spot of Boabdil's final moment of reflection on his beautiful, lost capital lies on the road south to the coast and became known as *El Puerto del Suspiro del Moro*—the Pass of the Moor's Last Sigh.

7

MUDÉJARS

It was a terrible event, even though they say the opposite in the schools. An admirable civilisation—a poetry, astronomy, architecture, and sensitivity unique in the world—were lost.[1]

This was the verdict, in the twentieth century, of modern Granada's most celebrated son, the poet Federico García Lorca, on the fall of the city into Christian hands. The sentiment most certainly was not that of the conquerors of 1492, however, who saw the event as a divine blessing. Bells rang out in cathedrals across Europe at the news, praising God for the defeat of the last 'infidel' state in Western Europe.

The Moors of Granada thus became Mudéjars—the term long used for Muslims living under Christian rule in other parts of the Iberian Peninsula. Following years of hardship, as they watched their deposed emir, Boabdil, and his entourage leave the city, the arrival through the gates of Christian troops would have been a fearsome spectacle, particularly so given the fate of Moors in other parts of the emirate, such as those of Malaga, who had been sold into slavery at the fall of their city. Yet the Treaty of

Granada, drawn up between Boabdil and the Catholic Monarchs, appeared generous to Granada's inhabitants. It allowed them to retain their customs, practise their religion, and in many ways continue their lives as they had before, only under new rulers. The treaty stated that:

> Their Highnesses and their successors forever shall let [the Moors] live under their own law, and they shall not allow anyone to take away their mosques or minarets or muezzins ... nor shall they interfere with their ways and customs.[2]

In a sign of good faith, as Christian troops took possession of Granada, supplies were sent into the city, bringing an end to months of hunger. The Moors were able to begin trading with the Christians, even, as the anonymous Arabic source that chronicled the events reveals, going down to the camp at Santa Fe to do so.[3]

Four days after Boabdil's departure, Isabella and Ferdinand rode into Granada, dressed in Moorish attire.[4] There was an air of excitement among the Christians as they finally got to see the fabled city for themselves. A letter to the Pope by one Christian eyewitness captured the admiration that the conquerors felt for their new territory, saying, 'Granada is the most distinguished and chief thing in the world, both in grandeur and power and the richness of its appointments. Seville is nothing but a peasant's house compared to the Alhambra'.[5]

It was the Royal Palaces that captivated the new rulers the most. They spent their days exploring the Alhambra before returning in the evenings to the camp at Santa Fe, still cautious about the possibility of rebellion—a concern that led Ferdinand to make some immediate alterations to the defences of the Alhambra itself to ensure security. Perhaps, at least in the beginning, it had been the intention of the Catholic Monarchs to honour the surrender agreement. A famous pragmatist, Ferdinand was put under pressure early on to forcibly convert his new subjects to Christianity, but he demurred given the potential for such a course of action to lead to uprisings. He was keen to ensure stability in this new corner of his realm and to turn his military focus instead towards issues along the borders of his lands in Aragon and in the Italian states.

Despite the trepidation of the Moors, the monarchs' early actions therefore demonstrated a desire for a smooth transition in adherence to the clause in the surrender agreement that promised to subject them only to sensitive administrators:

> The judges, officials, and governors [that] Their Highnesses shall appoint in the city of Granada and its surrounding areas shall be persons who will honor the Moors and treat them affectionately, and shall observe this treaty; if anyone should do anything improper, Their Highnesses shall order them to be replaced and punished.[6]

One of the most sympathetic of the officials to be tasked with the role of governing the city on behalf of the monarchs was Íñigo López de Mendoza, count of Tendilla.[7] This soldier and diplomat was a member of the powerful Mendoza family that had been key allies of Isabella and Ferdinand during the civil war in Castile at the beginning of their reign. A humanist and a Renaissance man, in his position as captain general of Granada and governor of the Alhambra he was tasked with commanding the city garrison at the Alhambra and given jurisdiction over the fortress itself. Over time, in many ways he came to act as a viceroy of the city,[8] taking a great interest in the Nasrid Palaces as well as in Granada as a whole, and from the very start, he worked to develop good relations with the remaining Muslim nobility. He would pass on this support for the Moors and their heritage to his descendants. Accompanying him in those early years were the archbishop of Granada, Hernando de Talavera, who was to oversee the city's spiritual development, and the royal secretary, Hernando de Zafra, who supervised the legal and administrative aspects of the city. A key task for the trio was to prevent any revolt from amongst the newly conquered subjects.

One way they sought to ward off rebellion was through incorporating willing Moors into the city's elite. Of course, not all of the former nobility were welcome, and to prevent the possibility that the people might regroup around their old rulers, encouragement and assistance were given to many of these influential figures to leave instead for North Africa. In autumn 1493, Boabdil himself bade farewell to his small estate in the Alpujarra and joined some 6,000 of his ex-countrymen in going into exile. Like his uncle and rival, al-Zaghal, before him, Boabdil saw out the final years of his life across the strait. This exodus left the Nasrid aristocracy much reduced in number, yet not all availed themselves of the opportunity to leave, and those who remained generally co-operated with the Castilians, taking up positions in the upper echelons of the new society. One of the most prominent of these was Yahya al-Najjar, a grandson of Yusuf IV who prior to the fall of Granada had been the governor of Baza in the east of the emirate. During the brutal siege of his city, al-Najjar had persuaded his people to surrender to Isabella and Ferdinand rather than prolong their terrible suffering. Unbeknownst to his fellow citizens, however, he had already been in secret negotiations with the Christians for a number of years, providing them with support against his fellow Muslims. After the conquest of Baza, al-Najjar was baptised as a Christian in King Ferdinand's tent and took the new name Pedro de Granada.

It was not only the few remaining former Nasrid nobles such as Pedro de Granada who were to choose the path of integration. The reduction in number of the former aristocracy in Granada also provided an opportunity for members of the middle classes to make their mark if they chose to collaborate with the new regime. The names of those who made up the city's first Ayuntamiento, or city council, which would soon establish itself in the magnificent setting of Yusuf I's Madraza, were all Moorish,[9] many of them from the city's merchants and religious elite. In the beginning, to have Muslims undertake much of the administration of the city made sense, since the population was almost entirely of that faith and enough Moors were happy to participate in exchange for the improvement in their social position.

However, whilst the upper stratum of Nasrid society either left Granada or began to integrate, most ordinary citizens deeply resented the new overlords and were begrudging in their obedience to these Christian usurpers. Yet, it was also impractical for them to move overseas to places they had never visited and where they would be viewed as outsiders. In addition, it was simply an economic impossibility for many without means. French-Lebanese writer Amin Maalouf's novel *Leo the African* portrays well the debate that must have gone on within families in those early years about whether or not to move to another Muslim country. Families in the Albaicín district are portrayed in their struggle between those who argued in favour of leaving and others who felt that the only way to restore the Islamic kingdom at some future opportunity would be for Muslims to remain. There were, however, some very strong voices arguing against remaining, with some Islamic lawyers proclaiming the impracticability for a good Muslim of living under Christian rule, insisting their duty under such circumstances was to emigrate to another, Islamic, realm.

Maalouf's novel captures the psychological effect on Granada's citizens of suddenly finding themselves in the position of having to defer to their former enemies, as Christian soldiers and officials appeared on the streets. Despite this, in the beginning it appeared that there would be no compulsion for the majority of the Moors to leave. Mudéjars had lived under Christian rule in other areas of Spain for centuries in those territories taken in earlier periods of the Reconquista. Although they were generally regarded as second-class citizens, they were often valued by Christian landowners for their agricultural expertise and as a source of cheap labour; in places such as Aragon and Valencia, their community was a significant presence. There was hope, therefore, that the Mudéjars of Granada too could live some semblance of their former lives.

Nonetheless, even if some held on to this hope, the Moors could not have failed to notice the precarious lot of religious minorities under Castilian rule when, on 31 March 1492, Isabella and Ferdinand issued the Alhambra Decree, ordering all Jews in Spain to either convert to Christianity or leave the country. The reasons for the expulsion of the Jews lay in the history of Castile, and this act was almost certainly on the cards before the fall of Granada. In the fourteenth century there had been an explosion of violence against the Sephardi Jewish community across cities such as Seville, leading many of its members to convert to Christianity in order to save their own lives. Despite this, widespread paranoia grew over the next century that these so-called *conversos* were continuing to practise their old faith beneath a Christian façade. The aim of the Inquisition, established in Castile in 1478, had been to uncover such *conversos*, for whose perceived lack of adherence the blame was laid at the feet of Jews who had refused to convert. The expulsion decree claimed:

> [E]very day it seems that the Jews increasingly pursue their evil and harmful mission wherever they live and converse—and because there can be no place for offending our holy faith ... [it is necessary to expel] the Jews from our kingdoms.[10]

This Castilian issue was, tragically, now to impact on Granada. Whilst Jews had been expelled from the city in Almohad times, under the Nasrids the community had been re-established, although as was common under Muslim rule, they always faced restrictions such as those placed on them under Ismail I of wearing a sign on their clothes to distinguish themselves from Muslim subjects.[11] Yet, despite these restrictions, records show the Jews of Granada to have had a strong presence as traders in Granada's silk market,[12] although estimating the size of their community in order to understand the effect of expulsion is difficult. Hieronymus Münzer, a German visitor to Granada two years after the event, claims that as many as 20,000 Jews had lived in the city, although recent research suggests this might be something of an exaggeration, with around 3,000 across the emirate as a whole being a more likely figure.[13] Unfortunately, archaeological evidence on this point is minimal because all traces of the Jewish presence were quickly erased. The Jewish quarter of the Nasrid era, which had been located around today's Calle San Matías, at the entrance of what is now the Realejo district,[14] was soon cleared and covered with new Christian buildings.

The expulsion of the Jews was traumatic. Whilst the Alhambra Decree claimed to offer them protection as they sold off their properties and possessions, in effect, the hurried nature of these sales drove down market prices and forced those who chose the path of exile rather than conversion to accept crippling financial losses alongside being stripped of the right to live in their homeland. In addition, as a taste of what was to come much later for Granada's Muslims, the Jewish expulsion demonstrated the brutal side of human nature. Jewish families trekking across Spain to move into exile in Portugal or across the sea suffered robbery, rape, murder, and even kidnap by slave traders.[15] This banishment on the grounds of non-conformity to the dominant religion must have formed part of the debate taking place among the Mudéjars over whether to stay or to leave under the reasonably good conditions of exile offered to them at the start of Christian rule.

Despite the option to leave, most Mudéjars chose to remain, and for some years after the fall of Granada to the Christians, the city remained almost completely Moorish in character. This is illustrated by the account of Münzer. A German physician, he passed through in 1494 while travelling around Europe, and his account is unfortunately only brief and possibly suffers from bouts of exaggeration.[16] What is clear, though, is that at the time of his visit, Granada remained predominantly Muslim, with Moorish culture continuing to dominate. His observations of the nature of the city included descriptions of being overwhelmed at each call to prayer by the clamour of its mosques, which he visited to observe the customs. His descriptions of the Albaicín suggest an incredibly densely packed area, and he expresses admiration for the advanced dedication to hygiene exemplified by the complex water systems, so different to those found elsewhere in Europe:

> [The Albaicín] has such built-up, narrow streets that the houses' upper storeys mostly touch each other, and in most one ass can hardly pass another except in the better-known streets ... The Saracens' houses are mostly so cramped and shabby on the outside but so pretty inside that you would hardly believe it. They mostly have water pipes or cisterns. The pipes and channels are duplicated. Some are for clean drinking water while the others are for taking away waste and sewage, etc. The Saracens are well-versed in this. In all the streets there are open drains for waste water, and if any house lacks its own drains because of the difficulty of the site, the waste is thrown out into these drains at night. They do not have many sewers. However, the people are very particular.[17]

Coming so soon after the fall of the Nasrids, his description of the Alhambra is, however, frustratingly fleeting. He details the marble and the fountains, including the Patio de los Leones; however, he disappointingly concludes that it is impossible for him to review everything, but that the reader would think it paradise. In addition, he speaks well of Mendoza, who showed him around the palaces and provides an indication of the admiration felt for the complex by its new custodians. He also notes the splendid homes of the Moorish nobility, 'with halls and gardens and fresh water and other amenities.'[18] He adds that the Moors delighted in their gardens and speaks of the comparative sophistication of expertise in their techniques of cultivation.

Yet, despite the fact that Granada was clearly still overwhelmingly Muslim at the time of Münzer's visit, work had already started to Christianise the city. Streets were being widened and churches were beginning to appear, Münzer noting that the peal of the church bells that could now be heard was totally foreign to the ears of the Muslim inhabitants. Whilst early immigration by Christians into the city was relatively slow—the promises contained within the Treaty of Granada to protect the Moors' property rights meant there was little real estate for newcomers to purchase at the beginning—this was soon to change. Attracted by the economic opportunities this newly added territory presented, Christian settlers began to move into the city, though these were not necessarily the pious types the Catholic Monarchs would have wished to attract in order to convince the native population of the superiority of Christianity. Ironically, given the recent expulsion of the Jews, some new arrivals even appear to have been *conversos* coming from other parts of Spain to evade the watchful scrutiny of the Inquisition, which had not yet been established in Granada. The soldier and writer Luis del Mármol Carvajal, who grew up in the city, tells of more dubious characters who saw a chance to advance themselves in this land of new opportunities, saying, 'The majority of those who came to populate it were men of war or upstarts, there being among them many who were ... uncontrollable in the evils that military life brings with it'.[19] Many settlers came for economic reasons, seeking work in the silk industry or—a more exciting prospect— attracted by rumours of concealed hordes of gold buried by the Nasrids as they left the city, in the hopes of retrieving it when one day they could return.[20] Diego Hurtado de Mendoza, the youngest son of the count of Tendilla, would later recall the economic draw for certain undesirables:

Like all newly colonized places, Granada had had to draw her citizens from here, there and everywhere. A large number had been ne'er-do-wells or beggars who had come to make a new start, others had come simply to try and make their fortunes as quickly as they could ... it was inevitable that many unstable characters should be attracted to the place, for stable people tend to stay where they are born.[21]

Over time, as Christian migrants began to settle in the city, there was a desire to segregate Granada's two communities. This led, in 1498, to a division of living space, with the top of the Albaicín hill designated a Moorish quarter, whilst the lower part of the city was defined as the Christian area. A mixed population remained in the lower areas of the Albaicín, in the former Alcazaba.[22]

Keeping an eye on his flock and the slightly unsavoury newcomers was Talavera, although his primary role from the start had been to convert the city's native population to Christianity. This deeply spiritual man, who had been for many years Queen Isabella's confessor, had at his own request been created the first archbishop of Granada. Renowned for his belief in peaceful means of conversion, his place in the history of Granada is that of an almost saint-like figure, a brief glimmer of hope for the Mudéjars of a destiny that could have been very different.[23] He was in his sixties at the time of the Reconquista and in his role at the Castilian court had been a long-time opponent of the Inquisition. He believed that education and persuasion were far more effective tools than force, torture, or the threat of execution in bringing to the Church those whose lack of belief, he argued, most likely stemmed from a lack of understanding. Münzer claims not to have met a man more learned in theology and philosophy in the whole of Iberia and considered Talavera to be, 'another Jerome, because he has so mortified himself by his abstinent life and by continual study ... that you can count the bones which are covered over only by skin.'[24]

Talavera's method was to educate and lead by example. He was one of the few to understand the links between language and social harmony, realising that effective rule over the Mudéjars could not be exercised without an ability to communicate with them in their own language. He commissioned a Castilian–Arabic grammar book and, despite his age, learned some Arabic and encouraged the clergy who moved into the city to do likewise.[25] Sixty years later, Francisco Núñez Muley, an early convert to Christianity who had been one of the archbishop's pages as a young boy, recalled how Talavera had even allowed his Arabic-speaking congregation in church to respond to the Latin in their native tongue.[26] However, with the poor standard of literacy among so many of the clergy across Spain, in the short time that Talavera's methods held sway in Granada, this attempt was to bear little fruit. Still, his philosophy of gently assimilating the Moors into Christianity was in stark contrast to what came later. For example, he preached in person on a daily basis to invited notables of the city in the hope of creating a trickle-down effect in terms of conversions, establishing meeting houses in the Albaicín to assist in this process. He also demonstrated a great interest in Moorish culture, being particularly impressed with Muslim alms-giving and charitable work. Although as a man of his time his ultimate goal was to bring the heathen into the fold, his methods were generally peaceful.

Through Talavera's influence, forced conversion of the native inhabitants was therefore not yet on the cards in the early years of Christian rule. However, his strategy of gradual assimilation proved to be remarkably slow, with few choosing to convert beyond those nobles who saw it as a means of social progression. In hindsight it does not seem unreasonable that this approach had so little effect during the first ten years. Cultural change is slow to occur and likely more effective when undertaken over generations than in just a handful of years. Nevertheless, the

Reconquista had in many respects been a religious crusade, with part of its funding coming directly from the Vatican. Thus, the conversion of the Moors was a high priority for many among Castile's religious community, not to mention for their deeply devout queen. In the final year of the fifteenth century, seven years after their conquest of Granada, Isabella and Ferdinand returned to the Alhambra and were reportedly shocked by the lack of progress made in converting the Moors. Although Christians from Castile had begun to move in, the call to prayer could still be heard five times a day, and the Mudéjars continued to dress in their traditional costume, speak in Arabic, and practise the customs and religion they had for centuries.

With the population of 'Old' Christians (a term used to differentiate those born as Christians from those 'New' Christians who had converted to the faith) growing in the city, calls to convert the native people grew louder. It would be another of Isabella's confessors, the archbishop of Toledo, later cardinal, Francisco Jiménez de Cisneros—who accompanied the king and queen to Granada in 1499—who would finally take the approach to conversion in a radical, new direction. Perhaps it was the astonishment that in seven years so little progress had been made by Talavera that led Isabella and Ferdinand to accept Cisneros's calls for a redoubling of efforts. Cisneros was given permission to work alongside Talavera with the aim of bringing the Mudéjars over to the 'true faith'. Yet the two archbishops could not have differed more in their attitudes on how to achieve this. Whilst Talavera had gone to great lengths to bring Christianity to the Mudéjars through their own language, Cisneros felt his Arabic translations had little merit. Taking inspiration from the Bible's Book of Matthew to demonstrate his contempt, he is claimed to have compared teaching the Moors the Word of Christ with throwing pearls before swine.[27] For Cisneros, conversions—by force if necessary—were essential for Granada.

Cisneros set about his conversions in two ways. One was to shower influential Mudéjars with valuable items of clothing such as silks and velvets, essentially bribing them to change their faith. The other, and one that was to become notorious, was to use more brutal means of persuasion. Cisneros's secretary and later biographer, Juan de Vallejo, records how he took prisoner a descendant of one of the branches of the Nasrid royal family, a man named by Spanish sources as Zegrí Azaator.[28] As Nasrid royalty, Zegrí was a man of distinction and known around Granada for his upstanding morals—exactly the type of man Cisneros needed to make an example of to the rest of the city. Accordingly, we are told, Zegrí found himself brought under God's command by force and was set upon in his cell by a henchman named Pedro de León, who—making a pun of his name—tortured him with the ferocity of a lion until he begged to be brought before Cisneros. Brought so low by this suffering over many days, his former pride destroyed, Zegrí purportedly claimed, 'Señor, I wish to be Christian, and I do so of my own will, as I have had a revelation from God that he commands this of me.'[29] Pleased with the results of his methods, Cisneros baptised this Nasrid noble with the new Spanish name Gonzalo Hernández.

Whilst this attack on a Nasrid noble appears to have frightened some Mudéjars into seeking conversion, Cisneros had other tactics up his sleeve to ensure they would do so in greater numbers. One of the first groups he chose to target were Christians who had converted to Islam prior to the fall of the city. These were the *elches* whom Boabdil's translator Baeza had mentioned in terms of the importance they had been given in the treaty negotiations between the Christians and the Moors. The Treaty of Granada had specifically prohibited the harassment of this group:

> It shall not be allowed for any person to mistreat, by deed or by word, any Christian man or woman who, previous to this treaty, has converted to Islam; and if any Moor has a wife who is a renegade [a

Christian who converted to Islam], that person shall not be forced to become Christian against her will, and she shall be interviewed in the presence of Christians and Moors, and her will shall be followed.[30]

Cisneros's use of such 'interviews' therefore sparked the first major act of rebellion against the new rulers in Granada. He sent two officials up into the Albaicín to bring a woman who was the daughter of an *elche* in for questioning. However, the woman refused to submit willingly to this outrageous treatment, and, while being escorted across the square beside the Bab al-Bunut—the Gate of the Standards, located in what is now the Placeta de Abad—she began to cry out to alert the neighbourhood to her abduction. Within moments the area was filled with angry Muslims who gathered to protect the woman. The crowd began to shout and manhandle Cisneros's agents, and as the violence intensified, a rock was dropped onto the head of one of his men, killing him instantly, the second man only saved by a local woman who hid him under her bed.[31]

The initial altercation fuelled a wider, seething discontent that now erupted across the whole of the upper Albaicín. Mudéjars began to barricade the area, weapons appeared, and the first serious threat to the stability of Granada since the Catholic Monarchs took control began in earnest. The municipal governors cannot have been particularly surprised that a rebellion such as this should break out, considering the tensions caused by Cisneros's utter contempt for both the spirit of the 1491 treaty and the legal obligations owed to the Moors under its terms. Unsurprisingly, as the revolt gathered momentum, his own house further down the hill in the Alcazaba was surrounded by the mob. Cisneros was advised to leave for the safety of the Alhambra, but as a show of defiance against the rebels and with a deep belief in the righteousness of his own cause, he chose to remain in the area. It was soldiers from the Alhambra under the command of the count of Tendilla who would come to Cisneros's rescue and set about trying to pacify the rebellion unleashed by his actions.

A number of days passed before the uprising was quelled, and it was done so not through force of arms, but rather by strength of character and reconciliation. The count of Tendilla and Archbishop Talavera, both of whom had expressed their opposition to Cisneros's methods of forced conversion, demonstrated the rapport that they had built up with the Mudéjars. They are said to have approached the crowd unarmed. At first bombarded with stones by the people behind the barricades, they were then allowed to negotiate with the rebels, in a sign of the high regard in which these two leaders of the city were held by the local population. Tempers were cooled and order was restored, the count of Tendilla even installing his wife and youngest children in a house in the Albaicín as a sign of good faith between the two communities. Even so, this manifestation of popular dissent did nothing to move Cisneros; nor did it dent his zeal to forcibly convert Granada fully to Christianity. Although 1492 marked the end of Muslim rule, 1499 heralded the beginning of the overt persecution of the city's Moors that would lead, just over a century later, to their ultimate expulsion from Spain, just as had been the fate of the Jews before them.

Undeterred by the anger he was rousing, Cisneros continued his conversions with renewed fervour, no longer focusing only on recent converts to Islam, but now targeting all its adherents. Such was the scale of these forced conversions that candidates were herded in crowds and sprinkled with holy water in a kind of collective baptism, rather than being received individually at the font. A relief created in the 1520s that can be seen inside Granada's Capilla Real portrays vast huddles of Mudéjars waiting for their mass initiation to Christianity. For some, such as Talavera, these events were entirely the wrong way to bring people to the religion, yet others hailed Cisneros for his efforts.

Pope Alexander VI congratulated the cardinal on his having baptised 60,000 souls.[32]

The forced baptisms were not the only outward signs of the persecution. Cisneros also ordered the infamous burnings of all Arabic books in the city. Only those works considered by the Christians to have practical merit, such as medical texts, escaped the flames, and these were collected and sent to the future cardinal's own University of Alcalá. The exact date of this immolation of centuries of thought and wisdom is not known for definite, but it is believed to have taken place in what is now the Plaza de Bibarrambla. Cisneros's secretary described the comprehensiveness of this attempt at cultural obliteration:

> To eradicate everything ... of their perverse and evil sect, their community leaders were ordered to take all of their Qurans and all of their other special books, as many as they had, which amounted to 4 or 5 thousand volumes ... and make very large fires to burn them all.[33]

Some of those involved considered keeping a selection of the parchments to make further use of them and noted the sheer value of the silver coverings of many. However, Cisneros expressly forbade anyone from saving anything from the fires. Vallejo concludes: 'thus everything was burnt, leaving no memory ... except for the medical books, which were great in number ... and these today are in the library of the University of Alcalá.'

Whilst the city of Granada might have been subdued in the aftermath of the rebellion of 1499 and its citizens forced to convert, those whose anger remained unassuaged left the city to regroup and continue the fight in the mountainous Alpujarra region, where they warned their fellow Muslims in the remote villages that they too would soon be forced to convert. Angered by the threat to their way of life and roused by the news from the city, another insurrection arose here in the middle of January 1500, far more violent than that witnessed in the Albaicín. Putting to the sword the Christians who had moved into the area, as well as any Mudéjar who had collaborated with the infidel rulers, the rebels readied themselves to fight to the death. So serious was the situation now that the army sent to respond was led by King Ferdinand in person. Reprisals by the Christian forces were swift and horrifying. Fighters in rebel villages were thrown from clifftops; countless women and children were sold into slavery; and, in the town of Andarax, hundreds were blown up along with the mosque they had gathered inside to seek shelter.[34]

The Catholic Monarchs were furious with Cisneros over the Alpujarra rebellion. As an indication of how vital it was that their newly conquered province remain peaceful, Ferdinand is said to have chastised his wife for her unwavering faith in her confessor, saying, 'What do you think of the mess your archbishop has got us into now? That which the kings our predecessors have won with so much effort and blood ... we have endangered in a single hour for his cause.'[35] But Cisneros remained unperturbed, and as the anger of the king abated, he persuaded the monarchs of the great work he had done in the city by saving so many souls. Now, he argued, the terms of the 1491 surrender treaty had been broken through the rebellion of the Moors, and steps could be taken to take conversion measures even further.

Cisneros's vision for a completely converted region won the day. In 1502, the Edict of Forced Conversion was signed, and the Mudéjars of Granada, followed some years later by those who had lived for centuries in other parts of Spain as Muslim subjects under Christian rule, were given the choice to either convert or leave the country. The vast majority chose conversion, many conceding that an outward show of conformity did not equal an internal acceptance of a faith. For a great number of them, there was no real choice but to convert in view of the obstacles placed in the way of exile. Any who chose to leave were prohibited from taking with them any gold or silver, or even their young children, and they were permitted to depart only from certain ports, inconveniently located in the north of Spain. Indeed, so onerous were the proscriptions that it is almost certain these were designed to discourage the Moors from electing for the option of exile.[36] Mudéjars were seen as an invaluable labour force, and their mass exodus at that time would have devastated the population of the region and destroyed its agricultural system. Conversion to Christianity was in reality the only option, not just for the victims of this policy, but also for its architects.

8

MORISCOS

The forced conversions of the Mudéjars began a new era in the history of Granada, now essentially considered a Christian city. These converts would henceforth be known by the pejorative Castilian term 'Moriscos' and would continue to be deemed inferior to the 'Old' Christians who settled in the city.[1] There are records of Morisco letters written to the Ottoman sultan in Constantinople and the Mamluk sultan in Cairo, lamenting the desperate misery and indignity of their treatment.[2] Yet, despite these appeals to potential allies in the Muslim world, the Moriscos were to find themselves very much alone. Indeed, to prevent any potential foreign intervention in the situation, Isabella and Ferdinand had themselves already dispatched an ambassador to the Mamluk sultan in Cairo, who was more persuaded by the Catholic Monarchs' promises of support against his Ottoman enemies than any pleas he might have received from his co-religionists in defeated Granada.

The Moriscos were therefore left to seethe with anger. Forced to make an outward show of their adherence to Christianity, their continued commitment to Islam had to be, from that point on, undertaken behind closed doors. As the locally born historian Mármol Carvajal recalled, the Moriscos were forced into a state of pretend conformity, observing Christian practices on the outside, whilst hating the new faith on the inside. They would attend church on Sundays and feast days to avoid punishment by the authorities, yet on Fridays, behind closed doors, they would perform their ablutions and carry out their Islamic prayers. Mármol Carvajal describes how they would have their children baptised, then:

> wash them secretly with hot water to clean off the chrism and the holy oil, undertake their circumcision ceremonies, and turn them into Moors; the brides, who were made by the priests to wear Christian clothes to receive the Church's benedictions, would take them off when back in the house and dress themselves as Moors, celebrating their weddings in the Morisco way with the instruments and the banquets of the Moors.[3]

Despite the clear hypocrisy that the Moriscos were forced to live with, the conversions were widely supported by the Old Christian immigrants. Only Talavera seems to have questioned the sense of these mass events and, indeed, whether any of the conversions could be considered genuine given the force involved. But the archbishop's ability to influence or propagate a pragmatic approach towards the issue was coming to an end. As a sign of the unruly behemoth that the Inquisition had become across the rest of Spain, it would soon bring in for interrogation this high-ranking clergyman who had always opposed its imposition and had kept it out of Granada. The Pope and even Cisneros both called for Talavera's release, which was eventually granted; however, this tireless promoter of tolerance died a few years afterwards.

Perhaps even for Cisneros the exertion of the past few years had been too much, because, in 1501, whilst staying at the Alhambra, he fell seriously ill. Queen Isabella, deeply concerned for her confessor, had him transferred to the quieter Generalife, and though his doctors seemed unable to do anything for him, in a twist of great irony it was the wisdom of the Moors that saved his life. Cisneros's secretary relates how the future cardinal was told of an elderly Moorish woman with great healing powers. He agreed to meet her, and she visited his room at the Generalife in secret over a period of eight nights, administering herbal treatments. On the eighth day she succeeded where Christian physicians had failed: the fever finally broke and Cisneros recovered his strength.[4] Perhaps this awareness of the medical knowledge of the Moors is what had prompted him to spare the medical treatises from the flames in the Plaza de Bibarrambla.

With the mass conversions, Granada was able to increase its pace of change towards becoming physically Christian, and the drive to urge Old Christians from across the rest of Spain to move into the city continued apace. This encouragement to immigrants was given a huge boost by the transfer of Castile's royal appellate court to Granada. The Real Chancillería, whose headquarters would, over the next few decades, be established in the newly constructed Plaza Nueva, gained jurisdiction over the whole of the south of Castile, and being located in the recently conquered Granada, it provided middle-class Castilians with opportunities for social improvement that they lacked in other cities dominated by an established nobility. This led to the arrival in the city of numerous ambitious and upwardly mobile clerks and lawyers, who tended to view the Moriscos with disdain.[5]

These Old Christian newcomers tended to be highly supportive of the royal decrees against Moorish customs that started to be issued from the beginning of the sixteenth century. It was clear that the newly converted had overwhelmingly become so on the surface only, yet the decrees themselves did little other than turn the Moriscos even more against the faith that had been imposed on them. This is because, whilst in theory the decrees were issued to ensure the Moriscos integrated with Old Christians, in many ways the effect was to make life incredibly difficult for them by forcing them to rely on the Old Christians who were moving into the city to oversee crucial aspects of their lives. For example, in spite of having converted to Christianity, Moriscos were banned from being named as godparents at baptisms; instead, an Old Christian had to be found to undertake the role. Halal butchers were outlawed and Moriscos were prohibited from slaughtering animals unless an Old Christian were present to oversee it. These measures were, of course, open to abuse by Castilian settlers, who could demand exorbitant fees to perform these services, or simply withhold them completely. Essentially, the limitations precluded the converts from integrating with the Christian society of which they were now supposedly part. They were, instead, treated as second-class citizens.

Yet, despite the hardships, influential members of the Morisco community became adept in the early years at achieving relaxations of some of the decrees, at least those made against the cultural practices deemed so abominable by the Castilians. This they achieved by offering to pay extra taxes.[6] The result was that Granada's Moriscos continued to speak Arabic, wear Moorish clothes, and invest in traditional silks and jewellery for their women for the next half century. Paintings from the 1520s by the German artist Christoph Weiditz clearly show just how distinctively from the Castilians the Moriscos continued to dress even two decades after the forced conversions. Meanwhile, another suspect practice in the eyes of the Castilians also continued: the frequenting of the public baths, of which a number of examples still survive around Granada, most notably those on the Carrera del Darro. At that time, the Moriscos were supported by the powerful Mendozas, governors of the Alhambra. When Íñigo López de Mendoza died in 1515, his son Luis took over the position, as well as inheriting the newly acquired family title of marquess of Mondéjar, bringing to the city the same respect and support for the Moors as his father had shown them.

In 1526, this second captain general of the Alhambra had a chance to demonstrate his love for Moorish culture when his city received its first royal visit in over two decades. The grandson of the Catholic Monarchs, Charles I—better known outside of Spain as the Holy Roman Emperor Charles V—made his one and only visit to Granada as a six-month honeymoon with his beloved bride, Isabella of Portugal. Entering the city through triumphal arches, the couple were greeted by enthusiastic displays of Moorish music and dancing. The city was to make a great impression on Charles and on a number of his entourage, including the Venetian ambassador, Andrea Navagero, whose letters home to Italy describe his fascination with Granada and in particular with the Alhambra: 'From so many ruins of delightful palaces, one can judge that those Moorish kings did not neglect anything that contributed to a pleasant and contented life.'[7] However, he also deplored the degradation of the city and its surroundings, adding, 'the country was much more beautiful in the time that it was in the hands of the Moors than it is now. Now there are many houses in ruin and gardens gone to ruin, which under the Moors were maintained so that they grew.'[8]

The display of Moorish music and dancing was intended to capture the hearts of the royal couple. Unlike many of the Christian immigrants to the city, Charles was well-travelled and would have been aware that not every Christian across Europe dressed the same way, spoke the same language, or practised the same customs. There was therefore a chance that the Moriscos could win him round to supporting the cultural practices that they had managed to preserve despite the earlier decrees. Indeed, it appears that the traditional dance, the *zambra*, pleased the royal couple.[9] Taking heart from this, a few days later Morisco leaders from the Ayuntamiento approached Charles with a list of complaints about the abuses their community had been facing at the hands of the immigrant Christian population, and, it seems, Charles was sufficiently concerned by these reports to commission an investigation. The Old Christian leaders of Granada, however, were in no mood to be criticised by the native inhabitants. Fighting back, they argued that the greatest problem in the city was not their abuse but rather that the Moriscos persisted in practising their old faith even then, twenty years after their mass conversions. In order to reach a resolution to the conflict between the two communities, Charles allowed the investigations to take place before making his own pronouncements on the situation.[10] His judgements were presented later that year against the backdrop of the resting place of both his parents and grandparents, the recently inaugurated Capilla Real. Unfortunately for the Moriscos, the result was far from what they had hoped for when first petitioning the king. Although Charles chastised the churchmen of Granada for their misdeeds and expressed concern about the need for clerical reform, the main issue to arise from his judgement was his desire for the prohibition of Moorish cultural practices. His measures extended earlier decrees that included the proscription of the dress worn by Morisco women and rules on the method for slaughtering animals. And they went further still, banning the use of Arabic—including Arabic names—as well as the use of Arab baths. Moriscos were further ordered to keep their front doors open on Fridays, to show that no secret Muslim ceremonies were taking place, and the men were prohibited from bearing arms.

The restrictions were harsh, but as usual, the Moriscos could count on powerful support. The marquess of Mondéjar upheld his family's tradition, and the Mendozas again allied with key members of the Morisco community to plead with the monarch to relax the rules. Once more, their calls would be heard; as had happened before, a cash-strapped monarch was receptive to a bribe in the form of extra tax revenue. At that moment, Charles was in need of funds for a project that would leave his indelible mark on Granada. While residing at the Alhambra he had decided, as so many Nasrid rulers had before him, to make his own signature addition to the complex: a building that would dominate the rest; a palace worthy of an emperor.

The Palacio de Carlos V dwarfs all else within the Alhambra today, just as originally intended. The king faced instability and rebellion across his vast European empire, and not least of his worries was the threat of further unrest in Granada, which brought with it the risk that the Moriscos might ally with his Ottoman enemies. Being so often absent from Spain, Charles intended the palace to act as a local reminder of his authority. Built in a Renaissance style that emulated the clean, monumental architecture of ancient Rome, it also acted as a cultural challenge to the intricate and delicate palaces of the vanquished Moors.[11] Charles was never to stay at the palace, and in fact the building remained unfinished into the latter half of the twentieth century. However, he needed money for his project and, in an expedient relaxation of earlier decrees, offered the Moors a forty-year moratorium during which they would be able to retain many of their customs in exchange for an annual levy put towards the cost of his vanity project.

The four-decade respite ensured that for the middle part of the sixteenth century, Granada would again manage to maintain much of its Moorish character, even though—in theory at least—the people were now all Christians. Of course, many Moriscos secretly retained their old faith, yet as time moved on, there would have been great difficulty in continuing to practise some aspects of Muslim tradition properly. The law robbed them of their teachers, and books would have been hard to obtain, especially copies of the Quran. And as well as the difficulties the

Moriscos had in maintaining their old religion, there were still plenty of obstacles to their accepting the new one. One of the most significant, as Archbishop Talavera had understood, was that the newly converted needed to be educated in the ways of the unfamiliar faith. This led, in 1531, to the founding of the University of Granada on Charles's orders, to ensure a high level of training would be available for those tasked with educating the Moriscos about their new faith, and also to enable younger members of that community to study for themselves the religion into which they had been born.

Several among the Moriscos to attend the university, born many decades after the Reconquista, went on to achieve important positions. Two would come to be forever associated with the last-ditch attempts to save their community from expulsion later in the century: Alonso del Castillo and Miguel de Luna, both of whom had been medical students. Another early alumnus was Juan de Albotodo. This son of a Morisco blacksmith was spotted for his intelligence by Christian leaders when he was a young boy, and he was encouraged to study at the city's newly founded university. His education and a genuine belief in Christianity that set him apart from the vast majority of his community would eventually lead him to the Jesuits, evangelicals who were far more tolerant of New Christians than the majority of church orders. The Jesuits, like Talavera before them, were conscious of the fact that education of the Moriscos would likely be most effective if undertaken in their native language. Part of the problem with early attempts at such education had been that the clergy of Granada generally spoke little or no Arabic. As an Arabic speaker, Albotodo was given the task of educating the children of the Albaicín as the head of the Jesuit Casa de la Doctrina, which was located opposite what is now the Plaza Aliatar and began its work in the 1550s.

Albotodo's school provides one example of how some movement was made towards integration during the four decades after

Charles's pronouncements. And whilst there has been a tendency amongst historians to view society in sixteenth-century Granada as a binary division between Old Christians and Moriscos, with little intermingling between the two communities beyond the assimilated former nobility and those who had joined the original administration of the city, it is likely that the situation was much more complex. In the letter in defence of Morisco culture that he wrote in 1567, Núñez Muley emphasised how Morisco men conducted business with Old and New Christians alike and dressed as the Castilians did, except that they were banned from carrying weapons. He also noted that there were Old Christians in the city who, like the Moriscos, attended the bath houses, and even some who worked there.[12] In terms of dress, in the early decades of the sixteenth century, a number of surprising decrees were issued ordering Old Christian women to stop wearing the Morisco *almalafa* garment,[13] something they had perhaps taken to doing for modesty when outdoors.

Evidence seems to suggest, then, that within the city of Granada, the Morisco community was adapting to the new conditions in many ways.[14] The livelihoods of traders and artisans, for example, would have depended on day-to-day interactions with the Old Christians of the city, and this would have required speaking Castilian and understanding the rules they were expected to obey. This is not to suggest that the Moriscos dropped their culture in the city—far from it—but rather that they adapted in a way that was not to filter through to the much more conservative and traditional surrounding countryside. There, the situation was different. Many villagers would have been largely removed from everyday interactions with Old Christians, and it would have been far more natural for people in the countryside to continue living by ancient traditions. Another feature of the countryside that made it far less receptive to Christianisation was the presence of the *monfíes*—Moors who had escaped to the mountains and continued to practise their religion, living as bandits and developing a fearsome reputation amongst Christian settlers. The difference in the willingness of Moriscos in the city versus those in the countryside to adapt to Christian rule was to play a major role in the events that took place during the reign of the next king of Spain, Philip II.

For the better part of four decades following Charles's visit to the city, no serious attempt was made to reopen the question of the Moors of Granada and their cultural practices. This would change, however, under Philip in the latter half of the sixteenth century. To understand why Philip returned to this issue, it is necessary to view the situation of Granada within the wider political context of Spain during the early years of his reign. Since the time of Charles V, Spain had seen itself at the forefront of the battle to protect Catholicism, fighting on the one hand the spread of Islam through the expansion of the Ottoman Empire, and on the other that of Protestantism in northern Europe. To give just one example, in 1566 Spain became embroiled in a revolt in the Netherlands that over the following decades would see it dragged into other conflicts, including against England. Significantly, the troubles that Philip faced abroad burdened Spain with a colossal expense. In Granada, this was felt through vast increases in tax on the silk industry; in 1561 alone, the levy on silk was increased by 60 per cent, with terrible consequences for the local economy.[15]

On top of the economic consequences for the Moriscos of Philip's international campaigns, there was also worry about the security of Spain's own Mediterranean seaboard. In the 1560s concern was increasing over raids being carried out by the Barbary Corsairs, particularly around Valencia but also along the shores to the south of Granada. A large population of angry and bitter refugees who had left their homes in al-Andalus and fled across the sea to North Africa were said to be using their local knowledge of the coastline to aid these Muslim pirates and privateers in their success.[16] To make matters worse for Spain, the western Mediterranean was fast becoming a new battleground against the Ottomans, who had allied themselves with those corsairs based in Algeria. Facing these threats, Philip became increasingly concerned that Spain was vulnerable through a potentially disloyal Morisco population who could aid his enemies in an invasion. Conveniently for the king, the seeds of these suspicions were being sown at around the same time as his father's forty-year grace period on Morisco customs was drawing to a close.

Belligerence characterised the mood of Spain in the 1560s. Granada's archbishop, Pedro Guerrero, had been one of the leaders of the Spanish delegation to the Council of Trent, convened in order to establish Catholic policy to counteract the threat posed by Protestantism. This high-ranking church reformer was said to be highly confrontational towards the other countries represented at the Council, and on returning to Granada he was determined to pass through the controversial reforms that had been agreed by the Church. He also now resolved to eradicate Moorish tradition from his own archdiocese and organised a local synod to determine how to accomplish this in the face of all opposition. By now, the municipal leaders were in a much better position to enforce an end to Morisco practices than they had been decades earlier, owing to the great demographic change that had taken place. Whilst the surrounding province remained predominantly Morisco, immigration into the city of Granada meant that by the beginning of the decade, the Old Christian population stood at some 30,000—double that of the Moriscos, who numbered only around 15,000.[17]

Like their church leaders, Christian immigrants to Granada were generally contemptuous of the city's original inhabitants and desirous of stamping out Moorish ways. Therefore, there was widespread support when Archbishop Guerrero's council proposed the implementation of all of Charles's 1526 mandates, thus bringing an end to the accommodations. These reforms also included a greater drive for Moriscos to be subject to the Inquisition, which had been established in Granada in 1526 but had had little meaningful impact in the intervening four decades.[18] This was because the original aim had been to convert the local population and, as influential sympathisers to the Moriscos had pointed out at the time of Charles's mandate, the Inquisition could hinder such a goal. Therefore, penalties against Moriscos had been moderate in comparison to those meted out to Protestants or Jewish *conversos* in other parts of the country.

Times were now changing. As Christian immigrants took up positions of power as city officials, the Moriscos found themselves less and less protected against those who saw them as a fifth column within Catholic Spain, despite having the continued support of those such as the Mendoza family. Many early immigrants had indeed had some respect for the Moors, acquired through their experience of fighting against them during the Reconquista, but the more recent settlers tended towards having a much lower opinion of them. Tales of bullying were rife and Moriscos were subject to continual harassment by some Christian officials; instances included the planting of weapons and incriminating books in their houses. This persecution was particularly strong in the countryside, where land was confiscated from peasants who were either unable to prove ownership or unable to understand the Castilian legal system that was, in any case, weighted heavily against them.[19]

Not only did these recent immigrants scorn the Moriscos, but they also resented the power long held by the Mendoza family. The marquess of Mondéjar had become increasingly involved with matters of importance away from the province and had therefore handed the captaincy general of Granada to his son

Íñigo. However, this third Mendoza to take command at the Alhambra lacked the diplomatic aptitude of his father and grand-father. As resentment built amongst the new factions in the city in the 1550s, the Ayuntamiento, with the support of the Real Chancillería, began to send complaints about him to the court in Madrid, using his support for the Moriscos against him.[20] Íñigo thus gradually found himself being sidelined. This became most apparent when an ecclesiastical panel in Madrid approved the recommendations of Guerrero's church council, and on 7 November 1566, Philip issued an extremely harsh pragmatic against the customs of the Moriscos, banning all aspects of their culture as identified in Charles's decree of 1526. In a sign of what was to come for supporters of the Moriscos, the king sent an avowed enemy of the Mendozas, supreme councillor of the Inquisition Pedro de Deza, to Granada to take up the powerful position of president of the Real Chancillería. This future cardinal was to become for the Moriscos, as he was for the Mendoza family, a true villain of their history.

On arriving in Granada, Deza ordered that Philip's new prag-matic be read out around the streets on the significant date of 1 January 1567, seventy-five years to the day since Boabdil had allowed Christian troops into the Alhambra. Íñigo, the once-powerful captain general who had succeeded to the title of marquess of Mondéjar on the death of his father the previous year, was now so out of favour that he did not become aware of the pragmatic until after Deza's arrival.[21] Outraged at the harshness of the restrictions on the Moriscos and seeing him-self undermined by the Real Chancillería, he did his best to plead in person with the king against the pragmatic. But at the court in Madrid, he got no further than Philip's powerful min-ister Cardinal Espinosa. Though he argued strenuously that the enforcement of the rules would only lead to rebellion and that he was not resourced to handle such an outcome with only his

Alhambra garrison, the marquess failed to move the cardinal and was denied a royal audience.[22] This outmanoeuvring of the mighty Mendozas was to play an important role in the events to follow.

Whilst Mondéjar was making his case at the court in Madrid, perhaps the most impassioned plea against the pragmatic was being written in Granada by one of the Morisco nobles of the city, Francisco Núñez Muley. As a young boy, Núñez Muley had been a page to Archbishop Talavera and had almost certainly been a convert to Christianity in the very earliest years following the Christian conquest. Indeed, Núñez Muley was an old man when he took it upon himself to write to Deza at the Real Chancillería to strongly oppose the decree. His letter sets out compelling arguments as to why the cultural prohibitions should not be enforced, stating that most of these had no connection with religion and were merely expressions of regional differences in lifestyle. For example, in arguing against the ban on Morisco clothes, he claims:

> The style of dress, clothing, and footwear of the natives cannot be said to be that of Muslims ... It can more rightly be said to be clothing that corresponds to a particular kingdom and province ... All the kingdoms of Castile, and all the other kingdoms and provinces, have their own styles of dress that is different from the others, and yet they are all Christians. In like manner, the style of dress and clothing of this kingdom is very different from the clothing of the Moroccan and Barbary Muslims.[23]

Likewise, he contends that the Arabic language has 'no direct relationship whatsoever to the Muslim faith', pointing out that the Christians of both Jerusalem and Malta quite happily used Arabic as part of their Christian faith, even in church.[24]

His arguments range from the economic, demonstrating that the banning of writing in Arabic would have an immediate and debilitating effect on the silk and the tanning industries, whose workers were illiterate in Castilian, to appeals to historic precedent whereby earlier monarchs had taken a much more accommodating approach to allowing cultural practices to continue. At times he appears to struggle to hold back his frustration at the royal court's irrational mentality towards entirely reasonable practices, in particular towards public baths. Noting the infrequency with which the Castilians bathed as a consequence of their belief that such hygiene weakened both the limbs and people's ability to fight in battle, Núñez Muley points out that the Moriscos were barred from going to war and that many undertook some of the dirtiest jobs in the city and therefore needed a place to bathe. Added to this, the Inquisition also persisted in its contrarian view that for a Morisco to bathe at home constituted a sign of Islamic worship. Addressing another widely held Castilian conjecture that public baths were places of immorality, he demonstrates the strict segregation of men and women:

> Let us say for the sake of argument that such women ... get the awful idea to meet their lovers for sex. It would be easier for them to do so while going on visits, or visiting churches, or attending jubilees and plays where men and women regularly interact with one another.[25]

If Núñez Muley provides history with a Morisco voice, arguing vehemently in favour of the retention of the cultural practices emanating from the time of the emirate, his voice was not alone. Although their numbers were dwindling because of old age, there still remained Castilians who could remember the first few decades after the Reconquista and who continued to love the unique culture into which their families had moved. Most notable amongst these was Diego Hurtado de Mendoza, the uncle of the marquess of Mondéjar. This youngest son of the first governor of the Alhambra had grown up in the Nasrid Royal Palaces before becoming one of Charles V's most trusted diplomats. A fall from favour at Philip II's court had led to his return to his hometown in the late 1560s, where, now in old age, he wrote an account of subsequent events. *The War in Granada* is highly sympathetic to the Moriscos and deeply critical of the bureaucratic types who had moved to the city to work at the Real Chancillería and who treated the original inhabitants with such disdain. He speaks of them and the decisions they would subsequently make with scorn:

> they all seem to fancy themselves as military men. They all seem to believe that their legal training gives them a knowledge of things both human and divine which amounts to a scientific understanding of right and wrong. They are quite sure that they have answers for everything. In Granada, they approached every problem from a most superior stance and used their authority to commit the most appalling blunders which lie at the root of the troubles.[26]

But these bureaucratic immigrant Old Christians now had the upper hand in Granada, and at the Real Chancillería they now had a powerful champion in Deza, who was unmoved by the pleas made by those who knew and loved the city well. Instead, this future cardinal began to enforce the law without concession. Tensions in Granada rose to a level not seen since the rebellion of 1499, with the whole city aware that civil unrest could break out again at any moment. An example of these frictions came in April 1568, when the torches of night watchmen in the Albaicín were mistaken for signals for battle. An alarm bell was rung at the Alhambra and armed Christian men from the lower part of the city stormed up into the Albaicín, intent on destroying the rebels, only to discover that their fears on that day had been unfounded. But each community remained aware that trouble was brewing, although the Old Christians could never be sure when it would boil over. Hurtado de Mendoza notes the remarkable ability of the Moriscos to keep their planned rebellion secret:

> One of the most remarkable things about the beginning of this rebellion is how many Moors of the middling sort, who are ordinary sociable enough people and love nothing more so much as to chat

and gossip in the market, managed to keep this secret for so long, even though it had to be shared amongst so many and even though they were very closely watched indeed by agents of the Inquisition and the Civil Powers, whose function was to sniff out rebellion.[27]

The city then was on edge, and on a bitterly cold Christmas Eve in 1568, the anticipated uprising finally began. As Hurtado de Mendoza tells it, Farax aben Farax, a former silk dyer from the city, slipped into the Albaicín with 150 other rebels; 'blowing hornpipes and playing musical instruments',[28] they attempted to rouse the city's Moriscos to action. Hurtado de Mendoza suggests the reasoning behind the choice of date:

> What better time to attack than Christmas night itself when all the people in all the towns would be in church and their houses would be empty and all men's minds would be on prayer and the Holy Mass? At that time of the year we would be off our guard and disarmed, torpid with cold, our thoughts entirely on religion: how easy it would be then for a lively, well-armed, experienced body of men, hardened by years of outlawdom and highway robbery, to destroy us.[29]

With Christian minds on other matters, Farax aben Farax and his men roamed the streets of the Albaicín entreating people to join them. They also tried to break down the door of the Jesuit Casa de la Doctrina, calling Juan de Albotodo a renegade dog for his genuine conversion to Christianity.[30] The Moriscos of the city, however, were unwilling to rebel. Perhaps, suggests Hurtado de Mendoza, this was because many of them had a realistic appreciation that a rebellion would ultimately fail with such relatively small numbers of Morisco fighters pitted against the might of Philip II's Spanish forces. As had happened seventy years earlier, those with the most anger inside them had no recourse but to flee, alongside Farax aben Farax and his men, to the hills of the Alpujarra to begin the fight against the Christian rulers there.

One of these angry men of the city had fled to the Alpujarra two days prior to the attempt to rouse the Albaicín and would be instrumental in events to come: a Morisco town councillor, Fernando de Válor y Córdoba. Born into a family claiming descendance from the Umayyad dynasty that had become part of the administration of Granada after 1492, this young man was already known for his volatile temperament, having recently pulled a dagger on his colleagues at the Madraza and consequently been put under house arrest. Struggling with debt and unable to leave the country as he had intended, instead he left for the Alpujarra. There, in acknowledgement of his noble birth, he was proclaimed king by the rebels; he renounced his Christian name and took his family's ancestral one: Aben Humeya.

Under the leadership of Aben Humeya, the Alpujarra rebellion was to be one of the most brutal civil wars of the sixteenth century.[31] This would almost certainly not have been the case had it not been for the great enmity of Deza towards the Mendoza family. Very early on in the war, the marquess of Mondéjar and his Christian troops gained the upper hand in the fighting, and there was every reason to suspect that through his good relations with the Moriscos in general, he would have been able to bring the rebels to the negotiating table. However, he was consistently thwarted by his persistent adversary Deza, who sent in another Mendoza rival to fight the Moriscos in a separate part of the region, leaving the rebels no option but to continue fighting. Despite their best efforts, the rebels were in many ways very much alone in their fight. Against expectations, they received no aid from the Ottomans, who were too involved in conflicts elsewhere in the Mediterranean, although a few willing volunteers did come across from North Africa without official backing.[32]

Whilst battle raged in the mountains, life in the city was turned upside down, despite the fact that the city's Moriscos had, on the whole, remained relatively passive. Hurtado de Mendoza describes how fear of what was happening in the mountains and its potential to spread to the city at first led to businesses being closed down. Old Christians spent more time praying in churches, and those families who could afford it moved their households into the Alhambra complex for greater safety. Over time, however, the city began to fill up with Christian families from elsewhere in the province seeking a safer place to see out the war.[33] And it was not long before the population expanded further as troops from around Spain descended on Granada, where they were billeted before being dispatched to their positions in the mountains. Tensions already high, the population of the city became even more heavily weighted towards an Old Christian majority, and the Moriscos of the Albaicín, despite having not rebelled, found themselves under constant suspicion.

It would be that suspicion that would lead to an event described with anger both by Hurtado de Mendoza and by the soldier Mármol Carvajal, another chronicler of the Alpujarra wars: the massacre of Morisco prisoners held in the back of the Real Chancillería.[34] Some of these prisoners were considered potential rebels who wished to escape the city for the mountains, although many, claims Hurtado de Mendoza, were businessmen who could never be conceived of as a threat to the peace. Such was the paranoia in the city, though, that many believed these prisoners were plotting a breakout to attack the Old Christians and then join the fighting in the mountains. The stories of how the subsequent massacre began differ between the accounts of Hurtado de Mendoza and Mármol Carvajal, yet both agree that one evening, fears of an escape reached a crescendo and officials at the Real Chancillería handed out arms to Old Christians, who then broke into the cells to attack the Morisco inmates, the latter using whatever they could lay their hands on to defend themselves. For hours the rioting raged inside the prison, with the Moriscos burning mats and whatever they could find, causing concern that the fire might spread from the gutted prison and threaten the entire building. Eventually, the blaze was put out, and amidst the ashes and the smoke it was discovered that almost all of the Moriscos, defenceless against the weapons provided to the Old Christians, had been slaughtered.

The prison massacre was just one brutal act in a war characterised by brutality beyond the city in the Sierra Nevada. Divisions under the command of the Old Christians, created out of Deza's hatred for the captain general, Mondéjar, made negotiations impossible, and the fighting on both sides intensified. It reached such a height that Philip sent his half-brother, Don Juan of Austria, to Granada with orders to take control. He arrived in the city amid great fanfare worthy of the brother of a king and was greeted at the Alhambra by the count of Tendilla, whose Castilian cavalrymen were dressed in Morisco style.[35] Hurtado de Mendoza describes the Old Christians' fawning welcome for this inexperienced military leader, whose entrance was more pomp than substance and who made daily trips up into the Albaicín to inspect the troops keeping a watchful eye on the Moriscos. Yet this arrival of the king's half-brother provided a clear demonstration of how power had shifted away from the Mendozas, objects now of the petty jealousies of the bureaucrats who had moved into the city over the previous few decades. Now it would be with Deza at the Real Chancillería that power truly lay and there—not at the Mendozas' home at the Alhambra—that discussions would take place about how to end the rebellion in the mountains. Worse still, it would be there, in secret discussions between Deza and Don Juan, that plans would be drawn up for a longer-term solution to the Morisco 'problem' that would forever change the face of Granada.

The fighting continued for a number of months before Deza chose to put his plans for the wholesale removal of the city's Morisco population into action. When he finally did, the

Albaicín woke up to the price it was to pay for revolt, despite the fact that the vast majority had not joined the rebels in the mountains. On 23 June 1569, soldiers entered the district and went from door to door ordering all Morisco males aged between ten and sixty to gather at their parish churches. The people were frantic; panic swept through the streets. Those Christian leaders who had their respect, the captain general, the Jesuit Juan de Albotodo, and Yahya al-Najjar's descendent Alonso de Granada Venegas, were called upon to reassure citizens that their lives were not in danger and that measures were being taken merely to bring them under the king's protection during the ongoing war. But not everyone was convinced, and a number of men managed to evade the soldiers and escape to the mountains. The vast majority, though, were herded as ordered into the churches. There, they were confined overnight under armed guard, unaware of the fate that had been planned for them.

The next day, some 3,500 Morisco men, hands tied, were marched down from the Albaicín, through the Puerta de Elvira built by their ancestors, and into the grounds of the Hospital Real. Both Hurtado de Mendoza and Mármol Carvajal record the sheer horror of the situation, the latter writing, 'It was a miserable sight to see such men of all ages, heads low, hands crossed and faces covered in tears ... realising that they were leaving their comfortable homes, their families, their homeland ... and still not knowing if they would keep their heads.'[36] In a show of great cruelty, some of the soldiers escorting the traumatised men down to the hospital took the opportunity to increase their fear by suggesting that they were being led to their slaughter, with one holding a crucifix covered in a black veil, a sign of the Moriscos' imminent deaths. The women of the Albaicín, the wives, the mothers, the sisters, the daughters, screaming and shouting in absolute anger and desperation at the troops, watched in horror as their menfolk were led down the hill, not knowing if they would ever see them again.

Determined to implement his plan in an orderly manner, Don Juan reprimanded the soldiers who were physically harming the Morisco prisoners. He stationed men around the gates of the city to prevent anyone coming to the prisoners' aid. Meanwhile, the men of the Albaicín were ushered inside the walls of the Hospital Real, where a record was made of the name and age of every man to be presented to the district to which they would be transferred, a mark of Philip II's famously efficient bureaucracy. Those artisans and craftsmen considered essential for the functioning of the city were permitted to return to their homes, along with those whose connections with Old Christians meant that pleas were made in their names. The vast majority, however, were kept interned for another night, and the next day they would begin a long march out of their city to be dispersed across other parts of Andalusia.

The eviction of the Morisco men from the Albaicín was just the beginning of what would, over the next two years, turn into one of Europe's most systematic acts of ethnic cleansing. Morisco women were allowed to remain in the city for a short time after the men's expulsion in order to settle their families' affairs, before also being ejected, their hands similarly tied as they were led from their homes and marched away across Andalusia. Further purges of Granada's Moriscos occurred over the following months. Whilst conditions for those uprooted first were harsh, they deteriorated to reach a nadir in 1570. On 1 November, after the second Alpujarra rebellion had been ruthlessly crushed, and buoyed by his expulsion of the Moriscos from the Albaicín, Philip ordered the removal of the entire Morisco population of the former Emirate of Granada. These banishments took place during a bitter winter, with conditions travelling north particularly harsh. Thousands of men, women, and children died of exposure, disease, and exhaustion. Some were robbed and murdered by the guards who escorted them; others were kidnapped and sold into slavery.

For the 'fortunate' ones who survived to reach the destinations determined by Philip's bureaucrats, huge problems awaited. The Moriscos of Granada were frequently unwelcome among the locals in their new homes, arriving as many did after their forced marches in a pitiable state of health, suspected of bringing disease and illness with them. Issues arose in terms of how they assimilated, not only with the Old Christians but also with the former Mudéjars, most of whom now looked and spoke the same as their Castilian neighbours after having lived among them for centuries. The refugees from Granada stood out for speaking Arabic and having different cooking habits. The Mudéjars separated themselves from them, seeing themselves as closer to the Old Christians than to these newly arrived 'foreigners'.[37] Every Morisco was formally registered in their new settlement and prevented from leaving without the permission of local officials. Return to Granada was punishable by execution.

The effects of these events cannot be emphasised enough. Back in the city of Granada, large parts of the Albaicín became deserted, the only Moriscos to remain being wealthy, well-connected merchants, artisans, and workers deemed necessary for the city, as well as those who served in Christian households. Mármol Carvajal describes the sheer sadness of this now almost empty district that had once been full of the beautiful, lively homes and gardens of the Moriscos, which in such a short time had become desolate and fallen into a terrible state of ruin.[38] There were also severe economic effects for the city as a whole. The massive drop in population of the order of around 10,000 people[39] meant the distribution and supply of essential goods were so disrupted that necessities could no longer be obtained. For example, there were not enough people left in the region to continue the vital silk trade that had already suffered greatly from the taxes imposed earlier in the decade. Meanwhile, the emptying of the surrounding countryside and loss of agricultural expertise passed down through generations of Morisco farmers would have disastrous effects on local food production, which would go on to affect production levels for centuries to come.

For the few thousand remaining Moriscos in Granada, life was now full of fear and uncertainty. A small minority in the city, they no longer enjoyed safety in numbers. There were some, of course, who remained relatively unaffected. Some of the elite who had converted very early on and integrated themselves amongst the ruling classes of the new regime, such as the Granada Venegas family, were barely distinguishable from the new nobility of the city by the 1560s, having married into noble Castilian families and adopted Castilian habits.[40] These former Nasrid aristocrats actively fought against the Alpujarra rebels and helped with the expulsion of the Morisco community. However, other Moriscos, merchants and the servants of the Christians for instance, lived in a state of constant trepidation.

The 1570s marked the end of Moorish Granada. It would be another forty years before Philip's son, Philip III, signed the 1609 decree ordering the expulsion of all Moriscos from the whole of Spain. By this time, the ethnic cleansing that had taken place in the former Nasrid territories had been so effective that the final expulsions affected Granada far less than places such as Valencia, which saw around 120,000 citizens driven out.[41] The descendants of the Moors of Granada were, by this point, scattered across Castile, and many born after the 1570s had never seen their ancestral homeland, yet they too would be summarily ejected from Spain.

The expulsion of the Moriscos brought to a wretched end this community that had been living on the Iberian Peninsula for close to 900 years. The deportations across the sea brought many thousands of deaths; crews on board some of the vessels threw their passengers overboard and stole their possessions. Those who did make it to North Africa faced widespread suspicion, being Christian converts, many of whom would have lost any knowledge of Arabic. Tales abound of the homesickness suffered by people dropped in foreign lands they had never visited before. The number of Moriscos forced out of Spain is disputed, but it is believed to reach into the hundreds of thousands, some studies suggesting between 200,000 and 300,000 were expelled from their country.[42] There is some evidence of Moriscos managing to evade the expulsions, and not just among the former Nasrid nobility. Records of the Inquisition in Granada from the eighteenth century show a number of citizens still suspected of Islamic practices, and it seems likely that there were merchants and traders who managed to remain, be it through bribery or hiding their origins.[43] However, a recent genetic mapping exercise conducted in Spain suggests that today there is a lower prevalence of North African DNA stemming from the time of the Arab conquests to be found in eastern Andalusia than in other parts of the Iberian Peninsula, where around 10 per cent of the population have some Moorish genes. Indeed, the study claims that today more North African DNA is present in Galicia, a part of Spain barely touched by Muslim rule, than in Granada, which perhaps indicates the success of so draconian a process as the Morisco expulsion.[44]

By the end of the sixteenth century, Granada had become a predominantly Christian city, its population for the most part recent immigrant families from other parts of Castile. Now an economic backwater, it would take on a profoundly religious character, yet this Christianity would be built on mysterious Arabic texts, discovered after all but a handful of the Moors had already left this once great centre of Iberian Islam: the lead books of the Sacromonte.

9

A VERY CHRISTIAN CITY

Almost two decades after the vast majority of Granada's Morisco community had been expelled from the city and the surrounding province, work was underway to demolish the Torre Turpiana. This former minaret was one of the city's most prominent landmarks and part of Granada's eleventh-century former mosque; it was being pulled down as part of the ongoing process in the transformation of this site into what is now Granada Cathedral. But on 18 March 1588, work halted when surprised workers unearthed amongst the rubble a mysterious lead casket containing yellowed parchment, old bones, and a scrap of cloth. The writing on the parchment was at first incomprehensible—letters and words in two different colours, dispersed within a grid. Some appeared to be Castilian Spanish, but there was also what looked like Latin, a smattering of Greek, and, more puzzlingly, squiggles suggestive of Arabic. A team of experts in ancient languages was assembled to translate the document, among them two Moriscos: Alonso del Castillo, Philip II's Arabic translator, and the medical man and writer Miguel de Luna. This pair agreed that the squiggles represented Arabic but explained that it was rather different to its modern form: the script featured no diacritic dots, and letters not normally joined together were so in this unusual text. They suggested, therefore, that this might be an ancient form of the language.[1]

According to both the Arabic and the Latin translators, the document was written by the first-century saint Caecilius—known in Spanish as San Cecilio—and recorded as yet unseen apocalyptic prophecies of St John the Evangelist. These foretold the coming of Islam, the Protestant Reformation, and the end of the world. In addition to the part signed off by Caecilius, the document also contained a postscript seemingly added by one of his companions, giving the reasons for its concealment. These were that Caecilius had foreseen his forthcoming martyrdom under the Romans, and also to ensure that this important text remained hidden for the duration of the predicted occupation of Granada by the Moors. The bones were declared to be those of St Stephen, and the material a piece of a veil belonging to the Virgin Mary. Found on the site of Granada's new cathedral, these artefacts generated immense excitement among the local Christians, who had had no religious relics of their own to venerate before—a major embarrassment when comparing themselves with other communities across Spain who proudly proclaimed their ancient connections to the early Church.

In all the excitement surrounding these discoveries, however, an important inference was missed. If authentic, this document purported that one of the earliest Christians to arrive in Spain had been an Arabic speaker. And arriving, as the document suggested, in the first century, well before Arab Muslims came ashore 700 years later, it would suggest that Arabs were strongly connected with early Christianity too. Logically, it would follow that this could have major implications for the Moriscos, who, despite having been largely expelled from Granada, continued at that point in time to live across the rest of Spain. If a venerated

Christian martyr could speak Arabic and be true to his faith, surely it would be reasonable to assume that this could be the case for the Moriscos, who had converted to Christianity but continued to use their ancestral tongue.

Another discovery made seven years later, on 21 February 1595, brought even greater excitement and seemed to confirm the earlier findings at the Torre Turpiana. Two men were said to have been given an ancient book detailing treasure buried by the Visigoths prior to the Arab invasions of the eighth century, lying somewhere outside the Nasrid walls on the Valparaíso hill, now known as the Sacromonte. Riddled with caves, this was an excellent hiding place. However, it was not gold that the two treasure seekers found there. With the help of a local man named Fulano del Castillo, what they discovered were mysterious lead tablets also inscribed in strange letters, which on further investigation were deemed to be the form of Latin used by the Romans of Hispania Baetica. When one of these plaques was found to reference the casket hidden in the Torre Turpiana, excitement grew over what new details might emerge of early Christian Granada.[2]

Over the next few months many more lead tablets were recovered from beneath the Valparaíso hill, small and intricately inscribed in classical Latin. Others were also found written in the strange Arabic of the Torre Turpiana document. Again, these were interpreted by Luna and Castillo, the Morisco translators, and these new finds yielded a yet more fascinating revelation. It appeared that two brothers—Caecilius and Ctesiphon—both of Arab origin, had travelled to Spain after having been converted to Christianity by Christ himself, along with Spain's patron, St James the Greater. Here on this very spot, these most revered of saints had celebrated the first mass in all Europe. Caecilius had then remained in Granada as its first bishop, but had been burned for his faith somewhere in the caves within the hillside, along with his brother and five other Christian martyrs under

Emperor Nero. It was not long before corroboration was found for the martyrdom in the form of charred human remains discovered in catacombs nearby.

This evidence that the earliest Christians to arrive in Spain had not only passed through Granada, but had also performed the first sermon there on the Sacromonte and suffered martyrdom for their faith, suddenly catapulted Granada to the forefront of Iberian Christianity. No longer would locals have to feel ashamed of their city's Islamic past. Festivals proliferated around the site of the martyrs' remains; tales of the miraculous healing of the sick and insane spread far and wide. Thousands of processions honoured the relics, and the hillside became a forest of wooden crosses. For the worshippers, the discoveries at the Torre Turpiana and the catacombs of the Sacromonte were the much-longed-for evidence of Granada's sacred and, more importantly, Christian origins. No more would the city be spurned as having been the last bastion of Islam on the peninsula; instead the Reconquista would be seen as a restoration of Granada to its rightful place at the very heart of the true faith. And, as a mark of the importance of the site, a few years later, the new Abbey of the Sacromonte would crown the hill.

Despite the euphoria, however, the story told by the Torre Turpiana parchment and the lead books was not universally accepted. Detractors could be found both in Granada itself and more vocally in other cities across the country. Some pointed out the odd juxtaposition of modern Castilian and the supposedly ancient form of Arabic used in the documents. Others questioned the ink and the writing equipment used on the parchment, arguing these were not the implements of the early Christian era. There were calls, too, for all the discoveries to be sent to Madrid for authentication. Yet none of this dampened the enthusiasm of the local population, who became devoted to the new cult of the Sacromonte. The finds also provided

Granada's residents with an opportunity to rewrite its history; for example, a local historian named Francisco Bermúdez de Pedraza penned a revised chronicle of the city that portrays eight centuries of Muslim rule as a minor blemish on the character of an ancient and holy Christian settlement. Claiming that Granada had only fallen under the yoke of Islam through an act of divine punishment for its corruption during the Visigoth era, he alleges miracles had occurred on the Sacromonte even in Moorish times—clear evidence that the Christians had been assisted in capturing the city by the divine power of the lead books.[3]

Bermúdez de Pedraza's usage of the lead tablets to reinvent Granada's history was mirrored by the importance acquired by the Sacromonte as a destination of pilgrimage in the years after the discoveries, attracting devotees from far afield. In 1633, to make the route easier for the multitude of visitors, a holy path was created to the site and demarcated with stone crosses in place of the wooden ones that had sprung up in the final years of the sixteenth century. The pilgrimage's apparently unstoppable rise was, however, to meet an obstacle. In 1623, after a great deal of pressure, the lead books were finally sent to Madrid for the authentication many scholars had demanded since the first discoveries during the 1588 destruction of the Torre Turpiana. They were then sent on to the Vatican and finally, in 1682, declared by papal bull to be complete forgeries.

In a haunting reminder of how tens of thousands of Granada's Muslims had been converted to Christianity and later expelled from their homes, it is believed that the lead books were the work of educated Moriscos desperate to save their people from this fate. Suspicion naturally fell on the Arabic translators, Luna and Castillo, both long dead when the forgery was declared, and a connection was made between Alonso del Castillo and the mysterious guide with the same surname who had helped the treasure hunters in their search. The fraud was an extraordinary one, and unlikely to have been perpetrated by just two or three people, considering the work that it entailed. Indeed, the depth of knowledge required to compile the content of the lead books, the creation of realistic fake scripts, and the actual physical production of the artefacts have led some to conclude that the conspiracy involved a substantially wider group of local people, possibly including descendants of the former Moorish nobility who had remained in Granada after the expulsion of the city's Moriscos, such as the Granada Venegas family, and even, potentially, some Christian sympathisers.[4]

There is something incredibly sad about a story of forgeries being made by Moriscos to create links between the Arabs and Spanish Christianity in an attempt to be allowed to remain in their homeland unmolested. Ultimately, though, their plan failed. Sadly, at the same time that the Sacromonte Abbey was under construction, the Moriscos themselves were being uprooted en masse from Spain. The attempt to link the two communities paradoxically led instead to the development of a deep and passionate Christian cult so strong that even the papal condemnation of the ruse did not stop the pilgrimages to the site. Indeed, as a justification for the cult of the Sacromonte, the Vatican rejected only the authenticity of the lead books and parchment of the Torre Turpiana, and perversely not the bones of the martyrs that they pointed to. Today, on a tour of the Abbey, where the parchment from the Torre Turpiana and copies of the lead books are displayed, guides explain that although the documents themselves are fakes, the stories about the martyrs are nevertheless true, and Granada continues, for some, to be a fundamental part of the history of early Christianity in Spain.

In many ways, the story of the lead books highlights Granada's move away from being essentially Moorish in culture at the beginning of the sixteenth century to being profoundly Christian at the dawn of the next. The transformation of the Valparaíso hill into the major pilgrimage site of the Sacromonte followed a whole host of changes that had been made to Granada since the Reconquista. These had begun in the early years when the expulsion of the Jews and the emigration of many of Granada's nobility freed up land for development in the lower part of the city. Here, veterans of the Granada wars, rewarded with land, began to build majestic houses in the Christian style so alien to the Muslim city. Many examples of Christian architecture from that period continue to dot the city, including the Casa de Castril, which today houses Granada's Archaeological Museum, and the Casa de los Tiros in the Realejo district, which would later become home to the Granada Venegas family, descendants of Pedro de Granada. Over time, transformations were made to more areas of the city. Roads were widened and squares were created more in keeping with traditional Spanish culture than the narrow, winding lanes of the old city. A prime example was the Plaza de Bibarrambla, designed in the style of the typical Spanish *plaza mayor* to hold key ceremonies and festivities in the city. Another key feature to disappear in the early years of Christian rule were the Muslim cemeteries, which had greatly impressed Hieronymus Münzer on his visit in 1494. The cemetery that lay just outside the Puerta de Elvira, for example, was completely transformed with the building of the Hospital Real, destined at first to be an infirmary for syphilitics but redesignated in the 1530s as a lunatic asylum to replace Muhammad V's Maristán in the Albaicín.

However, it was the building of numerous religious establishments, from small churches to large monasteries and convents, that led to Granada's most obvious transformation into a Christian city.[5] The first building to be used as Granada's cathedral, consecrated within days of the handover of the city, was the mosque inside the Alhambra complex, later knocked down and rebuilt as the Church of Santa María de la Alhambra. Then, in the mid-

1490s, the location of the cathedral was moved to what is now the Capitanía General on Calle San Matías, behind the Plaza de Isabel la Católica. However, with the forced conversion of the Moors, new plans were laid down to use the space then occupied by the former main mosque to build a new cathedral worthy of the city. From the destruction of the Muslims' central place of worship eventually sprang three Christian ones: the Capilla Real, Granada Cathedral, and the Church of El Sagrario.

The first building to be erected on the site was the Royal Chapel—the Capilla Real. The decision by the Catholic Monarchs to build this was of great moment since it allowed for both the queen of Castile and the king of Aragon to be entombed together at the heart of their most prized conquest. When Isabella died in 1504, her body was laid to rest in the Convent of San Francisco at the Alhambra as she had decreed, the site still marked today inside the building that is now the Hotel Parador. Ferdinand continued to reign over his own kingdoms and later as regent of Castile until his death in 1516, whereupon he was interred in Granada beside his wife. By this point, the construction of the Capilla Real was nearing completion and, in 1521, the royal remains were transferred to their final resting place in a solemn ceremony arranged by their grandson, Emperor Charles V. The bodies of Isabella and Ferdinand, their daughter Queen Joanna and her husband, Philip, as well as their grandson Miguel, who died in infancy, lie today under ornate marble tomb effigies decorated in Renaissance style, in contrast to the simplicity of the Late Gothic surroundings of the building that houses them.

Over the next few years, it would be Charles who would have the most impact on the site, not only in overseeing the final stages of the Royal Chapel but also, in the 1520s, by ordering the construction of the huge Renaissance cathedral.[6] It is said that when Charles visited Granada in 1526, he was underwhelmed by the Capilla Real as a royal mausoleum and decided, although this would never actually be fulfilled, that his own tomb would reside in this new cathedral. As with his palace at the Alhambra, Charles's cathedral was designed to dominate what had once been a focal point of the Moorish city, and was constructed next to the building that before 1492 had been Granada's main mosque. Building work had already begun in 1523 under the same architect that had built the Capilla Real, but Charles replaced him with Diego de Siloé. Siloé's architectural designs and sculptures were to have an impact on many of Granada's most important buildings of the sixteenth century, and with the cathedral he changed the original style from Gothic to Renaissance. A key feature of his influence can be seen in the Puerta del Perdón, the north entrance of the cathedral. Meanwhile, the Baroque façade would be the work of a later local architect, Alonso Cano.

The building that had been Granada's eleventh-century main mosque continued to exist until the eighteenth century, albeit converted into the Church of María de la O, and it became the city's main place of worship whilst the cathedral was under construction. It also acted as a place of burial for some of the most distinguished of Granada's post-Reconquista citizens, including the Morisco noble Pedro de Granada and, of course, Hernán Pérez del Pulgar—the soldier who had surreptitiously pinned the Ave Maria to the door of the building during the siege when it was still a mosque. Under its new name, the former main mosque retained its architectural features for many years, though Christian altars, tombs, and church decorations were added. Sometime in the eighteenth century, the decision was made to pull down the original building and reconstruct it as the Church of El Sagrario that stands on the site today.[7]

The majority of the city's minor, local mosques were also for a number of decades after the Reconquista still standing but converted into churches, meaning that after the forced conversions,

Granada's Moriscos were forced to attend Christian services against the backdrop of Islamic décor within their former places of worship. It would take time before these were demolished and new churches built in their place. As churches went up across the city, some retained elements of the mosques that had preceded them. Two prime examples of this that can still be seen are the bell tower of the Church of San José, which was converted from a Zirid minaret, and the inner courtyard of the Church of El Salvador, both in the Albaicín. Other churches were built in the Mudéjar style using the architectural knowledge of the Moriscos, one being the Church of Santa Ana in the Plaza Nueva, completed in the 1560s.

The post-Reconquista years also saw the establishment of substantial monastic institutions. Some of these were built within the city walls, transforming large parts of the Moorish city. One of the earliest was the Convent of Santa Isabel la Real, founded right in the heart of the most populated area of the city, inside the old Alcazaba in the Albaicín, to act as an ever-present reminder to the Morisco inhabitants of Queen Isabella's victory. Other monasteries were founded on land that became vacant in the 1490s. The area around today's Calle San Matías was completely remodelled following the expulsion of the Jews and many monasteries were erected in the area. One of the most important of these was the Convent of San Francisco Casa Grande, the site that today houses the Capitanía General, an army barracks. Nearby was the Carmelite convent where now stands the Ayuntamiento building. Further into the Realejo district, in the grounds of the Moorish palace today known as the Cuarto Real, the Convent of Santa Cruz was constructed, along with its magnificent Church of Santo Domingo.

In addition to these religious houses within the city walls, other land was acquired beyond the original municipal boundaries for more remote residences. Two of the most important of these, established in the sixteenth century, were the Monastery of San Jerónimo and the Charterhouse or, in Spanish, La Cartuja. San Jerónimo was founded in 1504 and became the resting place of that great hero of the Reconquista, Gonzalo Fernández de Córdoba—El Gran Capitán. The long, straight road that led from the walls to the monastery is named Calle Duquesa after his wife, who resided in a palace in the area whilst the monastery was under construction.[8] Further out, La Cartuja in the early sixteenth century lay well removed outside the city on horticultural land presented to the Carthusian order by El Gran Capitán. Navagero, the Venetian ambassador who had accompanied Charles V on his visit to Granada, declared it to be one of the most beautiful and happy spots it was possible to find, with its stunning views and secluded location away from the people.[9] This is not easy to imagine today; La Cartuja now sits incongruously amidst the modern architectural styles that characterise Granada's urban sprawl and is hemmed in by a 1970s-era university campus.

Meanwhile, as Granada was physically Christianised in the sixteenth century, even prior to the expulsion of the Moriscos, the city began to attract its fair share of religious leaders.[10] The Jesuit Casa de la Doctrina, run by the Morisco convert Juan de Albotodo, is a testament to the prominence of this group of church reformers, who sought to counter the ignorance of the regular clergy and their inability to connect with the native population. In this endeavour, the Jesuits often found themselves at odds with the establishment. With their evangelistic approach to spreading Catholicism, they would preach in the narrow, winding alleys of the Albaicín in order to reach out to the Moriscos, although with somewhat limited success. They were also far from ignorant of the unbecoming behaviour of the Old Christians, preaching in areas such as that just outside the walls around what is now Calle Recogidas, where prostitutes plied their trade, and in the fields surrounding the city, where local people slipped away on Sundays to gamble and engage in non-religious pursuits.[11]

Foremost amongst a number of celebrated holy men whom Granada was home to in the sixteenth century was João Cidade, later canonised as San Juan de Dios. Of Portuguese origin, Juan began his spiritual journey whilst fighting as a soldier in Charles V's army in North Africa. His first biographer, Francisco de Castro, tells of Juan's battle with his faith; it is said that these troubles almost allowed the devil to convince him to convert to Islam, but through prayer and the words of a Franciscan friar, he was persuaded to escape temptation and return to Europe, where his struggles to be close to God continued.[12] It would be after his arrival in the still predominantly Morisco city of Granada that his ambitions would be achieved. Juan first set himself up in the city as a bookseller under an arch connected to the Puerta de Elvira, which now houses a small chapel. But his true spiritual conversion took place in January 1537, when he ascended the Mauror hill to hear the preaching of another future saint, the peripatetic Juan de Ávila, at the Chapel of Los Mártires. Castro describes the tremendous effect the sermon had on the bookseller:

> As the sermon ended, he left there as if beside himself, crying out to God for mercy, and in contempt of himself ... threw himself on the ground, banging his head against the walls, and pulling out his beard and eyebrows, and doing other things that made everyone suspect that he had lost his mind. And jumping and running and continuing to shout out, he entered the city, followed by many people, especially boys, shouting, 'crazy man, crazy man!'[13]

With the youths of the city following at his heels, he returned to his bookshop, where he set about ripping up any of his books that were not devoted to God and giving away all those that were. He then stripped himself down to his shirt and breeches and ran out, crying to be allowed to follow the naked Jesus. As his biographer records:

Wishing to be held and esteemed by all as crazy and bad and worthy of all contempt and dishonour, in order to better serve and please Jesus Christ, ... he went to the Plaza de [Bibarrambla], and he threw himself into a muddy hole that was there, and covered himself in [the dirt], and putting his mouth in the mud, began in a loud voice to confess in front of all who looked on (there were a great many people), how many sins he remembered [committing].[14]

Juan's seeming madness continued for days, and he became a major object of fun for the youth of the city, who would torment him and encourage him to return time and time again to kissing the mud on the ground. Finally, judged completely insane, he was taken to the Hospital Real, where his treatment consisted of having his hands and feet bound and being repeatedly flogged. But, with the spiritual guidance of Juan de Ávila, who came to visit him in his cell, he was eventually able to leave the asylum, having, during his own suffering, resolved to dedicate his life to the poor and destitute. He began by collecting firewood and distributing it to the needy in the Plaza de Bibarrambla, and soon, devout observers of his good works provided him with the means to set up a hospital for the sick and impoverished in a house near the fish market. He would walk the city's streets with a large basket on his back, begging his fellow citizens for alms, saying, 'Who does well for himself? Who wants to do well for the love of God?'[15]

Over time, Juan was able to shed his reputation as a madman and gain the respect and admiration of both the Old Christians and the Moriscos of Granada. Before long, he was provided with a much larger building to house his hospital, just below the Alhambra on the Cuesta de Gomérez. Meanwhile, many heroic deeds were accredited to him, including risking his life to save patients when a fire broke out one night at the Hospital Real, carrying them out of the flames engulfing the institution that had once imprisoned him. When he died in 1550 in a house behind the Real Chancillería that is now home to a museum in his name, such was the admiration for this local figure that the whole city came together to mourn him. Later proclaimed San Juan de Dios, he was honoured with a basilica, although undoubtedly this man who had devoted himself to the sick and the poor would have taken more pride in the founding of the Brothers Hospitallers of Saint John of God, an order created in his name, which continues to work to provide health and social services for the poor around the world.

Another who brought fame to the city was Fray Luis de Granada. Luis was born in 1504 to a destitute mother and spent his early years begging at the door of the Church of Santo Domingo, outside which today stands his statue. It appears that he was adopted as a child into the household of the governor of the Alhambra and thus was able to gain an education from some of the humanist scholars whom the count of Tendilla invited to educate his own sons. This learning was to have a profound impact on Luis, who, on joining the Dominican order as an adult, went on to become internationally famous for his books of devotional prayer, in particular his 1554 *Book of Prayer and Meditation*. Although his work took him far away from the city of his birth, his chosen name as a friar kept him forever associated with Granada.

One further holy man whose story intertwines with that of sixteenth-century Granada is San Juan de la Cruz (St John of the Cross). A friend of the mystic Teresa de Ávila, Juan joined in her attempts to reform religious orders across Spain. Venerated for his mystical writings, he was sent by Teresa to Granada, where he became prior of the Monastery of Los Mártires on the Mauror hill. It is said that here he wrote one of his most celebrated poems, *La noche oscura del alma* (The Dark Night of the Soul), which describes the intense draw of mystical union with Christ and begins:

On a dark night,
Inflamed with love and yearning,
Oh, what happy adventure!
I left without being seen
My house still in deepest sleep.[16]

And ends with his union with his beloved:

I stayed and surrendered myself,
My face resting against the Beloved,
Everything stopped, I let myself go,
Leaving behind my cares,
Forgotten amongst the lilies.

Whilst spiritual figures and the construction of monasteries and churches were transforming Granada into a Christian city throughout the 1500s, there was also a great transformation in the administrative and commercial aspects of the city. The mercantile centre, in particular the silk market, continued to be of vital importance, although now with the addition of Old Christian traders, as well as those who had decided not to flee the city after its fall. The Genoese, a major presence since the time of the Nasrids, continued to have a significant influence in the new era. It was they who demanded and achieved the construction of a new customs house, the Lonja de Mercaderes, which was constructed prominently next to the silk market and the main commercial street, Calle Zacatín. It also had the advantage of being across the square from the Ayuntamiento, then housed in Yusuf I's Madraza, a building extensively remodelled over the years, the complete transformation of its Nasrid façade into the Baroque style occurring much later in the eighteenth century. Meanwhile the establishment of the Real Chancillería in Granada had brought about a transformation of that most important axis of the city, the river Darro, through its being partially covered over to form the Plaza Nueva.

Another institution of great importance to the post-Reconquista city was the University of Granada that Charles V had founded in 1531 to improve the educational level of those tasked with evangelising amongst the recalcitrant Moriscos. The university's first home reflected the religious nature of much of its teaching, facing the cathedral in a building that today constitutes one half of the Archbishop's Palace, although this location initially prompted protest given that it also overlooked the Plaza de Bibarrambla, the centre of Granada's festivities throughout the year. Concerns were raised that students would be distracted by the bull fights, the processions, and the executions in the square, but these apprehensions were dismissed. Later, towards the end of the eighteenth century and following the expulsion of the Jesuits, the main centre of the university was moved into that order's former college, a building in today's Plaza de la Universidad that now houses the Faculty of Law.

By the late sixteenth century, then, Granada was becoming physically more Christian. And, with the expulsion of a vast proportion of the Morisco population, the overwhelming majority of its citizens were now either second- or third-generation Christian immigrants. Yet, by this point the city had lost much of its attraction to ambitious Castilians. The energy of the early post-Reconquista days when people had flocked to Granada to make their careers or fortunes had all but disappeared; where once an aspiring, educated member of the Castilian middle class could move to Granada and rise through the ranks to join the elite, by the end of the 1500s the membership of both the Ayuntamiento and the Real Chancillería had become fixed. And despite the financial incentives offered, such as tax breaks, and the abundance of vacant property, it would take many years to replace the displaced Moriscos. Figures highlight the sheer scale of the impact of expulsion on the city's population. From a population of some 45,000 in 1561, the expulsion saw such a decline in numbers that even forty years later, at the turn of the seventeenth century, the population hadn't recovered, leaving a city with fewer than 40,000 inhabitants.[17] In just over a hundred years, Granada had gone from being one of the most densely populated cities on the Iberian Peninsula and the capital of a kingdom, to a city of minor importance in terms of Spain as a whole.

This depopulation had an even greater impact on the surrounding countryside. In 1494, Münzer had extolled the rich and bountiful agriculture of the Vega, claiming that the fields were so full of cottages and towers that they appeared to be an extension of the city. A century on, the picture was greatly changed. The Moriscos had gone, and those brought in to replace them from other parts of Castile lacked the better part of a millennium of local agricultural expertise accumulated by the Moors. Agriculture went into a rapid decline, taking centuries to recover. There were other economic ramifications of the expulsion, too; the silk industry was severely affected and would take decades to return to anything approaching the production levels of the Morisco period.[18]

Within the city itself, the biggest impact of the expulsion was on the Albaicín, which now lay partly deserted. Yet one feature of the city, much celebrated today, that actually emerged out of the depopulation and the ghost town that the Albaicín became was the development of that most locally distinctive style of house, the *carmen*.[19] The name originates from an Arabic word meaning vine, and, in many respects, the hidden-away and inward-facing character of these houses recreates the atmosphere of the way of life of the Moors. The local-born, seventeenth-century poet Pedro Soto de Rojas wrote a poem inspired by his own *carmen*, which he had created by joining together a number of vacant Morisco houses. The title, *Paraíso cerrado para muchos, jardines abiertos para pocos* (Paradise Closed to Many, Gardens

Open to Few), conveys that sense of an intense privacy and idyllic space that a *carmen* provides. Essentially, behind high walls that obscure it from the public view, an ideal *carmen* consists of a house on the highest point of the slope of the hill, with balconies providing breathtaking views over the Alhambra or the Generalife. Below this lies its garden, at the foot of which is the *huerta*, or vegetable garden. Through the use of running water and aromatic plants, each part flows harmoniously into another to create a beautiful, seamless whole.

With its depopulated Albaicín district and having now become something of a backwater in Spain, seventeenth-century Granada immersed itself in Christianity, the depth of its religious devotion seen most vividly in its festivals—the year-round calendar of religious events generally celebrated in the streets.[20] The most prominent of these was the observance of Corpus Christi, which had received encouragement from the very start of the Christian era as Isabella and Ferdinand sought to change the Moorish character of the city. In an attempt to attract the Moors to Christianity in those early years before forced conversions, Archbishop Talavera had allowed Moorish dance and music to be performed during the festivities, providing a distinctive air to the local festival. Over time, the celebrations became entrenched in Granada's social life. The exuberant atmosphere of Corpus Christi seen in modern-day Granada is a mere shadow of what it once was, much of the revelry having been moved to the outskirts of the city near the bus station. In centuries gone by, this would have spread throughout the centre, most notably around the Plaza de Bibarrambla.

Easter processions were as popular in Christian Granada as elsewhere in Spain. Organised by the *cofradías*—religious brotherhoods made up of members of the lay community—they co-existed, often uneasily, with the established Church leadership.[21] Processions during Holy Week, or Semana Santa, were not the highly co-ordinated events seen in modern-day Granada, which only really took hold in the early twentieth century. Instead, early Semana Santa processions were popular local expressions of religious devotion, some aspects of which were frowned upon by the church. An example was the night-time procession on Maundy Thursday that Archbishop Guerrero attempted to ban in the sixteenth century out of a desire to have all religious displays fall within the purview of his archbishopric.[22] Later, in 1604, one of his successors in that office attempted to prohibit certain Easter processions because they had become too bloody, the participants flagellating themselves with gusto in penitence for their sins. The whips they used would tear the skin off their backs and blood would be made to flow, the wounds allowed to heal only on the penitent's return to the church. Yet the religious authorities generally felt that a belief in redemption through self-flagellation might prompt sinners to opt for this route rather than atoning through the mediation of the priests by attending services and confession. Ultimately, the Church got its way and processions became less sanguinary, instead putting greater focus on the parading of religious images around the city.[23]

The *cofradías* were not only responsible for organising processions during festivals. They were also paid to accompany funeral processions, and collectively they helped poorer families with the cost of these observances. They also raised money for crafting the images of Christ and the Virgin Mary that would be paraded around the city during the processions. One of the most popular of the brotherhoods to emerge in the sixteenth century was that of the Church of Nuestra Señora de las Angustias, whose devotional image—the Virgin holding the body of her crucified son in her arms—became a popular symbol of the city. The popularity of the Virgen de las Angustias as an icon gained an early boost when Don Juan of Austria became a member of the *cofradía* and prayed to her image for success in his Alpujarra campaign. The importance that this image continues to have for the city is demonstrated in a procession that still takes place every September, with the front of the church adorned with flowers.

Across large parts of western Europe in the seventeenth and eighteenth centuries, there was a gradual movement towards Enlightenment ideas and a focus on scientific endeavours. This was not the case, however, in now tiny, insular Granada. If the city had entered the seventeenth century jubilant at its 'discoveries' of the early Christian martyrs on the Sacromonte, on the eve of Napoleon's invasion of Spain, the city was in many ways even more deeply immersed in religion. Indeed, within Granada the belief in the lead books and their prophecies had never truly disappeared despite the Vatican's condemnation, and it was this legend and the local people's continued longing for their authenticity to be re-established that proved one of the driving motivations for the fraudulent archaeologist Juan de Flores to begin his excavations in search of a pre-Islamic settlement in the Albaicín in the 1750s.

Flores was an amateur archaeologist as well as a lay cleric at Granada Cathedral.[24] His house is purported to have been full of antiques, including coins, inscriptions, and sculptures, and some of these, it seems, had been found in the underpopulated Albaicín. Visitors to Granada had made mention of Roman finds in the city before the time of Flores; however, in the post-Reconquista years, Granada's early history had also been blurred by the desire of the locals for the city to have Roman origins, which tended to produce legends rather than actual concrete evidence. Nonetheless, in the 1750s, the newly created Casa de Geografía in Madrid was calling for greater investigations to be undertaken into Spain's ancient history. It was in response to this that, in 1754, Flores began his excavations around the Cuesta de María de la Miel, in the former Alcazaba, where he

Fig. 1: The Fuente de Aynadamar (Fuente Grande) at Alfacar—this is the reservoir that fed Granada, enabling it to develop into one of the major cities of al-Andalus.

Fig. 2: An example of an *aljibe*, one of a network of cisterns to store water when it reached Granada from the Fuente de Aynadamar.

Fig. 3: The remains of the Bab al-Difaf, a Zirid-era sluice gate enabling the flow of the river Darro to be controlled.

Fig. 4: The bell tower of San José Church, a converted Zirid-era minaret.

Fig. 5: The eleventh-century Zirid/Almoravid walls of the old Alcazaba.

Fig. 6: The fourteenth-century Nasrid walls, built to protect the enlarged city that housed refugees fleeing areas of al-Andalus conquered by the Christians.

Fig. 7: The Alhambra—since its foundations in the thirteenth century, the complex has continuously evolved. This view shows how Charles V's palace deliberately dominates over the more delicate Nasrid Palaces.

Fig. 8: The ruins of the 'new' Alcazaba, the first part of the Alhambra to be completed.

Fig. 9: The Palacio del Partal, one of the earliest surviving palaces within the Alhambra complex.

Fig. 10: The Patio de los Leones in 1910, showing Rafael Contreras's addition of an anachronistic domed roof.

Fig. 11: The Patio de los Leones today with the dome replaced by a more authentic style of roof.

Fig. 12: Carved motif on the walls of the Alhambra showing the Nasrid crest and motto.

Fig. 13: The Puerta de Elvira—originally Zirid-era, this important gate was completely remodelled during the reign of Yusuf I and large parts were later destroyed during the French occupation.

Fig. 14: The Corral del Carbón, a Nasrid *alhóndiga*, the Andalusian equivalent of a caravanserai.

Fig. 15: The Madraza—built in the fourteenth century, this building was given a Baroque facelift in the eighteenth century.

Fig. 16: The Capilla Real, resting place of the Catholic Monarchs, beside La Lonja, the sixteenth-century mercantile exchange where business was transacted, including that of the essential silk trade.

Fig. 17: The Real Chancillería—established in Granada by Queen Isabella, the court attracted many opportunistic Christian immigrants to the city, seeking social improvement.

Fig. 18: The Hospital Real, the city's Christian-era insane asylum, which was home for a time to San Juan de Dios.

Fig. 19: La Cartuja (The Charterhouse), described in the sixteenth century as one of the most beautiful and happy spots it was possible to find.

Fig. 20: Granada Cathedral, commissioned by Charles V to dwarf the neighbouring eleventh-century former main mosque.

Fig. 21: The Abbey of the Sacromonte, built following the discovery of the lead books and the charred remains of St. Caecilius.

Fig. 22: The Arco de las Orejas in c. 1830, showing the original position of the gate.

Fig. 23: Mariana Pineda, freedom fighter and inspiration for one of Lorca's plays.

Fig. 24: Mariano Fernández Santiago, 'King of the Gypsies', better known as Chorrojumo.

Fig. 25: The Azucarera de San Isidro, a sugar refinery built as that industry boomed in the nineteenth century, bringing great wealth to a handful of Granada's inhabitants.

Fig. 26: Calle Ángel Ganivet, a wide, straight road bounded by colonnaded buildings, built on the site of a traditional area and bizarrely named after one of the nineteenth century's staunchest critics of this very destruction of the old city.

Fig. 27: The Alhambra Palace Hotel—built in 1910 to cater to wealthy visitors, it is still visible throughout the city today with its dome referencing Contreras's contribution to the Patio de los Leones.

Fig. 28: The Huerta de San Vicente, the summer home of the Lorca family.

Fig. 29: The Albaicín in 1878, a much less built-up area then than it is today.

Fig. 30: The Albaicín today with the towering Church of San Nicolás and, to its right, Granada's modern-day main mosque.

had received reports that some Roman inscriptions had recently been uncovered.

Modern-day researchers into Granada's pre-Islamic past believe it is likely that Flores's early finds were indeed authentic, and from recent excavations it is clear that he was even conducting his digs on the actual correct site of Roman Granada. Yet, whilst he may have hit upon the actual spot of a Roman administrative centre, just one month into his excavations, his first forgeries were produced. Possibly his motivation to go to such lengths to falsify historical artefacts was born out of a deep desire, shared with so many in the city, to authenticate the legend of the lead books. Indeed, one of his earliest forgeries was a sheet of lead inscribed with details of the parchment from the Torre Turpiana and the Sacromonte finds, which he held up as evidence for the authenticity of the original discoveries. Flores was also intent on proving that Granada had been the meeting place of the Synod of Elvira, the fourth-century Church council known to have been held somewhere in the region. To this end he produced other spurious artefacts, including the base of a column inscribed with what purported to be the date of consecration of a church on a former temple dedicated to Apollo.

In the way history so often repeats itself, much about Flores's deceptions mimics the forgeries of the lead books from a century and a half earlier. It is not only Flores's desire to prove a certain history that links the two plots; there is also a similarity in the collaborative nature of the conspiracies. In the same way that it is believed that the Moriscos Luna and Castillo could not have concocted so complex a plot alone and were almost certainly helped by others in the city, Flores too was only able to perpetrate so intricate a fraud with a great deal of assistance. His co-conspirators included local artisans, who assisted him by fabricating a wide range of counterfeit artefacts: vases, sculptures, coins, pieces of jewellery, historical documents, and even an altar dedicated to Hercules. However, it was not only crafts-men skilled at working in stone, bronze, and lead who aided his deception, but also members of prestigious institutions in Granada and beyond. Most prominent among these was Luis Francisco de Viana y Bustos, a canon of the Sacromonte Abbey who, like Flores, was determined to restore the reputation of the lead books. Others who collaborated were members of the very panel tasked with authenticating the discoveries. This was of great significance as there was genuine scepticism about the find-ings in some quarters and many academies refused to endorse them. Yet one accomplice, Cristóbal de Medina Conde, was a member of Barcelona's Academia de Buenas Letras, and this establishment accepted all of the discoveries as genuine.[25]

In 1763, the excavations came to an end, possibly, it appears from a text found later in Flores's house, owing to the rogue archaeologist's having had an attack of conscience about the fraud he was committing. Some years later, Flores and his co-conspir-ators were tried and convicted of their crimes. Flores was ordered to pay for the filling in of the excavation sites and his fakes were destroyed. Today all that remains of those years of great excite-ment is the name of a small square in the Albaicín—the Placeta de las Minas—named after the passageways underneath the square where many of the excavations took place. However, even the trial and the public disgrace of Flores and his gang could not bring an end to Granada's continued debate about the authentic-ity of the lead books. This raged on amongst some religious scholars well into the twentieth century, and the conjecture over Granada's importance in Roman times even continues today, the controversy caused by Flores and his fellow conspirators having done much to harm the discovery of the truth.

Flores's aim had been to strengthen the city's claim to a very Christian heritage. Yet within fifty years of his excavations, Napoleon's *Grande Armée* would arrive in the city, bringing in its wake a change in focus. Future generations would be more interested in the archaeological evidence of Moorish history, in particular the glory years of the Nasrid dynasty. Here, as Granada entered the nineteenth century, it was once again to find itself embroiled in international affairs, even if it played a somewhat minor role in the Spanish theatre of the Napoleonic wars. The impact of the French on the city would prove profound and Granada would be shaped by a new character on the scene, a Corsican general passionate about all things Oriental and whose personal ambitions would start to drag the Moorish city out of the obscurity it had fallen into over the previous two centuries. Moreover, this temporary foreign leader of the city would act as the catalyst for a new age of international interest in this last kingdom of the Moors in Spain.

10

HORACE I, KING OF GRANADA

At three o'clock in the afternoon of 28 January 1810, Horace Sebastiani, a general in Napoleon Bonaparte's *Grande Armée*, rode into Granada through the Puerta de Elvira in triumph, watched by a crowd of wary onlookers.[1] Like Napoleon himself, Sebastiani was a Corsican who, as an energetic and charismatic man, had risen through the military ranks in the years following the French Revolution. Even before his arrival in Granada, he had developed a passionate admiration for all things Oriental from his time as French ambassador to the Ottoman Porte in Istanbul. His dominance in Granada lasted a mere eighteen months, but in this time, his love of Islamic art and architecture inspired this French soldier to make some quite radical changes to the city in the name of both historical conservation and revolutionary modernisation.

By the time of Sebastiani's arrival, the city had spent almost two years preparing itself for a likely French invasion. Andalusia had fallen late in Napoleon's peninsular campaign and, as elsewhere across the country, the region was outraged when the emperor removed the Spanish royal family to exile in France and later replaced them on the throne with his own brother Joseph Bonaparte. This anger was fuelled in particular by the violence the French had unleashed in Madrid in May 1808, famously depicted on canvas by Francisco Goya. The general mood of the country was restive and especially hostile to anyone thought to be harbouring ideological sympathies with the French. Across unoccupied parts of Spain, cities began to prepare to repel further attacks by Napoleon's forces.[2] Granada was no exception, and it set about organising its own defences.

Large parts of the country were in revolutionary mood and, exasperated that so little was being offered by way of resistance to the invaders by the traditional authorities, some began to establish alternative governing councils, or Juntas, around the country to prepare defences.[3] In Granada, the Junta set about acquiring both property and money to create barracks for soldiers and stores for artillery, as well as to ensure there were enough supplies to feed both the local population and the defenders. Yet this newly founded body was frequently frustrated in its efforts to acquire resources, because the city's established elite at both the Ayuntamiento and the Real Chancillería tended to look down on the local, mid-ranking notables who made up the Junta as upstarts and showed little enthusiasm in co-operating with them. The Junta was also seen as a threat to the privileges of the clergy, calling, as it did, for the secondment of religious property for the war effort. The French position against religion was widely known, yet ecclesiastical officials were often half-hearted in their approach to co-ordinating their efforts with the Junta, despite owning vast properties across the city which could have been used.[4]

In spite of the obstacles, preparations for a French invasion went ahead, though the atmosphere was strained. Robert Semple, an American travelling through Spain in 1809, described this tension in a city resonating with a deep hatred of the French; places of recreation such as the theatre and the bullring had been closed down, and the heads of alleged traitors could be seen hanging in cages above the Puerta de Elvira.[5] Local men were sent to the front alongside soldiers from the rest of Spain, and people at home waited with trepidation for news of their loved ones and updates on the French advance on the region. In the first few months of the war came terrifying reports of the sacking of nearby Cordoba, as French troops marched into Andalusia to attack the Spanish navy based at Cadiz. Yet this was followed by a period of euphoria when, on 19 July 1808, word came that Spanish forces had triumphed at the Battle of Bailén in the north of the region—the first defeat Napoleon had suffered on the open field anywhere in Europe. Granada erupted in celebration of what was already being dubbed the beginning of the liberation of Spain, perhaps even Europe, with processions and revelry taking place throughout the city.

Despite this victory, the building of defences continued, while Napoleon, furious at the humiliating defeat at Bailén, now took personal command of the *Grande Armée* in Spain, reasserting French dominance through a devastating campaign. Details of this would have reached Granada from its sons on the front line, leading to greater worries about the potential invasion of the city. The Junta's problems in trying to raise money from the elite continued; nevertheless, historic buildings such as monasteries and colleges began to be converted into buildings for the war effort. These included parts of the Alhambra, where the Alcazaba was turned into a prison for the French. During his visit to the Nasrid Palaces, Semple expressed his surprise at finding that many of the French incarcerated on the Sabika hill, far from being Napoleon's troops captured in battle, were actually long-term residents of Granada, married to Spanish women and who had spent most of their lives in the city:

> Their sole crime was that of being Frenchmen by birth, for they certainly did not appear to be such in any other respect. Some of

them were engaged in various games, some conversed, whilst others mounted on the highest platform of the tower, looked down upon the city, where they might with ease discover the roofs of their own houses from which they had been so cruelly torn. It does not appear possible by any sophistry to justify the act of seizing and imprisoning men reposing in all the security of citizenship.[6]

Whilst French-born locals languished in the Alhambra prison, defence preparations continued. Morale was low as stories flooded in from other parts of Spain of the terrible reprisals being meted out to cities that had held out against Napoleon, such as Zaragoza and Girona. This had a major impact on the way that Granada's defence was organised, as many, in particular among the upper classes, wanted to avoid risking the same fate befalling them. This meant that, despite reassigning many of the city's buildings to new purposes, Granada's Junta avoided building up the city's fortifications beyond installing a few cannon.[7] The emphasis instead was on preparing people for battle in the open.

In early 1810, French troops entered Andalusia. Soldiers guarding the Sierra Morena north of Jaen were overwhelmed, and, fearful of reprisals, few cities offered an effective check on the advance, preferring instead self-preservation. As General Sebastiani marched on Granada, easily overcoming the forces fielded to halt his progress, all resistance within the city crumbled. Members of the Junta fled, and those among their townsmen who refused to surrender, like others from across Andalusia, followed in the footsteps of the Moriscos of three centuries earlier and headed for the mountains. The resistance regrouped in the Alpujarra, where they were to continue their fight throughout the period of French occupation as outlaws, joining with other guerrillas from the hills of Murcia to the east of Granada province to fight a war of attrition against the invaders.

Back in the city, however, local leaders from the Real Chancillería and the Ayuntamiento chose to submit without a fight, seeing this as a price worth paying to avoid the destruction wrought on other cities across the country. Members of the ruling classes went out to greet the French at Pinos Puente, claiming that by doing so they were maintaining order and saving Granada from the horrors of anarchy.[8] Later, Sebastiani entered the city and assembled his troops at Triunfo, the large space just outside the Puerta de Elvira, where local leaders, who had felt so humiliated by the Junta, went to great lengths to ingratiate themselves with the occupying forces. In the evening a *Te Deum* was sung in Granada's cathedral to give thanks for the delivery of the city. Perhaps, in those early days of occupation, the rest of the local population also felt some relief at the possibility of the restoration of order after two long years of preparing for war and waiting for news. But any relief that was initially felt would be short-lived as Sebastiani began to assert his dominance over the city.

Eyewitnesses who knew Sebastiani differ in their conclusions about his effectiveness as ruler of Granada. One particularly scathing account of the general was written by his *chef d'état-major*, Louis de Bouillé, whose disdain for his boss was so strong that he devoted seven pages of his memoir to a character sketch attacking him on every front.[9] According to Bouillé, Sebastiani had the airs of great importance that come from being born at the bottom of society, which led him to an arrogance that offended those around him, as well as to despotic tendencies that would come to the fore during his time in Granada. Another, though kinder, account of Sebastiani's character comes from Andrew Blayney, a British prisoner of war captured in a battle on the south coast. As a major general, Blayney was permitted the privilege of certain freedoms in captivity that allowed him to accompany Sebastiani around Granada and gain an insight into the mind of this temporary administrator of the city, whom he portrays as a gallant character at times, although generally he writes with a sense of irony about Sebastiani's motives.[10]

Despite the doubts of some of those around him about his ability to govern, Sebastiani himself almost certainly felt triumphant at taking Granada without a fight and, like many among the French, believed his 'enlightened' presence would win over the local population. An article in *La Gazeta de Madrid* interpreted the ease with which the *Grande Armée* prevailed over some of the large cities of Andalusia as a sign of a local populace tired of the chaos of the Juntas, keen to escape the oppression they had suffered, and aware of the benefits that the 'just' and 'liberal' French regime would bring them.[11] The reality is more likely that these cities had surrendered so readily to avoid the repercussions that would have followed almost inevitable defeat, and this in no way indicates that people welcomed their new, foreign masters.

Of course, not everyone in Granada was opposed to the new French rulers. There were some among the educated classes, for example, who embraced the arrival of novel and so-called enlightened ideas; however, these were a tiny minority. Others, particularly within the elite, made an outward show of normality under the French, continuing the polite society they had kept under the old regime. The duchess of Gor, a member of one of the noble families of the city, held popular social gatherings to which she invited both the local elite and the new occupiers, with Sebastiani a regular attendee. Yet, Bouillé suggests a more devious reason why the elite might have been happy to hold these events, and that was because Sebastiani was, allegedly, incapable of keeping anything secret when he was surrounded by people of titles as grand as 'duchess'. Bouillé suggests that Sebastiani was always letting French military secrets slip, allowing the Spanish to gain advance warning of French attacks.[12] Meanwhile amongst the ordinary residents of Granada, there was, generally, outright hostility towards the invaders. The working classes, including the peasants, worried about food shortages with an occupying army in the city to feed, and they remained relatively immune to the new ideas after prolonged exposure to anti-French propaganda going back to the time of the French Revolution. The clergy had much to fear with the arrival of the French, and in the days prior to the invasion, many monks fled the city.[13]

With such opposition to his rule, it was not long before Sebastiani's despotic tendencies began to emerge. Finding the majority of the people to be hostile to the French, he fostered a culture of fear within the city. Most locals supported the rebels, who were carrying on the fight from their mountain redoubt, and Sebastiani threatened severe punishment should anyone act to assist the guerrillas. A police force was set up to keep an eye out for signs of resistance, based out of what is now the Church of Perpetuo El Socorro, and Blayney wrote in his diary of the daily garrottings carried out at Triunfo, saying, 'Scarce a day passes without several similar executions, the sufferers being mostly those whom the French stigmatise with the names of rebels and brigands, but to whom the page of history will accord those of loyalists and patriots.'[14] Meanwhile, any potential for relief and an end to the hardships of the pre-war years quickly evaporated. Sebastiani had troops to house and feed, and very quickly imposed high taxes on the local population, ordering them also to provide billets for all French soldiers garrisoned in the city. He himself moved into the Archbishop's Palace, by the cathedral, the first of Granada's greatest buildings to accommodate his increasingly lavish lifestyle. As Blayney observed, 'In every respect the General's establishment is superb, and well calculated, not only to acquire the respect of the Spaniards, but also to maintain the dignity of his elevated situation with his own troops.'[15]

In effect, Sebastiani began to comport himself in Granada in the style of a king. However, at first, he was forced to take second place to an actual monarch who was touring the newly conquered Andalusia. On 16 March 1810, King Joseph Bonaparte arrived in

Granada and was welcomed by an artillery salute fired from the Alhambra and the sound of the cathedral bells.[16] His procession into the city halted outside the Hermitage of San Sebastián, on the banks of the river Genil, where the municipal leaders presented him with the keys to the city on the exact spot where over three centuries earlier Boabdil had performed the same ritual with the victorious Catholic Monarchs. The procession was then escorted over the Puente del Genil, where a magnificent triumphal arch had been erected to welcome the royal visitor.

The sycophantic pro-French press had staged a considerable build-up ahead of King Joseph's visit, praising him as a philosopher and highlighting his great virtues of modesty, beneficence, and faith without fanaticism.[17] This was a somewhat contrary portrait to that common to most Spanish people, who had nicknamed him Pepe Botella (Joe Bottle) thanks to his reputation for being a heavy drinker. Perhaps it was curiosity, then, about this supposedly great saviour that brought crowds out onto the streets to greet the new monarch. The press hailed how the faces of the people were lit up with 'the most sincere jubilation'[18] as Joseph passed through the city along streets strewn with flowers and leaves. More likely, however, the jubilation stemmed from the fact that as the king walked majestically along Calle Zacatín and through the city's squares, he tossed handfuls of coins to the waiting crowds.

King Joseph took up his lodgings at the Real Chancillería, the judges and magistrates having been moved out and the prison annex turned into a large kitchen. From here, he started as he meant to continue, with the intention of winning round the local population. One of his first acts, which won widespread support, was to order the French Tricolour flying above the Torre de la Vela to be struck down and replaced with the flag of Spain. Meanwhile, Granada's elite were keen to show their loyalty and honoured their new royal master with a host of events on

19 March to celebrate his saint's day. At the cathedral, he was showered with praise by the presiding canon, who gushed about how Joseph would re-establish great happiness and prosperity across the country.[19]

The day continued with the king undertaking tours of the city in an attempt to win the affection of its people. He visited the tombs of Isabella and Ferdinand at the Capilla Real and, understanding the great passion of the locals for bullfighting, arranged for the bullring at Triunfo to be cleaned up and reopened. Joseph's most personal desire, however, was to visit the Alhambra. There had recently been a growing interest in France in the history and legacy of the Moors, brought about in part by the accounts of a few intrepid eighteenth-century travellers to Granada, and this fascination was not lost on the man who had already shown his tendency towards the Romantic. The king would visit the complex many times during his stay in the city, and unable to ignore its state of dilapidation, he ordered that money be spent on its restoration.[20]

However, with the lack of available funds for anything else during the occupation, such conservation work was, in reality, nothing more than a fanciful notion at that time.[21] For the people of Granada, struggling financially after their efforts to defend the city over the previous two years and now forced to provide the resources to keep the French garrison housed and fed, this two-week visit by the king and its attendant pomp, ceremony, and constant state of celebration must have been hard to countenance. Nevertheless, it seems they may have got off lightly. Before reaching Granada, Joseph had initially suggested a prolonged stay in this famous, historical city, and plans had been mooted to move the court there for a period of some months. However, Granada was no place for even a temporary court, being so open to continued guerrilla attacks from the surrounding mountains and close to a coastline dominated by the British Royal Navy.

Unfortunately, the end of Joseph's visit did not signal an end to the costs associated with the upkeep of a royal household. Sebastiani relished the regal lifestyle, and becoming ever more seduced by the city over which he now exercised complete control, he began to adopt the mannerisms of a monarch and to surround himself with the trappings of royalty. Louis de Bouillé later described in his memoirs how generals fighting in other parts of Spain envied the pleasant situation Sebastiani had established for himself in Andalusia, mocking him with the moniker of '*Horace I, Roi de Grenade*' (King of Granada).[22] Meanwhile, in the style of many a vain autocrat, *le Roi Horace* surrounded himself with sycophants who lavished on him constant praise, and he strove to great lengths to live in the style he imagined his dignity to command. Beginning with the period of his residence at the Archbishop's Palace, he expected the Ayuntamiento to wait on him and would throw grand parties, inviting along all the notables and aristocracy of Granada. In the autumn of 1810, in emulation of the king, he moved his residence to the Real Chancillería to avail himself of its more sumptuous atmosphere. But it was at the Alhambra that Sebastiani felt most in his element, hosting visiting dignitaries in the Royal Palaces, seated upon satin cushions like an Ottoman pasha.[23]

Here, under Oriental architecture that he had learned to love so much at the court of the sultan in Constantinople, his passions could really take hold. History provides us with mixed reactions to Sebastiani's restorations of the Alhambra's Royal Palaces. Washington Irving, for example, was later to hold him in high esteem for saving the buildings from ruin:

> With that enlightened taste which has ever distinguished the French nation in their conquests, this monument of Moorish elegance and grandeur was rescued from the absolute ruin and desolation that were overwhelming it. The roofs were repaired, the saloons and galleries protected from the weather, the gardens cultivated, the water-

courses restored, the fountains once more made to throw up their sparkling showers, and Spain may thank her invaders for having preserved to her the most beautiful and interesting of her historical monuments.[24]

Yet other writers were less impressed by the French attitude towards the Alhambra, suggesting some of their touches changed the character of the Nasrid Palaces. Blayney, who lived as a prisoner within the complex, complained:

> Some of the apartments have been fitted up in the modern style by Sebastiani, which certainly is no proof of his good taste, for a Parisian salon or boudoir in a Moorish palace five hundred years old, is almost as absurd as dressing an antique statue in the costume of a modern *petit maître*.[25]

Whether Sebastiani improved the Royal Palaces or was just one of many who caused unnecessary alteration to the Nasrid architecture, it is certain that the buildings were in a terrible state when the French arrived in Granada. Three centuries earlier, in the years after the Reconquista, the Alhambra had been a site of fascination for Isabella and Ferdinand, as well as for the governing Mendoza family, which ensured it had at first been kept in good condition. That is not, however, to say that the beauty of its Nasrid architecture had been maintained in a state of pure preservation. On the contrary, vast changes had been made in those early years, with Charles V's palace only the largest and most noticeable. Other modifications included the conversion of one of the Royal Palaces into the Convent of San Francisco, the destruction of the main mosque and its replacement with the Church of Santa María de la Alhambra, and the morphing of other areas into buildings more suitable to the tastes, culture, and religion of the Castilians. Charles V, for example, had converted the bath house of the Palacio de Comares to make it more amenable to Western-style bathing.

Whilst the complex was maintained in those early years for royal visits and as a home for the governing family, the deterioration of the Alhambra began with the decline in fortune of the Mendozas following the Alpujarra wars and the expulsion of the Moriscos. Although the family retained the governorship for more than another century, they lost some of their other positions through the machinations of their enemies, such as Deza, president of the Real Chancillería.[26] In 1717, the marquess of Mondéjar was finally stripped of his governorship of the Alhambra by Philip V in retaliation for his having supported Philip's rival in the War of the Spanish Succession. The Nasrid palace that the Mondéjars had long called home was destroyed, bringing to an end the relationship between the Mendoza family and the Alhambra.

Yet it was not just the diminishing influence of the Mendoza family that had led to the state of dilapidation of the Alhambra by the beginning of the nineteenth century. A fire in a powder magazine down by the river Darro in 1590 had been an early indicator of the fragile nature of the Royal Palaces. However, although there was some immediate destruction to decorative features of the buildings closest to the northern walls, such as the shattering of windows, the impact was less than it could have been, and the structures themselves fortunately remained intact.[27] The complex had also, over time, become home to an assemblage of different people. As its military necessity diminished following the expulsion of the Moriscos, the Alhambra lost its original garrison and became home to an invalid corps, providing housing to soldiers injured in battle and their families. Meanwhile, the security of the fortress also declined, and people from other parts of the city moved into its buildings. Little was done to prevent the deterioration that resulted from this new domestic use. The Alhambra had also served down the centuries as a space for entertainment, such as bullfighting, with people pouring in from the city and clambering onto the roofs of some of the monuments surrounding the Plaza de los Aljibes in order to gain a good view of the spectacles.[28]

Even if credit can be given to Sebastiani for taking some care over the Royal Palaces of the Alhambra, without doubt, he and his troops added greatly to the devastation across the vast majority of the rest of the complex. Early on in the occupation it became clear that the war in Spain was far from over, and that it was not going to be of the conventional kind. All across the country, particularly in Andalusia, French troops were coming under frequent attack from guerrillas hiding out in the mountainous regions, generally supported by the people living under occupation in the surrounding cities. It would not be enough, therefore, to simply rebuild city walls when attacks could take place inside them. So Sebastiani chose the Alhambra, with its exceptional strategic position high above the city, as the location for his garrison.

A huge programme of fortification building began, not only at the Alhambra, but across the whole of the Sabika hill, causing irreparable damage to this area of such archaeological importance. For example, the site now commonly known as the Silla del Moro, a former Moorish watchtower overlooking the Acequia Real, was turned into a major outpost supporting more than 100 cannon.[29] The site of Muhammad V's Palacio de los Alijares, brought down by the earthquakes of the fifteenth century, was also turned into a gun battery, leaving few remains of this once magnificent Nasrid palace for future archaeologists to study. However, it was at the Alhambra that the greatest damage was done. The fortress was too old and in too fragile a state to be put to the modern use that Sebastiani had in mind for it. At various times it housed between 150 and 600 troops, together with their horses, and this wrought havoc on the structure. Not only did the weight of the numbers cause this destruction, but also the behaviour of the troops. Living all over, from Charles V's palace to the Convent of San Francisco, French soldiers themselves ruined large parts of the Alhambra, for example burning wooden doors and religious objects for firewood during the long, cold Granada winters. It is likely that a great many items of significant religious importance were used as fuel to keep the French fed and warm during this period.[30] Elsewhere in Granada, further injury was done to its historic legacy; the Hermitage of San Miguel Alto was destroyed and its materials used to build a fortification on that hill too. The present building is a replacement erected in a Neoclassical style after the departure of the French.

Worse still, the ravage brought upon the Alhambra by Sebastiani's brutal refortification was, sadly, just a foretaste of what was to come when the French later abandoned the city. And it reflects another aspect of the despoiling at the hands of the invaders. The looting of the city's monasteries led to the loss of much of Granada's Christian art and architectural heritage. Some of this pillaging took place under the hypocritical guise of liberating Spain from the yoke of the Church. On a visit to La Cartuja, Blayney noted with some sarcasm how Sebastiani went about justifying to himself his growing collection of plunder:

> While viewing the valuable articles of church furniture collected here, Sebastiani declaimed on the oppressive taxes the Spaniards must have borne, to furnish religious ornaments alone, and the advantages that must result from the abolition of monastic institutions. Here I could not help reflecting, that if plundering the churches was for the good of the country, the French had certainly taken a most lively interest in its welfare.[31]

In fairness to the French, before the arrival of Napoleon's army, groups of locals had already sacked a number of religious houses after many of their inhabitants had fled the city in fear of revolutionary anti-clericalism. Yet the French continued the process; within three days of entering the city, an order was issued for monks to leave their establishments within fifteen days. Nuns were treated less harshly simply because no-one could decide what, as women, should become of them.[32] Many cloisters were turned over for use as barracks, and as was the case at the Alhambra, much of the damage done was caused by the poor treatment of the buildings by the soldiers quartered within them.

One of the most famous cases of destruction of the monasteries of Granada was that of San Jerónimo. Although, like other monasteries, this had been looted even before the arrival of the French, it was subjected to a greater indignity by the arriving conquerors, who defiled the tomb of Isabella and Ferdinand's celebrated military leader, El Gran Capitán, in 'revenge' for the defeats he had inflicted on their countrymen back in the sixteenth century. The monastery was then used as a barracks for troops and a store for artillery. Another act committed at San Jerónimo that remains infamous among the people of Granada today was the destruction of the top of the monastery's tower, from which the stone was taken and later used to build new landmarks in the city of Granada, in common with materials taken from other religious structures ruined at the time.

Nevertheless, amidst all this devastation, Sebastiani continued to proclaim a passionate determination to improve the city. Alongside many of Napoleon's other generals, he was greatly influenced by the emperor's notions on the subject of urban reform and saw it as part of his mission to bring the 'light' of the philosophy of reason to the less advanced cities of the conquered nations. As early as March 1810, his plans were laid out in the *Gazeta de Madrid* for bringing a new form to Granada and thereby turning it into a centre of beauty and elegance in just a few years. His plans included clearing away the obstacles in the street that impeded the flow of people, for example by moving the multitude of crosses and symbols of religious devotion that littered the city, returning the fountains to being springs of health, and improving the conditions of the marketplaces, which he saw as noisy and chaotic.[33] In this he became the first in a line of the city's leaders who, over the next two centuries, would become resolved to change the look and character of the still fundamentally mediaeval Granada in the name of progress.

One of the most visible of Sebastiani's changes to the city was the landscaping of the gardens alongside the river Genil, in today's Paseo del Salón. This area had been a recreational space since Moorish times, legend suggesting that gardens on the spot had been the regular meeting place of those thirteenth-century poet-lovers Hafsa and Abu Ja'far at the time of the Almohad invasions. Now, Sebastiani laid it out in gardens in the French style. And there, on the river, a new entrance to the city was created by the building of the Puente Verde, famously using the masonry pillaged from the tower of San Jerónimo. This eased the flow of traffic passing over the Puente del Genil, which had since Zirid times been the main point of entry to Granada from the south.

Elsewhere in the city, other projects were initiated to ease movement. Again, many of these caused irreparable damage to some of Granada's most important historic landmarks. For example, the Puerta de Elvira was remodelled. Since the time of Yusuf I, this had been a large and important fortress guarding one of the major entrances to the city, but under Sebastiani, changes were made that left standing only the gateway that remains to the present day.[34] Further up in the Albaicín, buildings were demolished in order to widen some of the streets and improve circulation. There was also a major drive to clean up the streets, especially the markets, and to ensure burials took place in cemeteries outside the municipal boundaries. One significant project that had enjoyed little success prior to the arrival of the French was the improvement to the city's street lighting. This, of course, had the benefit of helping French patrols to monitor the eleven o'clock evening curfew imposed upon the residents.[35]

One cultural undertaking completed in Napoleon's time but that sadly no longer exists today was a theatre, which had been started in 1802 but remained unfinished due to a lack of funds and the outbreak of the war. Perhaps, more than anything else, this theatre symbolised the desire of the French occupiers to move Granada towards modernity—greater than that enjoyed by any previous administration, mired as they generally were in their religiously conservative mindset. Located in what is today the Plaza del Campillo, the new theatre was inaugurated in November 1810 and named Teatro Napoleón, after the emperor. This would later be renamed the Teatro Cervantes, before being pulled down in 1966 to make way for a 1970s commercial and residential block.

Of course, Sebastiani's changes to the city came at a financial cost, and the brunt of this was borne by a local population already stretched to the limit paying for the upkeep of the general and his men. The Peninsular War was also an increasing burden for the French, as they fought a battle of attrition against the guerrillas in the mountains, who were supported by the British. Finally, it was not only the cost of the modernisation works that brought them to an end, but also the loss of their most significant champion. Sebastiani left in a convoy for Madrid on 25 June 1811, from where he returned to France. Bouillé, ever uncharitable to his commander, claims that, 'he was not regretted either by the city nor the province of Granada, which he had tired by his despotism and his arrogance, and which he had exhausted by his fantasies and his greed.'[36]

Sebastiani was replaced by Jean François Leval, whose command would be short-lived given that the tide was beginning to turn against the French in the war. By the spring of 1812, the huge cost of the conflict, combined with a concerted effort by British and Spanish troops, had started to make an impact in Andalusia and required the new commander to recall troops from around Granada province to reinforce the city.[37] By the summer of that year, people had become worn down by illness, fighting, hunger, and the crushing tax levy of the French. Then, as the allied British and Spanish forces began to bear down, Joseph Bonaparte ordered a complete withdrawal from Andalusia. This was done slowly, with the French taking care to blow up fortifications as they left to ensure they would be of no further use to their enemies.

In the early hours of 17 September 1812, the imminent departure of the French troops was announced to Granada by the sound of explosions coming from the Alhambra and across the Sabika hill. People awoke to discover that major landmarks, including the Silla del Moro and the recently built outpost at San Miguel Alto, were no more. Perhaps beyond anything else, the destruction of large sections of the Alhambra's defensive walls demonstrates the devastating impact of the French occupation of Granada. Local legend has it that the damage would have been much worse had it not been for the heroic efforts of a member of the Invalid Corps named José García, who managed to snuff out the fuse and prevent further detonations with his own body, later gaining recognition for his heroism with a plaque on the walls of the complex he saved, close to the Alcazaba.[38]

To get some idea today of the extent of the destruction of the Alhambra's fortifications, walk around the outer wall from the Torre del Cabo de la Carrera, near the top of the Cuesta de los Chinos, clockwise through the Alhambra woods in the direction of the Puerta de la Justicia, noting just how many of those towers and gatehouses are reconstructions. Not only did the dynamiting affect its intended targets, but the shockwaves from the blasts also seriously damaged or destabilised other parts as well, most notably the Palacio de los Abencerrajes, which now lies in ruins. Furthermore, the violence of the explosions and the debris that was flung out from the Alhambra by the force of the blasts also damaged numerous other buildings in the surrounding area.

Later that same day, the French forces gathered at Triunfo to begin their departure from the city in the same spot where they had arrived less than three years earlier. Off to fight in parts further north, where the war would continue for many more months, they left Granada, carrying off much that had been looted in the city during the occupation, along with romantic tales of the Alhambra and Granada's Islamic past. These stories and legends taken back to France and other parts of Europe would soon bring a new set of invaders to the city, armed with the pen and the brush in place of the gun and the sword, to usher in a new phase in its history—the Romantic artists and writers of the nineteenth century.

11

DREAMS OF THE PAST, VISIONS FOR THE FUTURE

Although now the mock of Europe, which once grew pale at her name, Granada is still the chosen land of romance, where the present is forgotten in the past.[1]

This excerpt, from the English travel writer Richard Ford's *Handbook for Travellers in Spain*, sums up much of the prevailing feeling among foreign visitors for whom Granada was a must-see stop on the Grand Tour during the early nineteenth century. As Napoleon's troops withdrew, the era during which Granada had tried to assert itself as the most Christian of cities was well and truly coming to an end. Visitors from northern European countries and America had no interest in Granada as a centre of Catholicism. Instead, they came to see the Moorish influence of the past—the mystique of the Orient so tragically destroyed, as they saw it, three centuries before, in 1492.

Many of these visitors, not least Ford, disparaged the contemporary inhabitants of Granada for their disdain for the city's Moorish past, and seeing the dilapidated state of the Alhambra, they were quick to blame both Spain and Catholicism for what they deemed the decline of a once regal city. Contrasting a negative present with a glorious past, Ford claims:

> Few parts of the Peninsula present a sadder contrast between the past and the present. Under the Moors Granada was rich, brilliant, learned, industrious, and gallant, now it is poor, dull, ignorant, indolent and dastardly. The Spaniards, have, indeed, laboured hard to neutralise the gifts of a lavish nature, and to dwarf this once proud capital down to a paralysed provincial town.[2]

It is true that, in the three centuries since the end of Moorish rule, Granada had indeed become a provincial city, playing little role in the wider events in Spain. However, Ford's contempt for nineteenth-century Granadinos is not entirely fair. The French army had left behind a vast trail of devastation, reducing the defences at the Alhambra to rubble and destroying a number of buildings on the Albaicín hill, and the people of the city were left to face many of the same debilitating problems as the rest of the country at that time.[3] When Napoleon's troops withdrew, the disrupted harvests meant great hunger for many of Granada's inhabitants; there were frequent outbreaks of disease, and travelling in the region was perilous owing to the banditry that was rife. Even within the city itself, there were issues with safety and security, and this was not helped by the fact that the Peninsular War had left Spanish society deeply divided.

Whilst the French had left the city in a terrible state, under the new constitution drawn up during the war in unoccupied Cadiz, the local councils of Spain now had increased powers that they could put to use for improving the cities in their charge. Unfortunately, in Granada the lack of resources meant that for a number of years some of the innovations brought in by the French were reversed. The street lighting, for example, became neglected, and many streets were plunged once again into darkness at night. Meanwhile, following the end of the occupation, the new constitution was met with antagonism by both the clergy and the nobility across the whole of Spain. This allowed the recently restored Ferdinand VII, in May 1814, to abrogate the constitution and re-establish absolutist rule. In Granada, as elsewhere, those who supported Ferdinand paraded through the streets in triumph, a huge bonfire was made of symbols of the Constitution of Cadiz, and later an extravagant celebration was staged in the Madraza in honour of the king.

As the new regime took effect, there was also a bid to undo many of the secular changes brought about by the French. Granada's newspapers were closed down, and later a new archbishop was installed who was a strong supporter of absolutism and the restoration of the Inquisition. Efforts were made to reinstall in their previous locations around the city the crosses and devotional alcoves removed under the occupation. Monasteries were reopened, religious processions were revived, and one of the cofradías rebuilt the Hermitage of San Miguel Alto, which had lain in ruins since the French departure. However, this drive to return Granada to its eighteenth-century state was not a complete success, and it left the city with many traces of the secularisation brought in by Sebastiani. Indeed, across Spain as a whole this reversion to absolutism was to prove only a temporary phenomenon, and as the mid-century approached, modernity was clearly coming even to provincial backwaters like Granada.

Throughout the nineteenth century, Spain would experience continual upheavals, as political struggles took place between supporters of liberalism and the traditionalist forces made up predominantly of the Church, the monarchy, and the aristocracy. For the most part, however, Granada was merely a small city to which little attention was paid in comparison to the scenes being played out in the capital and other, larger population centres. Nevertheless, as elsewhere in the country, there were highly charged conflicts of ideology between supporters of the authoritarian monarchy and those who continued to fight for a constitution as first proposed in Cadiz. And one local woman, later immortalised in a play by Federico García Lorca, would become a symbol of the political struggles of the time: Mariana Pineda.

It is difficult to extract the true Mariana Pineda from the fictional character Lorca portrayed. Like many a great playwright before him, Lorca was less concerned with historical accuracy and more interested in using Pineda to convey his theme, in this case the incredible power of love. He depicts Pineda's allegiance to the liberal cause as stemming from her love for her cousin, a man who, in the play, is totally undeserving of such ardour. As Lorca himself acknowledged, he was portraying Pineda as a 'Juliet without a Romeo'.[4] Yet this Pineda, a romantic stereotype of womanhood, engaged predominantly in embroidery, and acting out of affection rather than reasoned political beliefs, is one that lingers. This is shown in Lorca's opening to the play, which sees a child singing a rhyme about the heroine:

What a sorrowful day for Granada,
Oh! the stones from the pavement could cry
just to know that Mariana,
for silence, has to go on the scaffold to die.
Marianita, she sat in her bedroom,
thinking thoughts that were always the same!
'If Pedrosa should see me embroidering
on this banner in Liberty's name.'[5]

The real story behind Pineda's involvement in the liberal cause, though, shows us a courageous woman who, far from sitting by the hearth embroidering, was intimately involved in the political struggles of the time.[6] Born in 1804 in a house in the Carrera del Darro, she married young but was left a widow with two small children at the age of eighteen. It was after this that she took up the liberal cause in Granada, first by becoming a central point of communication between liberals based in other parts of Andalusia and political prisoners incarcerated at the Real Chancillería, the latter of whom she visited to pass on messages. Long kept under surveillance by the authorities, who were suspicious of her actions, she achieved greater notoriety amongst the monarchists for her participation in a plot to free her cousin, the rebel soldier Fernando Álvarez de Sotomayor. This was the relative who legend, and later Lorca's play, would claim to be Pineda's true love. Whether or not there is truth in this, her support in enabling him to escape incarceration, dressed in a monk's habit she had smuggled in for him, allowed Álvarez to evade his sentence of death for conspiracy. Pineda ensured she had an alibi on that occasion but remained under suspicion, the authorities watching her every move. Her conviction would come in the end for something far more innocuous than aiding in the escape of a condemned prisoner: through the discovery of a flag that she had ordered to be emblazoned with the treasonous slogan, '*Ley, Libertad, Igualdad*' (Law, Liberty, Equality), and which was later found in her house during a police search.

The flag alone might not have been enough to convict Pineda, but the story goes that she had also spurned the advances of an official of the Real Chancillería named Ramón Pedrosa Andrade. In both the local legend and Lorca's play, Pedrosa is the true villain of the piece and responsible for her brutal death. Under his interrogation, Pineda showed her true heroism, refusing to furnish him with names of other liberals in exchange for her life. Frustrated by her silence, and following her own attempt to escape captivity dressed as an old woman, Pedrosa had her locked up in the Convent of Santa María Egipcíaca. This establishment, on Calle Recogidas, had long been used for the imprisonment of prostitutes and was later destroyed when the street was widened in the twentieth century. Here, behind closed doors, she was sentenced to be garrotted for conspiracy against the security of the state and the legitimate rights of the crown.

On 26 May 1831, Mariana Pineda was led through the city on a mule, flanked by monks, to the site of her execution at Triunfo, just beyond the Puerta de Elvira. Whilst many in the crowd that gathered to witness the spectacle expected her to relent at the last minute when confronted by the horror of the death awaiting her, she instead met her end with great dignity and with the distinction that her belief in liberty remained intact. As she had declared at her trial, 'The memory of my torture will do more for our cause than all of the flags of the world.'[7] Indeed, within five years of Pineda's execution, Ferdinand VII had also died and the political landscape in Spain had shifted; the liberals now had the upper hand and suddenly the heroine of their cause in Granada became a celebrated name in the city. The anniversary of her death began to be commemorated and the site of her execution was eventually renamed the Plaza de la Libertad. Her statue was erected in a central square that bears her name, and later a hall inside the European Parliament building in Strasbourg was also named after this crusader for liberty.

Yet the battle between conservative and liberal forces was far from over and it continued to mark the history of Spain for much of the next century, a foretaste of the civil war that would break out in the next. One issue that would court controversy throughout this period was the limitations the liberals wished to place on the power of the Church. In the mid-1830s, the vast influence of the religious establishment was challenged with the widespread confiscation of church lands known as the *desamortización*. These property seizures carried out by the state came about in large part as a means of repairing Spain's finances after decades of instability, through attacking the incredibly powerful and wealthy Catholic Church. The expropriations were widespread, and Granada was not immune; the *desamortización* impacted heavily on the look of the city, one prime example being the demolition of the Carmelite convent in what is now the

Plaza del Carmen, home of Granada's modern-day Ayuntamiento. A painting by David Roberts shows the convent prior to its destruction, towering over the river Darro running along what would later become Calle Reyes Católicos.

Paintings and lithographs by visiting artists such as Roberts provide a last glimpse, in the days before photography, of the mediaeval Granada that was about to undergo a huge transformation in its outward appearance. Roberts was one of the many foreigners who arrived in Granada in the years following the withdrawal of the *Grande Armée*, and he became captivated with this romantic vestige of the once magnificent al-Andalus. The city had long sparked the imagination of those with a romantic bent. As early as the sixteenth century, even as the Moriscos were being expelled from Granada, the Spanish writer Ginés Pérez de Hita wrote a highly sentimental portrayal of the noble Moors, romanticising the final years of the Nasrid kingdom in what is considered one of the earliest historical novels: *Guerras civiles de Granada*. Later, the poet and playwright John Dryden produced a play in seventeenth-century London called *The Conquest of Granada*, which tells a wholly fictitious tale of the final years of Moorish rule. Yet it was to be in the nineteenth century that a steady trail of visitors to the city would attempt to take this fanciful and heroic view of the past to new heights.

One of the earliest of these was the French writer François-René de Chateaubriand, who visited Granada prior to Napoleon's invasion. Captivated by the romanticism of Granada's past, he published his *Aventures du dernier Abencerage* almost twenty years after his visit. Using the legend of the Abencerrajes, Chateaubriand creates a tale of a descendant of that noble family returning to see his ancestral home a century after its fall to the Christians, and—as fate would have it—falling in love with a beautiful Spanish girl living in Granada. It allows for the portrayal of the end of Moorish rule as a romantic tragedy, presenting an idealised image of the Moors as embodying the values of traditional mediaeval chivalry, despite their adherence to Islam, whilst creating an essential connection between the Spanish inhabitants of the city and the Moors who had lived there in the past:

> When Aben-Hamet came in sight of the roofs of the first buildings in Granada, his heart beat with such violence that he was forced to stop his mule. He crossed his arms over his chest, and, with his eyes fixed on the sacred city, he remained silent and motionless. The guide stopped in his turn, and as all noble feelings are easily understood by a Spaniard, he seemed touched and guessed that the Moor was seeing his old homeland again.[8]

His descriptions of Granada capture what other artists would also later see, in particular the overly romanticised impression of the Alhambra. His hero expresses similar visions of the building to later nineteenth-century Romantics:

> Motionless and silent, he gazed in astonishment at that dwelling place of genies: he felt as if he was being transported to the entrance of one of those palaces described in the tales of the Arabs ... Something voluptuous, religious and warlike seemed to breathe in this magical building; a sort of cloister of love, a mysterious retreat where the Moorish kings tasted all the pleasures and forgot all the duties of life.[9]

Other writers such as Victor Hugo conjure up an equally quixotic portrait of the city. But perhaps Granada's most celebrated literary visitor in terms of the impact he continues to have on the city today was Washington Irving. In 1829, after a journey on horseback across the mountains in which he lost himself in the fantasy of the Moors and the pages of Cervantes, the American author of *Rip Van Winkle* and *The Legend of Sleepy Hollow* arrived in Granada. There, he was given permission to live in the apartments of the governor of the Alhambra, inside the Royal Palaces. He resided amongst the locals, who had returned to living in the complex following the withdrawal of Napoleon's troops, and describes the everyday uses to which they put the once opulent spaces, which included making fires for cooking whose smoke blackened the Nasrid decoration. He romanticises both the locals themselves and the history of the complex, incorporating many of the folk legends that prevailed at the time. His tales of his time at the Alhambra, swimming in the pool of the Patio de los Arrayanes, could only ever elicit the envy of other adventurers keen for similar experiences.

Irving's *Tales of the Alhambra* enjoyed broad appeal, influencing writers and artists as far afield as Russia. Alexander Pushkin based one of his later tales on a story contained in Irving's work, and one of the most prominent Russian composers of his age was to follow in the footsteps of Irving himself. Mikhail Glinka visited Granada in the 1840s and, renting a *carmen* next to the Torres Bermejas, he became captivated by flamenco. Transcribing the music of a local guitarist, he went on to create a movement called 'Symphonic Alhambrism', which features pieces inspired by the Nasrid Palaces.[10] Writing about his inspiration, Glinka paints a picture of the musical culture of the city:

> The melody and dance that predominate here in Granada is the fandango. The guitars begin and then each person present in turn sings a verse while one or two couples dance with castanets. This music and dance [are] so original that up until now I have been unable to capture the melody, because each one sings it in his own way ... here music and dance are inseparable ... Most of the melodies are Arabic ... I turn to the muleteers, the artisans, and the simple folk, to listen with great attention to their melodies.[11]

Arguably, though, the greatest impact of the nineteenth-century Romantic impressions of Granada is felt through the visual arts. Seduced by the dilapidated state of Granada's exotic Moorish ruins rising against the backdrop of vivid blue Andalusian skies, artists such as David Roberts and John Frederick Lewis conveyed the beauty of the Alhambra and perhaps did more than any others to attract visitors to the city. Both Roberts and Lewis were captivated by the monuments set amidst the decay of the city. Far from being accurate representations of the landscape, though, their lithographs distort the scale of the architecture to emphasise the majesty surrounded by decay—the crumbling walls, the sagging roofs, the damage to the decorative features of prominent buildings—highlighting the tragic nature of a lost civilisation. The local Spanish, in contrast, are frequently depicted in a manner which reinforces northern European stereotypes. They lie idly amongst the dilapidation, seemingly unaware of the grandeur and beauty of their surroundings, or else certain 'exotic' aspects of their culture feature prominently, such as Spain's deeply rooted Catholicism, or its passion for bullfighting and flamenco.

These Romantic portrayals of Granada were, in turn, to have a major impact on another artist of the nineteenth century, whose designs inspired by the Alhambra led to even greater fame for the monument. The architect Owen Jones arrived in Granada in the 1830s while undertaking the Grand Tour with another young architect, Jules Goury. The pair became fascinated by the geometrical designs contained within the decoration of the Alhambra and began to study the mathematics behind them, making plaster casts in the process in order to learn this lost art form. These studies, in particular of the use of colour, led to significant advances in modern design theory.[12] Their book, along with Jones's designs for the Great Exhibition in 1851 that featured an 'Alhambra Court' amongst the displays at the Crystal Palace, helped to increase the mania for the now hallowed monument that was already becoming ever more renowned amongst the upper classes across Europe.

Yet, despite the growing interest in the Alhambra, helped along by the works of Roberts and Lewis, the buildings were in a terrible state. The time the French had spent in residence and their dynamiting of the southern walls had left much of it effectively in ruins. Large parts were buried in the detritus left by the soldiers, and there had been attempts to loot anything that could be carried away, including, it appears, the Fountain of the Lions, some of whose very lions were left scattered on the floor.[13] Some 150 mattresses were left behind by French troops inside the Convent of San Francisco, a building that usually accommodated just twenty-five monks.[14] Meanwhile, even after the French withdrawal, the fortress continued to be used for military purposes, this time by Spanish troops, but, as the frontlines moved gradually northwards, normality returned. By the end of 1813, the Alhambra was no longer part of the war effort, although the Torre del Homenaje remained in use as a prison for some time afterwards.

Unfortunately, not every aspect of the building's sorry state was down to the French. As Ford was to note, the Alhambra had been neglected by the Spanish authorities and even the local population for centuries by this point. And, as Irving's tales and Lewis's paintings show, the wider complex was a town within a town, its inhabitants adapting the existing buildings for their own use. Despite the expulsion of these dwellers from the Alhambra by the French in order to allow for its use as a military stronghold, after the war they returned, even though many were to discover that their former homes were now little more than rubble. The residential part of the complex was soon rebuilt, and as absolutism once again took hold of the city, for a while the Alhambra became a place free of restraint for people from the city below. They came up to drink and visit prostitutes, until the complaints reached all the way to the government in Madrid, and the establishments of ill repute were finally closed down.[15]

Ford's *Handbook* may have denounced the local population for their treatment of the Alhambra, but the foreigners who claimed to idolise the place so much were not above causing damage of

215

their own to the fragile Nasrid décor. An illustration by the French illustrator Gustave Doré depicts a couple surreptitiously chiselling away at one of the palace walls to remove a piece as a keepsake. However, other outsiders were incensed by the neglect and petitioned the authorities. And their calls did not go unheeded, because as the nineteenth century progressed, there was a growing awareness within both local and national governing bodies of the money that was coming into Granada by way of these visitors from far and wide who wished to view the Nasrid Palaces. In need of the potential revenue, the politicians proceeded to take a keener interest in the building's preservation.[16] Yet, questions were asked about how Spain should set about promoting a building that had been constructed and enjoyed, as they saw it, by heathen foreigners who had occupied their Christian country for so long.

The solution to the quandary became apparent with Queen Isabella II's appointment of the architect Rafael Contreras to the position of official restorer of the Alhambra in 1847. Instead of recreating the monument in all its Nasrid glory, Contreras was directed to restore the buildings in such a way as to symbolise the triumph of Spanish history and to promote the standing of the present monarch:

> That he [Contreras] should work especially on the restoration of the decoration of this marvellous souvenir of Spain, bringing it back to the original form that it had at the time of the Conquest when the Catholic Monarchs waved the banner with the cross ... The Queen wishes to equal her ancestor Isabella I who conquered the Alhambra, becoming thus the Queen who restored it to its former glory.[17]

Tasked with creating an Oriental jewel that could be viewed as a triumphant monument within Spanish history, Contreras set about restoring the Alhambra. To him, this meant making profound changes to fit his own vision of what a mediaeval Oriental palace should look like, his ideas highly influenced, ironically, by the nineteenth-century visions of the past created by Washington Irving and the Romantic artists. In order to provide the building with this 'Oriental' character, Contreras did not shrink from making quite drastic alterations to entire rooms within the Nasrid Palaces and reimagining them based on his own ideas gained from the colour and design techniques developed by Owen Jones. An example of this is the Sala de las Camas within the Palacio de Comares,[18] at the time of writing often closed to visitors.

Perhaps Contreras's most infamous change, however, was his replacement of an original gabled roof of the Patio de los Leones with what he felt was more appropriate for an Oriental palace: a gaudy and anachronistic dome. Moreover, at the time of Contreras's restorations, so much of the plasterwork had been destroyed that he chose to recreate some of the decoration from scratch, his belief being that: 'It is better to make a small error of assessment than to unreservedly abandon a monument to its ruin.'[19] Yet, in effect, his errors were not simply ones of assessment—rather, they meant the creation of a new concept of Moorish design. In the tradition of Juan de Flores, who only a century earlier had attempted to show an ideal Christian past for the city, a Spanish architect was now, in a similar vein, constructing for the benefit of visitors to the city a past for the Alhambra that also had little basis in truth.

Nevertheless, this Orientalist homage to the past, based on little in the way of academic evidence, attracted the visitors. Indeed, to a certain extent this desire continues to exist, with visitors still coming to the Alhambra for photographs in front of what is often portrayed as a Moorish building frozen in time, rather than understanding the reality of what was, or the debates over what might have been. Fortunately, today's restorers are much better informed, and much more is done to provide an understanding of historical evidence than was the case in the nineteenth century. Back then, not only did Contreras make some quite drastic changes to the Alhambra, but he also established a lucrative business, selling models of his own images of the monument to rich tourists passing through the city. There is doubtless a beauty to these plaster models, examples of which can be seen in the museum of the Casa de los Tiros. However, in effect, Contreras was only providing the nineteenth-century visitor with what some guidebooks continue to relate to their modern-day counterparts: an ideal vision of what they seek, whether or not there is a true basis for the 'history' being promoted.

The dramatic changes to the way the Alhambra looked were to be reflected to a large extent down in the city below, although for entirely different reasons. Granada's ruling elite had come to the conclusion that the best thing for the city would be to push it into the modern age, and by this they meant completely changing its still predominantly mediaeval appearance.[20] Nothing highlights more clearly the drive towards that vision of modernity than the decision to cover over the river Darro. As with many of the changes about to be made, this decision to hide the waterway that had been the lifeblood of Granada since the eleventh century was made in the name of hygiene. Whilst it was certainly the case that there had been widespread epidemics in the early nineteenth century, to blame the river for these outbreaks of disease seems a little unfair. What appears to have been a greater spur for the changes was the way the elite looked with envy on cities like Paris and Madrid that enjoyed wide boulevards and open spaces, and they began to draw conclusions that what held Granada back from progress was its ancient street plan. The rhetoric they used was powerful: the air would be able to circulate better and make the city healthier; it would give easier access for transport, which would in turn improve the economy; and jobs would be created for the unemployed.[21]

The character of the city was to be changed significantly by the culverting of the Darro. Although in reality this process had begun shortly after the Reconquista with the creation of the Plaza Nueva, it was only in the nineteenth century that the major work to put the river underground took place. This fundamental feature of the landscape was hidden away beneath the street that became Calle Reyes Católicos, whilst the buildings so admired by those visiting artists such as David Roberts were knocked down and replaced with the townhouses that still exist today. The main thoroughfare of ancient times, Calle Zacatín, was relegated to being an unimpressive backstreet. Richard Ford, prior to the changes, describes it thus:

> The Moorish Zacatín ... is as antique as the Spanish Plaza Nueva is modern. In summer it is covered with an awning ... which gives a cool and tenty look. Go, without fail, ye artists, to the back part ... and sketch the Prout-like houses and toppling balconies so old that they seem only not to fall. Here is every form of picturesque poverty; vines clamber up the irregularities, while below maids dabble washing their red and yellow garments in the all-gilding glorious sunbeams.[22]

Like other Romantic visitors to the city, Ford was enchanted by the charm of grandeur amid decay, although this is something that naturally would have been less pleasant for those who had to live in such conditions at the time. Cities have to evolve, with people generally desiring an improvement in their lot, and one of the biggest criticisms made against the nineteenth-century Romantic artists and writers is that they placed a higher value on the picturesque appearance of the place than the environment of the people who lived in it. Yet the problem with the drastic changes that Granada's leaders set in motion was that in actuality, almost all of these were carried out in the interests of upper-class residents, whilst poor families saw themselves turfed out of certain areas, leaving the rich to benefit from the inevitable property speculation that ensued.[23]

Changes to Granada at the time involved the demolition not only of numerous Moorish buildings, but also of some of the city's early post-Reconquista layout. The Plaza de Bibarrambla, developed as the main site for public entertainment in the early sixteenth century, was extensively remodelled in the nineteenth.[24] This square had been central to Granada's festive occasions; for example, prior to the building of the circular bullring at Triunfo, it had hosted bullfights in the traditional format on horseback. The buildings surrounding the square had been designed with balconies for spectators to watch the festivities, whether these be the bullfighting or the Corpus Christi celebrations for which the square had always provided the main focal point. With the redesign in the gentrified style still in evidence, less consideration was made to its importance as a place of public spectacle.

Another dramatic alteration in the appearance of the Plaza de Bibarrambla, again made in the name of hygiene, was the destruction of the mediaeval gate known as the Arco de las Orejas, which had for centuries been the main entrance to the square. Legend has it that the name of this gate—the Arch of the Ears—stemmed from its being where parts of executed criminals' bodies had been displayed as an example to others. Despite the importance of the gate amongst the Moorish monuments of Granada, for which reason it had been declared a national monument, the Ayuntamiento was determined to remove it. A campaign, backed by the president of the republic, that lobbied for its preservation ultimately failed to dissuade a council hell-bent on its quest for modernisation. Insisting that restoration was now impossible and claiming a cholera risk, in 1884 the Ayuntamiento pulled down the Arco de las Orejas. The remains of the gate were, however, rescued and in 1935 reconstructed within the Alhambra woods, where the gate continues to stand in retirement today.

Whilst it appears the elite almost overwhelmingly supported the changes to the city, there was some vocal opposition. Among the foremost critics of the city's ruling bodies was Ángel Ganivet

García. One of Spain's greatest intellectuals in the latter years of the nineteenth century, this writer and diplomat from Granada penned a scathing critique of the way historical cities were being mutilated in the name of modernity. The book, *Granada la Bella*, was filled with examples from the city of how a local government could set about making irreversible changes to a city in the name of progress, and in the process destroy the beauty and heart of these truly magnificent places.[25] Setting out how cities are designed around their own particular climatic conditions and topographical features, he rued the trend across Spain of blindly emulating the layout or feel of cities in other, cooler parts of Europe. He noted that Granada's narrow streets had been designed to provide maximum shade in a city that often swelters in the sun, condemning the desire of the local council to cut wide boulevards that they perceived to be at the heart of progressive cities elsewhere. His criticism was particularly strong for the covering up of the river Darro, noting that the section still open to the skies at the time of his writing passed through the Puerta Real, where the houses were so far apart that they couldn't possibly provide shade to shoppers in the street. Sending the river underground would actually make the city less healthy, as the coursing water provided cooling freshness to counteract the oppressive heat.

Some of the changes made towards the end of the nineteenth century were spurred on by the sudden injection of wealth into the region through the discovery of the ease with which sugar beet could be grown in the surrounding Vega.[26] Juan López-Rubio Pérez, the owner of a chemist's shop on the newly created shopping street of Calle Reyes Católicos, was one of the first to experiment with the production of sugar beet, and the results of his experiments were to have a major impact on agricultural production in the Vega and would spark the building of factories for sugar production. The ruins of one of the most important of these factories, the Azucarera de San Isidro, can still be seen on the outskirts of the city. The sugar beet industry made fortunes for landowners in the Vega, and as the century drew to a close, this would become even more pronounced when Spain lost its colonies in South America, rendering imported sugar much more expensive and creating a lucrative market at home.

This newly created wealth for a relatively small section of society in Granada was the spur, then, for what would be considered by some as the biggest and most brutal folly yet: the construction of the Gran Vía de Colón. Conceived of as a majestically wide, traffic-friendly avenue through the centre of Granada, this grand thoroughfare cut a straight line across the heart of the mediaeval city and no building was permitted to stand in its way. Moorish houses, religious establishments, family neighbour-hoods—all were swept away without a trace, and the once har-monious street plan that had existed since the eleventh century was chopped in half. Whereas since the foundation of the city the Albaicín had been intimately connected with the flatlands below, now this hillside neighbourhood was set apart from the rest.[27] At the same time, in order for Granada to emulate the larger, more modern cities the elite held in such high esteem, rules were laid down mandating that building façades be in a classical style, thereby fundamentally changing the look of the city. Not only did this huge change affect Granada's physical appearance, but it also led to a greater divide between the living quarters of the middle and the working classes. Families who had previously lived around the centre of the city but could not afford the cost of the new accommodation were forced to move up into the Albaicín, thereby increasing the population of this working-class district. This would have major consequences for the politi-cal battles of the next century.

Despite all the changes and the claims that the Ayuntamiento made of the great benefits these would bring to Granada's citizens, there was little in the way of relief in terms of living conditions for the vast majority of the poor. The population was growing, but there was no desire on the part of the authorities to expand the city's boundaries to ease the pressure. Instead, more and more people moved into already crumbling buildings, some tumble-down former houses of the nobility, turned by the poor into tightly packed tenements for numerous families. The city, in turn, became less salubrious, and there were outbreaks of disease and problems with maintaining a clean water supply. It was in the Albaicín, and further out in the Sacromonte, where these conditions were among the worst.

Fortunately for the city, though, not all of the proposals made by the Ayuntamiento in the nineteenth century were ultimately realised. Ángel Ganivet mentions plans for further street altera-tions that would have involved the widening of Calle Navas from the Plaza del Carmen all the way through to the Plaza de los Campos in the Realejo district. At the time of his writing, that entire area, now behind the Plaza del Carmen and the main post office at the Puerta Real, consisted of narrow, winding streets. For a while, the zeal for street-widening ebbed after the creation of the Gran Vía. However, it would only be a matter of half a cen-tury before, following the Civil War, another council decided—again on the premise of improving the city—to cut another wide, straight road through existing, traditional alleyways. Although this thoroughfare today bears none of the traces of its past, home as it is to trendy tapas bars and jewellers' shops, in an irony seemingly lost on the town planners of the time and almost in mock homage to one of the few who attempted to alert Granada to its own destruction in the nineteenth century, this wide, grey street would carry the name Calle Ángel Ganivet.

These further facelifts were yet to come, however. By the turn of the twentieth century, Granada's look had already radically changed from the mediaeval one experienced by the early-nineteenth-century Romantic artists and writers. The new century, in its turn, would bring about something of an explosion of artistic expression in the city, with an increasing appreciation for Granada's local heritage, in particular that of the gypsies living in the caves of the unmodernised and untouched Sacromonte. And this short period before the Spanish Civil War broke out witnessed the rise of one of Granada's greatest home-grown poets, a man whose life and death are intimately entwined with the city itself: Federico García Lorca.

12

CREATION AND DESTRUCTION

If the seventeenth and eighteenth centuries had witnessed concerted efforts to portray Granada as deeply and innately Christian, and the nineteenth century witnessed a great romanticising of the city's Moorish past, the early years of the twentieth century were to be characterised by the idealisation of yet another of Granada's fundamental cultures. Surprisingly, given the vitriol so often directed towards them, this would be the gypsies of the Albaicín and the Sacromonte.

The Iberian gypsy community is believed to have arrived on the Peninsula sometime around the fifteenth century. Genetic mapping has shown that European gypsies originated from north-west India,[1] although the term 'gypsy'—or *gitano*, in Spanish—derives from the legend that they came from Egypt. Perhaps paradoxically, despite their being relative latecomers in terms of migration to the Iberian Peninsula, gypsy culture features prominently amongst the images most often associated with traditional Spain, with its major presence within the art of flamenco music and dance. Nevertheless, from the time of their arrival, the *gitanos* tended to be the subject of persecution by the

Spanish authorities, and numerous laws were enacted over the centuries banning them from nomadic life, leading large groups to settle in areas on the periphery of cities. This was particularly the case in Andalusia, where they were able to practise their customs and speak their own language outside the more orthodox communities. In the case of Granada, the places they chose to settle in were the depopulated Albaicín district and the caves of the Sacromonte.

Outsider interest in Granada's *gitanos* had begun with the nineteenth-century visitors. One with a particular interest in the gypsies of Spain was George Borrow, who in 1841 published a book describing their lives and traditions.[2] Arriving in Granada, he noted it had the appearance of the poorest city in the country and that the gypsies shared in the general state of distress. He sets the scene by describing how they inhabited the caves on the outskirts of the city, often working with iron, and he paints a vivid picture of their labours:

> To one standing at the mouth of the cave, especially at night, they afford a picturesque spectacle. Gathered round the forge, their bronzed and naked bodies, illuminated by the flame, appear like figures of demons; while the cave, with its flinty sides and uneven roof, blackened by the charcoal vapours which hover about it in festoons, seems to offer no inadequate representation of fabled purgatory.[3]

The most famous of Granada's nineteenth-century gypsies, whose statue stands today at the start of the Camino del Sacromonte, was Mariano Fernández Santiago—better known as Chorrojumo. *Un chorro de humo* means a stream of smoke in Spanish, and the nickname stemmed from his original profession as a blacksmith. His fame was to come when the Catalan painter Mariano Fortuny, while wandering the cave district of the Sacromonte, became captivated by the sight of three gypsies singing away to accompany their hammering against the anvil. The artist was particularly enchanted by the dark features and enormous sideburns of Chorrojumo, and he returned to the spot a few days later to persuade this striking *gitano* to sit for a portrait. Still at a time when image was more important than authenticity, Fortuny dressed Chorrojumo in the clothes of a bygone era in order to add to the romanticism of his painting. And such portraits were to prove popular given the growing fascination with the romance of the gypsies, turning Chorrojumo into something of a star. Styling himself *el rey de los gitanos*—the king of the gypsies—Chorrojumo rapidly achieved fame in Granada and beyond, swapping his life of toil at the forge in the Sacromonte district for the environs of the Alhambra, where he became a popular guide for tourists. His income increased substantially from the meagre salary of a blacksmith as he regaled visitors with myths and legends of Granada's history, whilst charging people to take his photo in prominent places amongst the picturesque surroundings of the Nasrid monument.

It was a good time to be making money from tourism. The publicity Granada had received thanks to the Romantic artists and writers of the 1800s meant visitor numbers had continued to rise. In 1909, the first tickets were sold to visitors for the Nasrid Palaces after the authorities realised the benefits that directly selling tickets for access to the monument could bring.[4] Indeed, the potential for yet more income from tourism was clear, in particular to one entrepreneur who was to make his highly visible mark on the city. Julio Quesada-Cañaveral, the duke of San Pedro de Galatino, was inspired by the influx of wealthy visitors and, conscious of the lack of luxury accommodation in the city, embarked on a project to provide Granada with a signature luxury hotel. Building began in the first decade of the twentieth century on what would become one of the city's most eye-catching landmarks. The Alhambra Palace Hotel dominates the Mauror hill, overlooking the Realejo district below. Its terracotta-coloured walls and mock-Oriental décor—including a dome mimicking the anachronistic one that Contreras had erected atop the Patio de los Leones during his nineteenth-century Alhambra restorations—provide one of the most striking focal points of the city. Constructed on a high point within the Alhambra woods, the hotel was designed to provide its affluent patrons with views across both the Alhambra and the Vega, not only providing lavish lodgings but also hosting prestigious events for local notables.

However, the duke's vision ranged far beyond just the city itself. He also perceived the potential of the, as yet, under-exploited Sierra Nevada, whose snow-capped peaks rise majestically behind Granada. Here, he built a sister hotel for the Alhambra Palace that later became known as the Hotel del Duque, and he also commissioned an infrastructure project of visionary proportions that was sadly closed down in the 1970s: a tramway connecting the city and the mountains. This route, built under the supervision of the engineer Juan José Santa Cruz, cut tunnels through the hillsides and passed over bridges high across gorges, eventually arriving in the village of Güéjar Sierra. Videos of the tram shot prior to its closure can be found on the internet, showing just how spectacular a ride through the landscape it provided. Over the years, as the Sierra Nevada ski resort was developed, ideas were proposed for a funicular to link up the tram with the pistes, though these concepts were never realised.

Meanwhile, as the tourism boom continued in the early 1900s, the beauty of Granada and the Andalusian light remained just as irresistible to artists as they had been in the preceding decades. These included local painters making a name for themselves across Spain, such as José María Rodríguez Acosta, who was to make his mark on the city's skyline with the construction of his studio just along the road from the Alhambra Palace Hotel. This striking, white *carmen*, which today houses the Rodríguez Acosta Foundation and displays the works not only of its namesake but also of other notable artists, sits high up above the Plaza del Campo del Príncipe in the Realejo district, where it contrasts with the bright, terracotta-coloured walls of the nearby hotel. Artists like Rodríguez Acosta continued to be inspired by the scenery and the *gitano* culture that had so delighted others like Fortuny. George Apperley, an English painter who moved to the Albaicín in the early twentieth century, was also fascinated by the beauty of the gypsies and fell deeply in love with one of his muses.

Portrayals of the *gitano* community on canvas most frequently focus on their characteristic style of music and dance, and it was for these characteristics that they would become most renowned, particularly outside of Spain. The flamenco music that had profoundly influenced musicians who visited the city, like Mikhail Glinka, had, by the early twentieth century, become popular beyond the borders. At the 1900 Paris Exposition, Spanish gypsies performed flamenco at the exhibit entitled '*Andalousie au temps des Maures*', though some commentators noted the anachronism of Spanish gypsy heritage being mixed into a celebration of the legacy of the Moors.[5] This melding of Spanish, gypsy, and Arab cultural influences into something purporting to be quintessentially Spanish was, however, already well-established by the turn of the twentieth century. Indeed, the popularity of flamenco with foreigners had actually sparked off something of a backlash at the time amongst Spanish intellectuals, who were keen to move the popular image of Spain away from such stereotypes and to establish the country as European in essence, rather than an Oriental offshoot.

Yet the romantic vision of Spanish gypsies, with their seemingly mysterious connections to the artistic traditions of the Moors, would continue to have a major effect on the artists, musicians, and writers of Granada into the 1900s. Two who stand out for their international fame are Federico García Lorca and his friend, the composer Manuel de Falla. The first of these to appear in Granada's story was the younger of the pair. Although he was born in Fuente Vaqueros in Granada's Vega, Lorca's family moved to the city in 1909, when he was eleven years old.[6] Residing in a house on the Acera del Darro, the young Federico had the good fortune to be living in Granada at a time of intellectual revival. First, he was to have a highly influential teacher at Granada University in Fernando de los Ríos, a man well-connected with intellectuals of an earlier generation across Spain and Europe as a whole, and who would later achieve prominence as one of Spain's foremost socialist politicians. In addition to his teacher, very much considered a friend, Lorca was surrounded by other intellectuals and artists emerging in the city who were to form a group known as the Rinconcillo.

This group met in the evenings in a little corner (*rinconcillo* in Spanish) in the back of the Café Alameda in the Plaza del Campillo, at the time of writing Restaurante Chikito.[7] The group of friends were initially involved in writing a magazine called *Granada*, but they continued to meet even after the magazine ceased publication, united in their passion for the city and desire to discuss and debate new ideas. The Rinconcillo consisted of writers, artists, and intellectuals, many of whom were to have a major impact on the city. These included Lorca himself; his brother Francisco, who later became a diplomat; Antonio Gallego Burín, an art historian who after the Civil War became Granada's mayor; Constantino Ruiz Carnero, a journalist and later director of the newspaper *El Defensor de Granada*; and the Cubist painter and later both friend and collaborator of Picasso, Manuel Ángeles Ortiz. These, along with other creative types living in Granada, would gather regularly at the café, most notably between 1915 and the early 1920s.

Other artists and intellectuals who were already recognised in their field beyond Granada would also attend whenever they were in town. The guitarist Ángel Barrios, who had already achieved success across Europe, was one. Another was a man of even greater celebrity, who would become a fundamental part of Granada's artistic scene when he moved there; this was the composer Manuel de Falla. Born in Cadiz, Falla had already become fascinated with Granada even before his first visit, setting one of his early operas, *La Vida Breve*, about a gypsy girl's love for a rich man, in the Albaicín. When Falla eventually came to Granada, his experiences had a profound effect on him. His ballet *El Amor Brujo*, for example, appears to have been inspired by an early visit to the *gitano* cave dwellings of the Sacromonte.[8] Then, in 1916, he performed his *Noches en los Jardines de España*—a piece inspired in part by the gardens of the Generalife—during a concert at the Palacio de Carlos V at the Alhambra. It was these early trips to Granada that persuaded him to move there on a permanent basis.

Before taking up residence in Granada, Falla had already developed a friendship with Ángel Barrios during their time living and working in Paris, and this induced him to initially find a new home close to his friend's. This was a good choice since Barrios's father ran a famous tavern within the Alhambra itself. Situated in Calle Real, on the site of a former Nasrid bath house, the tavern El Polinario had gained a reputation for its spontaneous musical performances that varied according to whoever happened to be in the tavern at the time. Falla took up lodgings at the Pensión Alhambra, on the same street, which allowed him to regularly attend the musical evenings at El Polinario. Then, with Barrios's help, he searched for an appropriate permanent residence, finally settling on a nearby *carmen* on Calle Antequeruela Alta, just along from the Alhambra Palace Hotel, where Falla went on to live for almost two decades. The house is now a museum dedicated to the composer.

Lorca and Falla appear to have met during the time when the latter was staying at the Pensión Alhambra, and they soon became friends. A mutual acquaintance later described their relationship as being one of 'two geniuses, two creators face to face. On the one hand order, obsessive neatness, and the serene inspiration of the maestro; on the other hand, the vitality, the extreme vigour, and the wonderful childlike ways of the young poet.'[9] Like many artists of the early twentieth century, Lorca and Falla had developed a fascination with the Albaicín. This was in contrast to some of the visitors of the previous century, such as Ford, who, whilst writing pages extolling the beauty of the Alhambra and the flatlands of the city around the cathedral, had in turn been rather dismissive of the Albaicín, mainly commenting on its poverty. He claims, 'The Albaicín suburb, busy and industrious under the Moor, is now the abode of idleness and poverty.'[10] David Roberts also tended to overlook the upper Albaicín in his lithographs, focusing instead on the Alhambra and the dilapidated convents along the river Darro.

This had now begun to change with artists such as Apperley setting up studios in the district. And for many of these artists, it was the very juxtaposition of grandeur and decay that made the Albaicín such an inspiring muse now that such contrasts had all but disappeared from the city centre through the gentrification of the previous decades. Early photos of the Albaicín clearly show it to have been somewhat different in the early twentieth century to the way it is today. Its population was largely working class, and many of its male inhabitants were casual labourers reliant on whatever work was available to them on a given day. As Ford had identified, the district was a far cry from its heyday in the time of the Moors; many of the old buildings had fallen down over the years, and those that were left were frequently packed tightly with families, the overcrowding having become worse with the destruction of the area now taken up by the Gran Vía. The area was also marked by its *huertos*—allotments for cultivating food crops or rearing livestock—giving the feel of a semirural area, somewhat separate from the rest of the city, and it was seldom visited by residents of the wealthier parts of Granada.[11]

For Lorca and Falla, however, the Albaicín and the Sacromonte were an inspiration, not least of all because of their cave-dwelling *gitano* communities, whose music was to awaken the muse in both men. For Falla, flamenco was part and parcel of what it meant to be Andalusian, an art form that flourished in the unique conditions of southern Spain with its meeting of three cultures: Spanish, Moorish, and that of the gypsies. Meanwhile, Lorca, who supported Falla's vision, gives the following description of the gypsies: 'the gypsy is the most distinguished, profound and aristocratic element of my country, the one most representative of its way of being and which best preserves the fire, blood and alphabet of Andalusian and universal truth.'[12] His fascination with the music of the *gitanos* would lead him to write two collections of poetry based on gypsy culture: *Romancero gitano* (Gypsy Ballads) and *Poema del cante jondo*.

It was this *cante jondo*—meaning deep song—emulated in Lorca's poetry that both Falla and Lorca considered to be the oldest and purest form of flamenco, as well as one of the defining characteristics of Andalusian identity, thereby placing gypsy tradition at the heart of Spanish culture. Yet both men believed this authentic interpretation to be in great danger of dying out. Whilst flamenco might have been popular in the taverns of southern Spain, the interpretation had become something more commercial in nature—watched, but not loved, by audiences whose only understanding of it was as a kind of cabaret act.[13] Their fears over the loss of this art form brought both Falla and Lorca to the idea of organising a great festival for the city: a *cante jondo* competition that would allow for the revival of the music of the gypsies in its most authentic form.

The *Concurso de Cante Jondo*, organised with great excitement by Granada's artistic circle, took place at the Alhambra during the

Corpus Christi celebrations of June 1922, in the Plaza de los Aljibes, the square between the Palacio de Carlos V and the Alcazaba. In a bid to try to remove some of the commercialisation that purists felt had entered the art form in the flamenco taverns, only amateur singers of the pure *cante jondo* form were permitted to compete. So stringent were the criteria set out for the event that criticisms were raised that the organisers themselves had become too elitist in their vision of purity, which ignored the way music evolves.[14] Nevertheless, the event was a triumph. The atmosphere was accentuated by the artwork decorating the square and by the crowds of women who attended dressed in their silks and their shawls. Even an unseasonable downpour, captured beautifully in a cartoon by the young artist Antonio López Sancho, could not dampen the festivities. Indeed, such was the success of the event, it would lead to the beginnings of a growing acceptance even amongst Spain's intellectual elite of the importance of this type of music to the country's cultural heritage.

The Alhambra had long been a space for entertainment, including bullfights and theatrical performances throughout the Christian period, and the *Concurso de Cante Jondo* in many ways followed the tradition of cultural spectacle staged amidst the grandeur of the complex. Later in the decade, another Rinconcillista, Antonio Gallego Burín, organised a quite different event on the same spot as the *Concurso*. A friend of Lorca and future mayor of Granada, Gallego Burín had been born into a relatively wealthy Granada family and grew up in a house in the Plaza de Santa Ana while it was still separate from the Plaza Nueva. He was renowned amongst those who knew him for his zeal for both his city's art and its history, and it was these that in 1927 inspired in him an idea for the restoration of a long-lost Spanish tradition: the *auto sacramental*.[15]

A form of religious theatre, an *auto sacramental* would traditionally be celebrated at Corpus Christi but had been banned across Spain in 1765. Given the importance of Corpus Christi to

Granada, these plays had once been a major feature of the festivities in the city. Gallego Burín's decision to revive this tradition, to be staged in the Plaza de los Aljibes, once again drew on the creativity of the Rinconcillo. Musical adaptations for the event were placed in the hands of Manuel de Falla, whilst Ángel Barrios was given responsibility for directing the orchestra. Other members assisted by creating stage sets. The play chosen was the seventeenth-century *El Gran Teatro del Mundo* by Pedro Calderón de la Barca, which takes for its theme the Catholic belief that man's life on Earth is a test for which judgement shall come in the afterlife. A number of Rinconcillistas took to the stage themselves, including Gallego Burín.

The revival of the *auto sacramental* in the 1920s coincided with the growth of another religious spectacle in Granada, one that every year draws in tens of thousands of visitors. The Semana Santa processions are descended from ones that had taken place from the sixteenth century onwards, although those that emerged 400 years later did so on a scale never before seen in the city. In earlier times they had been smaller, more intimate affairs, with each *cofradía* organising its own, and processions sometimes clashing as they traversed the city.[16] Occasionally, fights broke out over who had right of way down the narrow streets. In the eighteenth century a complaint was made to the archbishop of Granada about the processions:

> In the Semana Santa processions there are even greater excesses, such is the noise and uproar with which they start and finish in the churches where they come out, those being more deformed and deplorable in the churches whose processions take place on the Thursday till Friday, on which the Lord is on the monument. It is unthinkable the lack of attention and irreverence which on those occasions is given to such a blessed sacrament.[17]

The processions that were organised in the twentieth century were much more orderly and under much more centralised control than those of the past. Far more elaborate, with enormous *pasos*—ornate floats depicting religious scenes—being paraded through the city, they showed a greater similarity to the Holy Week observances that had become popular in rival Seville. Lorca was a particularly vocal critic of the emergence of these new and ostentatious parades around Granada, comparing them to those he had witnessed as a young boy when he recalled only one procession taking place, and only in the years when wealthy locals were happy to fund it. Contrasting Granada with the much more flamboyant Seville, well-suited to such events, he bemoaned the city's new proliferation, which had, in his view, been created purely for commercial reasons and posed a major distraction from the serious message he had known as a child. He issued the following plea:

> I beg of my fellow Granadinos that they restore that Semana Santa of old, and hide in the name of good taste that hideous procession of the Last Supper. And don't profane the Alhambra, which isn't and never will be Christian, with the circus of processions, where that which is believed to be good taste is vulgarity, and only serves for the crowd to burn laurels, trample on violets and urinate in their hundreds on the illustrious walls of poetry.[18]

But it appears Lorca's was a minority voice. There was generally great enthusiasm for these new and ostentatious displays. As the number of processions grew, much greater organisation was needed to keep things in check, to the point where today each must arrive at key positions around the city centre according to a strictly enforced itinerary in order to avoid the conflict and chaos of earlier centuries.

Whilst these early decades of the 1900s were marked in Granada by music, poetry, and increasingly grandiose religious spectacles, there was also a darker side to the city, in particular in the poorer areas such as the Albaicín, where poverty was a fact of life for the majority of its inhabitants. Over the past hundred years many of Granada's traditional industries, including the once famous silk industry, had practically disappeared, and many of the city's inhabitants were reliant on seasonal agricultural work in the Vega, the city at the time being still fundamentally connected to the surrounding countryside in a way that is difficult to imagine today. But in the first few decades of the twentieth century, the population of the city was to increase greatly from around 75,000 in 1900 to over 100,000 by 1920.[19] Jobs in agriculture weren't enough to provide full employment for migrants to the city, and instead, many turned to construction work paid on a daily basis. Yet, the insecurity of this type of work meant that these casual day labourers could be left facing long periods without pay during lulls in construction, leading to further suffering for families with no other means of financial support. The early twentieth century had seen plenty of opportunity in the area as the building of the Gran Vía progressed, but in the second decade this regular employment began to drop off, and this problem was coupled with rising prices for food and other essential items.[20] And, on top of high unemployment levels, the Albaicín lay far behind other parts of the city in terms of infrastructure. In many ways the Ayuntamiento had ignored the Albaicín in its development plans for the city, leaving the inhabitants with few of the modern amenities that by then were being enjoyed in other parts of the city.

One of the most significant impediments to progress in the Albaicín was widespread illiteracy, not surprising given that literacy levels across the country were amongst the lowest in Europe. Things had, though, started to take a turn for the better in the poverty-stricken Albaicín and Sacromonte back in the 1880s with the arrival in Granada of a priest from the north of Spain.[21] Andrés Manjón, inaugurated as a canon at the Abbey of the Sacromonte, was walking past some caves one day on his way down into the town when he heard the sound of children reciting the Ave Maria. On closer inspection, he discovered an old woman surrounded by ten little girls whom she was teaching to read and pray. Inspired by what he had seen, Padre Manjón first provided the woman with a bigger and better cave for her school, and later began himself to gather together the money to found a series of Escuelas del Ave María (Schools of Ave Maria) in buildings around the city. As he argued to his detractors:

> If such a teacher in such a location and with so few means has been able to organise a school for girls in the Camino del Sacromonte, which was amongst the most uncultured and poor [areas] of Granada, who can doubt that improving on all this will mean ending up with a school with everything that could possibly be desired?[22]

Manjón's efforts were to set in motion progressive ideas about education—including instructing children outdoors in nature and teaching them manual skills—that would soon spread with his school system across other parts of Spain. Yet, even with the help of charitable foundations such as the Escuelas del Ave María, the Albaicín continued to be desperately poor, particularly in times of economic hardship when construction work was scarce. This provided fertile ground for the new anarchist and socialist ideas that were beginning to spread across the country. These new political ideologies brought fresh impetus to the conflicts that had raged on and off in Spain since the start of the previous century between conservative forces trying to preserve the traditions of church and monarchy, and those of a more liberal bent who were by now calling for greater enfranchisement, improved workers' rights, and expansion and improvement of the education system.

Between 1916 and 1919, it was this growing political awareness, coupled with the ever-worsening economic situation for those on the bottom rung of the social ladder, brought about in large part by the drying up of construction jobs along the Gran Vía, that led to a series of at times violent street demonstrations in Granada. These became a rallying point for protests against the corrupt political system that existed across the whole of Spain, although of greater local significance was the graft within the city's own Ayuntamiento, which was dominated by a self-serving elite that refused to cede any power to wider society. Political influence in Spain continued to be organised from the top, with factions sharing out power amongst themselves with no consideration for the wishes or needs of any form of electorate. And, as elsewhere in the country, in Granada this elite controlled groups of armed thugs who could be paid to attack any potential election rivals on the streets of the city.[23]

Public protest against the powers of the Ayuntamiento, then, had ample potential to turn unpleasant. And this, indeed, is what happened. In February 1919, public demonstrations came to a head when a large group dominated by students gathered around the Plaza de la Universidad. As tensions mounted, the Guardia Civil opened fire, forcing many of the protesters to barricade themselves inside the university buildings. Those who remained outside were subject to further attacks, and one student was hit and killed by a bullet. The anger of the protesters increased significantly in response to this and rioting broke out across the centre of Granada. Windows were smashed at the Ayuntamiento building in the Plaza del Carmen and damage was caused to buildings in the Plaza de Bibarrambla. The Guardia Civil continued to fire on the protesters as the disturbances went on unabated in different areas of Granada over the following two days. Finally, the army was drafted in to patrol the streets; curfews were imposed and martial law was declared in the city. The two days of unrest had left three dead and hundreds more injured, but they had also prompted the beginnings of an investigation into the dealings of the Ayuntamiento. The much-hated mayor was forced to step down, and the commander of the Guardia Civil was charged over the deaths of the protesters. Meanwhile, a commission in Madrid uncovered extensive corruption and misuse of public funds by the former municipal leaders of Granada.

The ousting of unscrupulous politicians had been brought about by a temporary coalition of various opposing factions within the city from both the left and the right of the spectrum. Members of these factions, in particular the socialists, now called for free and fair elections and lent their voices to the calls being issued by political parties across the whole of Spain. Two local men whose political activism had been growing over the previous few years were inspired by events to stand for political office. Lorca's friend and former teacher Fernando de los Ríos was to win a seat in the general election, becoming Granada's first socialist deputy in the Cortes in Madrid. A year later, with his passion for Granada and desire for its reform, the art historian Antonio Gallego Burín stood in the municipal elections. However, this future mayor of the city was to lose in this first bid for political office.

The democratic period of the early 1920s proved short-lived. The journey to democracy in Spain had a somewhat shaky start in the early twentieth century and came to a shuddering halt just four years after these elections. The street protests in Granada had been minor in comparison to the agitation elsewhere in the country, in particular in Barcelona, where demands for workers' rights had spurred major violence over the previous few years. The turmoil was exacerbated when Spanish troops were ambushed by Moroccan tribesmen in North Africa in a catastrophic encounter that caused the loss of thousands of Spanish soldiers. The ruling classes began to fret about the country's stability and, in response to these problems, a military coup took place in 1923. This was led by Captain General Miguel Primo de Rivera and supported by the monarchy, and it established a dictatorship that would govern for the next seven years.

At first the stability brought about by the dictatorship received support across the country. And during these years, Granada would continue to be a place of enchantment for members of its intellectual and artistic crowd, even though many, like Lorca, had now dispersed to other parts of Spain, returning from time to time to their native city. The 1920s were to be a decade, too, of change and transformation at the Alhambra with the arrival of a new preservation architect, Leopoldo Torres Balbás.[24] At the time when Torres Balbás took on the role at the Alhambra, the complex was in a dismal state of disrepair. The buildings had suffered at various times complete neglect and at others, such as under the watch of Rafael Contreras during the nineteenth century, reconstruction work based often on little more than the Orientalist fantasies of the restorer himself. Torres Balbás had already made a name for himself in the field of architectural theory, and at the Alhambra he would pride himself on basing his restoration work on historical evidence obtained from documents and reconnaissance of similar buildings in Morocco in order to determine how the buildings should appear.

Torres Balbás's conservation projects had a profound impact on the vast majority of the Alhambra complex. Photographs from the time show parts, such as the Convent of San Francisco, in a state of utter dilapidation. Muhammad III's Palacio del Partal is a prime example of the architect's restoration efforts. For many years the building had been a private house, with the arches we see today filled in and adorned with modern windows. The transformation of this building back to something approximating what it would have been like under the Nasrids was undertaken in the 1920s. Nevertheless, despite the major drive to restore and conserve the Alhambra, Torres Balbás was not without his critics. Decisions had to be made about which of the periods of the Alhambra's history should take precedence, meaning that the architect's decisions were sometimes as difficult to make as those that had been made by past restorers. And there was a great deal of local controversy when he decided to take down the anachronistic dome looming over the Patio de los Leones to replace it with a roof that he felt was more in keeping with architecture from Nasrid times. Many local people had become fond of Contreras's Oriental additions and were furious when the dome was removed. It would take a campaign in the press led by the likes of Manuel de Falla and Antonio Gallego Burín to persuade people that it had been nothing more than an Orientalist fantasy to begin with.[25]

The dictatorship of Primo de Rivera came to an end in 1930, his popularity having diminished during his seven years in power. This event ushered in the Second Republic, and with that a return to the political battles of the early 1920s. Fernando de los Ríos made a return to politics, becoming one of the most prominent leaders of the first Republican government, which was heavily made up of left-leaning parties including from the socialist faction. This administration immediately set out on an ambitious programme of reforms in a country that was largely still very traditional. Among these reforms was bringing about the end of the monarchy, and Alfonso XIII soon followed Primo de Rivera into exile. Land ownership was to be reformed, the education system improved, and the traditional power of the Church challenged. The left-leaning newspaper *El Defensor de Granada* captured the excitement of the possibilities that lay ahead with this new political system that would recognise the voices of all the citizens of Spain: 'The Republic is a blank page on which all Spaniards will start to write. Let's reconstruct the life of Spain! Let's reconstruct the life of our city! Onwards all, with hearts full of optimism, enthusiasm, and faith!'[26]

Yet, despite the enthusiasm in many quarters for the newly established republic, almost immediately it found itself confronted with the battles it would face up until the outbreak of the Spanish Civil War, and Granada did not escape the turmoil. On the one hand were conservative forces, highly suspicious of reforms that they saw as an attack on Spain's traditional culture. They worried the country could stumble into a Russian-style revolution should the left go unchecked. On the other hand, the downfall of the dictatorship had precipitated the re-emergence of the anarchists and groups on the far left, suspicious of the government's agenda for reform and viewing it as merely a new vehicle by which to impose top-down control over the working classes, rather than allowing those oppressed by the political elites for centuries to gain any real power. The republic also had to contend with international circumstances far beyond its control. To implement any of the reforms needed to improve the lot of the vast majority of Spain's population, either those living in miserable conditions on the land or those reliant on irregular work in the cities, the republic needed a healthy economy to work with. In this regard, the Great Depression of the early 1930s proved a major obstacle. In the Albaicín, the plight of working-class residents continued; promises of improved conditions went unmet. Anger that had been simmering both there and elsewhere in Spain would intermittently boil over throughout the next few years, and it would manifest most visibly and controversially in attacks upon churches.

Opposition to the political sway wielded by the Church had been growing for decades across Spain. Large swathes of the lower classes saw the institution as a fundamental supporter of the oppressive landowners and governments that had done almost nothing to alleviate their plight for centuries.[27] As anarchist and socialist ideas entered the country, the hatred directed at the Church from some quarters increased dramatically. The first Republican government proposed major reforms to ecclesiastical power, including a greater separation of state and religion through the abolition of the traditional financial support bestowed by the former on the latter. The removal of the Church's hold over the education system was also mooted, as was introducing other anti-Catholic measures such as the legalisation of divorce. But these fundamental constraints were vehemently resisted by conservative elements, and the Church grew increasingly associated with right-wing opposition to the changes.

The first outbreak of left-wing agitation against the Church in Granada would take place only a few weeks after the declaration of the Second Republic, in response to a confrontation that had taken place between conservative and leftist forces on the streets of Madrid and that had also led to riots in other parts of Spain. A crowd of protesters gathered outside the Jesuit Church of the Sagrado Corazón de Jesús in the Gran Vía and eventually broke into the building and stripped it of many of its sacred objects, which were then piled up into a bonfire in the middle of the street outside and burned.[28] The protests spread to other religious buildings; monks and nuns fled for shelter elsewhere in the city. Up in the Albaicín at the Convent of Santa Isabel la Real, the sisters were evacuated and the keys handed to members of the Centro Artístico in a bid to protect its treasures. Posters were plastered over the walls of the convent begging the protesters to respect its artistic and monumental heritage.[29] Meanwhile, the offices of the Catholic newspaper *La Gaceta del Sur* were targeted in an early indication of the attacks on media outlets to come over the next few years.

Even after those early anti-clerical protests had abated, Granada remained on edge, with the Albaicín at the forefront of continuing agitation. But it was an attempted coup d'état by the right wing in Seville in August 1932 that led to much more violent action across the city.[30] It began as demonstrators surrounded key buildings that were the focus of popular ire over national events. The Casino Cultural in the Puerta Real—a social club for the wealthy and many who supported the right—was set ablaze, and a protest further down the street was met with gunfire from the security forces, which led to further panic and unrest. The following day, riots spread to the Albaicín, where the most prominent building to be attacked was the Church of San Nicolás, site of today's famous viewing point over the Alhambra. The door of the church was broken down and the interior stripped of everything made of wood, which was then piled into the centre of the nave, doused with petrol, and set alight. The fire brigade was unable to prevent the almost complete destruction of the building, leaving nothing but a burnt-out shell.

The destruction of the Church of San Nicolás was widely condemned on all sides in Granada, though this did not prevent further attacks on religious symbols at times of great tension. Later, in December 1933, more of the Albaicín's churches fell victim to an outbreak of arson; the Church of San Luis was never restored following this episode of violence and its ruins remain as a reminder of those troubled times, a reaction to events taking place throughout Spain. Even during periods without full-scale disturbances, attacks on religious symbols continued; these years also witnessed the destruction of many of the stone crosses that had been dotted around the city for centuries.[31] Yet whilst the targeting of churches spoke of the enmity felt by many at the bottom of society towards the oppression of the Church and its support for the right, it also had the effect of alienating many among the middle classes who might otherwise have come around to the government's proposed reforms. Much that was of traditional value to Granada's Christian history was damaged or destroyed in the early 1930s, and this iconoclasm was abhorrent to many of the city's economically better off. These swung to the right in the elections of the middle period of the Second Republic, bringing a coalition of right-wing parties to the fore against their left-wing opposition. This, and the fact that many of those involved in the earlier church attacks in Granada had now been imprisoned, led to a dwindling of church burnings, but an undercurrent of resentment and animosity remained, especially amongst the poor of the Albaicín.[32]

That middle period of the Second Republic would not last for long, and whilst tensions between left and right had been high throughout this period, violence was to reach new heights after the general election of February 1936. Across Spain, the leftist coalition known collectively as the Popular Front picked up the most votes; however, in Granada the right triumphed. Evidence was strong that people in rural areas had been intimidated by landlords into not voting for the Popular Front. The coercion included voters being turned away from polling stations for not wearing a collar.[33] The consternation of the left both in the city and across the province was extreme, and Fernando de los Ríos led calls in the Cortes in Madrid for the election results in Granada to be declared void.[34]

On 8 March, supporters of the left began protests across the city to challenge the authorities over the outcome of the ballot. On the following day things turned violent. Supporters of Spain's fascist movement—the Falange—took shots at protesters in the Plaza del Campillo, their indiscriminate firing leaving women and children amongst the injured. With Granada already a tinderbox, when a general strike was called on 10 March, the spiralling situation could no longer be contained. Those most enraged gathered to torch buildings associated with the right, including the Falange headquarters behind the Plaza de Mariana Pineda, the nearby Teatro Isabel la Católica, the offices of the pro-Catholic newspaper *Ideal*, cafés and social clubs where the wealthy would meet, and—once again—the city's religious establishments. This time, the Churches of El Salvador and San Gregorio Bético, both in the Albaicín, were the victims. The fury of the rioters did not go unnoticed in Madrid, and on 31 March, the February election results in Granada were declared void by the Popular Front government.

Granada was now on tenterhooks. The civil unrest wreaking so much damage on the city was also pushing sympathies towards the right, and when new elections took place on 3 May, they were boycotted by most right-wing voters. The inevitable, overwhelming victory for the left spurred more hostility amongst the middle classes towards the government in Madrid. Meanwhile, a revolving door of officialdom meant that it had become a constant challenge to keep Granada's political and military situation under control. At the end of June 1936, a new civil governor—the official government representative in the city—was appointed. With little experience of the city and therefore few ties with its key functionaries, César Torres Martínez found himself in an environment divided between groups who felt nothing but abject hostility towards one another. At the Ayuntamiento, battles raged over who should take up the position of mayor. It was not until 10 July, a mere ten days before the military was to rise up in the city, that it was finally decided to appoint the socialist Manuel Fernández-Montesinos, brother-in-law of Lorca, to the position. To make matters more difficult for the administration, workers responsible for a number of public services such as transport and rubbish collection in Granada had decided to go on strike.

Despite the administrative wrangling, however, in common with cities across the country, the major threat for Granada lay with the military. Concerned that the local army commander sympathised with suspected conspirators on the right, the government in Madrid replaced him in early July 1936. The new man appointed, Brigadier General Miguel Campins y Aura, was a friend of the military troublemaker General Francisco Franco, but was nevertheless believed to be a strong supporter of the Republican government. The government had been correct in its assumptions about the loyalties of both Campins and his predecessor, but they had failed to take into account the depth of antipathy towards the Republican cause among the rank and file of the army garrison in Granada. The Falange, whose membership had expanded locally in the wake of the rerun of the February ballot, began to actively conspire with discontented officers. Prominent amongst these was a Major José Valdés Guzmán.

Valdés was a member of the Falange and, like many in the military, had served in the Rif War in Morocco and felt disgruntled with the Second Republic. Gerald Brenan, a British writer who was living in the Alpujarra prior to the Civil War, described the way all Spaniards would sit in cafés expressing their dissatisfaction with politics, but how a member of the army would take this dissatisfaction further:

> [H]owever much the opinions of the café politicians may differ, they are all invariably agreed upon one thing—that the Government is deliberately ruining and dishonouring the country. But the captain also remembers that he belongs to the Army, to that noble and patriotic corps of officers which once gave orders to the politicians, and that he has men with rifles and machine guns under his command. And he begins to think of all the nice jobs and of all the prestige that come in Spain from government.[35]

Valdés had been in Granada for five years prior to the arrival of Campins and, unlike his new commander, knew the city well, particularly its right-wing supporters. And it would be this inability on the part of Republican leaders to understand the depth of feeling within the city that would have terrible consequences when, on 17 July 1936, news began to filter through of an uprising of the Spanish army based in North Africa.

13

CIVIL WAR AND DICTATORSHIP

When the news filtered through of the uprising in Morocco of the Spanish Army of Africa, General Campins, as newly installed commander of the Granada garrison, remained convinced that his men would continue to be loyal to the Republican government. Saturday, 18 July 1936 began as usual: a calm summer's day in the city. Yet as people began to hear about the rebellion, and with the growing realisation that many military districts across mainland Spain were also starting to rise up in support of the rebels, anger and panic began to spread.[1] Most worrying for Granada, given its geographical proximity, was the news of the rapid fall of Seville to the rebels. The soon-to-be-notorious General Gonzalo Queipo de Llano had swiftly seized the city, unleashing his troops on a spree of mass rape and murder across the working-class districts. By the evening of 18 July, Granada began to receive Queipo's infamous radio announcements glorifying the carnage taking place and boasting of the imminent fall of all Spain to the rebels. Confusion reigned, as families in the city listened to Queipo's claims that military columns were advancing at that very moment on other Andalusian cities, including

Granada, and that anyone who stood in their way would be hunted down like vermin.[2]

For now, though, Granada's authorities appeared to be sticking with the government in Madrid, but the widespread fear was spurring many in the city into action. As elsewhere across Spain, left-wing groups came out onto the streets of Granada to implore the authorities to arm them in preparation for any trouble. But this was something the government in Madrid was not willing to countenance. In those first couple of days of the uprising, the national government seemed more concerned about the potential for a Bolshevik-style revolution from the left if they armed the working classes than they were about the coup already underway and being perpetrated by the right, which they believed would be put down in a matter of days. The working classes were thus officially denied arms, and the way in which individual civil governors across Spain decided for themselves to obey this order would prove an important factor in whether or not a city fell to the rebels.[3] In nearby Jaen, the governor armed the anarchists and socialists, and the city remained on the Republican side for much of the war. In Granada, however, Torres Martínez chose to obey his superiors and refused to open up the armoury to supporters of the left. With reassurances from Campins, he firmly believed that the garrison was loyal.

Unfortunately, he could not have been more wrong. The conspirators inside the Granada garrison, with Valdés Guzmán amongst the leaders, were continuing to meet and plot in places around the city, behind the back of their commander. This involved ensuring that Granada's troops did nothing to help other areas of Andalusia that were falling to the rebels, most notably on 19 July when orders came through from Madrid that soldiers be sent to Cordoba to help retake that city, which had fallen the day before. Despite Campins's orders from Madrid, his officers managed to prevaricate, claiming their weaponry was not ready, thereby preserving their numbers in Granada. The next day, civilians from the left showed their willingness to take matters into their own hands. With the workers offering to form a militia to head to Cordoba and fight against the rebels, the government finally agreed to provide them with arms. But, again, Granada's armoury delayed, long enough to prevent a single weapon from getting into the hands of the left. It was by this point too late to save the city from rebellion.

At five o'clock in the afternoon of 20 July, the army in Granada rose up, forcing Campins to sign a declaration of war. The general would later be arrested and sent to Seville, where he was shot. As soon as the declaration of war was signed, the city changed dramatically into a place of fear and confusion. Within moments of the declaration, the army and Guardia Civil came out onto the streets, moving swiftly to take control of the city. Over the next few hours, they would seize the main municipal buildings. Valdés Guzmán entered the civil governor's headquarters—now the University of Granada's Law Faculty in the Plaza de la Universidad—and placed Torres Martínez under arrest. The town hall in the Plaza del Carmen was stormed and a group of soldiers arrested the mayor, Lorca's brother-in-law Manuel Fernández-Montesinos. With the city's leaders under arrest, the next step was to prevent resistance amongst the general populace. The captured Radio Granada, based on the Gran Vía, was of vital importance in allowing the rebels to control the spread of information and ensure confusion in the city. Here, the declaration of the state of war would be read out at regular intervals, and calls issued for the people to collaborate in the uprising:

> His excellency the General of the Military Command Headquarters invites all those who wish to collaborate with the cause of maintaining order for the good of Spain ... that they present themselves at the Command Headquarters building ... and there to say if their collaboration is personal and also if they desire to put at the disposition of the authorities means of transport (cars, trucks, etc.).[4]

This 'invitation' was a key policy of the rebels: forcing people to openly take sides. They were not only requested to collaborate but told to turn up for work and open their shops and bars the following day as they would have under normal circumstances, with harsh sanctions threatened for those who disobeyed. The radio announcement continued:

> I hope for the good sense of everyone not to alter anything about the normal life of the city, which we have to defend at every moment, applying the maximum rigour in punishing those who crazily try to disturb the peace which everyone requires and hopes for, after the sad days and the violent tension which have been gone through.[5]

The fear was palpable. With the rebels in control of the airwaves and having closed down the left-wing newspaper *El Defensor de Granada*, local people were now bombarded with one-sided reports. Alongside the continuing radio reports from the bellicose General Queipo in Seville, claiming the imminent victory of the rebels across the whole of Spain, the two remaining newspapers in the city were the Catholic *Ideal* and the Falangist *Patria*, whose articles confidently backed up Queipo's claims. Henceforth both newspapers labelled anyone against the Nationalists as part of a united bloc of either '*rojos*' or '*marxistas*', playing on the fears among the middle class of a Russian-style revolution in order to justify their actions in the city.[6]

But not everyone was prepared to accept the new order so easily. Those willing to fight the rebels made their way en masse to the Albaicín, where socialists, communists, and anarchists alike built barricades out of anything to hand, such as large items of furniture from nearby houses, or rubble and detritus from the streets. The main concentration of the resistance was around the recently inaugurated Escuela de Estudios Árabes on the Cuesta del Chapiz, where the inadequate supplies of guns and ammunition were doled out. The well-armed military, in the meantime, subjected them to artillery bombardment from vantage points above the district, including from batteries set up along the ramparts of the Alhambra. Ibn al-Ahmar's structure, built as a formidable threatening presence against potential rebellion in his capital seven centuries earlier, was pressed into service again with devastating effect, this time against the working-class resistance in the Albaicín. This resistance was heavily outgunned thanks to the reticence on the part of the authorities to equip left-wing groups for the fight, leaving them unable to mount an effective defence against attacks that came from all sides, including occasionally from the air.

The resistance managed to hold out for just three days. As surrender became inevitable Radio Granada announced that the women and children of the district should leave. Those who did so were rounded up and sent to concentration camps. The men continued to fight for a short while longer, in a valiant last stand against far stronger forces. As this stand eventually crumbled, their weaponry exhausted, white sheets were hung from balconies as a sign of surrender and the army stormed the district. In the panic that ensued, some fighters managed to flee over the hills to areas of the province still held by the Republicans, but the majority were rounded up and sent to the already overflowing prisons, many later to be shot.

For those opposed to the uprising who had remained in the city, there was to be no mercy. Almost as soon as the military took control, just as in other parts of Spain that had fallen under the control of the rebels, they implemented a campaign of terror to dissuade any potential challenges. This terror had been planned long in advance by the rebel conspirators to facilitate a rapid breakdown of any agitation.[7] Those who had held out in the Albaicín and later surrendered would join the left-wing officials and leaders of socialist or Marxist groups in the rapidly overcrowding prisons. Even those not actively involved in the resistance efforts could also find themselves caught up in the mass detentions, which aimed to scoop up anyone suspected of sympathy towards the left or progressive ideals, and these included many lawyers, university lecturers, and other white-collar professionals. They would initially be incarcerated in the prison to the north of the city, the population of which swelled throughout the course of the war to triple its capacity of 500 inmates.[8] Only the gatehouse of this institution exists today, on the Avenida de Madrid, still bearing its pre-war coat of arms of the Second Republic.

Those deemed dangerous to the success of the rebellion faced death. Such detainees were driven by the truckload along the Gran Vía, up the Cuesta de Gomérez, through the Alhambra woods, and on to the cemetery. Helen Nicholson, an American visitor to the city whose sympathies lay firmly with the rebels because of her obsessive fear of the potential butchery of 'the reds' against the middle and upper classes, was not too far gone in her support for the Nationalists to ignore the horror of the early morning processions of trucks of prisoners being driven past her residence and the subsequent sounds of the gunfire coming from the cemetery.[9] There, in the early hours of the morning, the prisoners were forced out of the lorries and lined up in front of a now notorious wall. It is estimated that between four and five thousand people were shot here both during the conflict and through the subsequent years of dictatorship.[10] The bodies during those early days were left until staff arrived at 9 a.m., when they would be removed to a mass grave inside the cemetery walls.

Meanwhile, down in the city, this oppression that had been implemented from the first moments of the uprising continued and was very far from being entirely imposed from the top down. Indeed, part of the rebel strategy was to ensure as much of the general population as possible participated in the violence. People were frightened; their own instincts for survival and for that of their families took precedence as the horror unfolded around them. Denouncing neighbours as 'reds' demonstrated loyalty to the new authorities and created its own sense of solidarity: people fighting together against a common enemy. Yet, whilst many made such denunciations out of fear and a will to survive, there were almost certainly those who did so out of envy or desire for revenge. All of this led to a desperate sense of trepidation in the city. This was heightened by the creation of citizen militias, in theory to keep a check on behaviour and quell dissidence, but which often became themselves perpetrators of violence. The most notorious of these was the *Escuadra Negra*, whose acts of terror included dragging suspected Republicans from their homes in the middle of the night up to the cemetery to be shot alongside those ferried out from the prisons. They also entered hospitals and took patients implicated as leftist sympathisers outside to be shot in the street.

Amidst the many thousands of executions that took place in Granada in those early days of the war, the best known would be the assassination of Lorca. Against the advice of many of his friends, the internationally renowned poet had returned to visit his family only three days prior to the mutiny in North Africa.[11] He had already ruffled feathers locally through a recent interview he had given wherein he had dubbed Granada's middle class the 'worst bourgeoisie in Spain' and accused them of causing trouble in the city.[12] During the first few weeks of the uprising, his family, who were staying at their summer home, the Huerta de San Vicente on the outskirts of the city, were visited a number of times by the military rebels now running the city. These visits led Lorca to believe that his life was in danger, and seeking a place to hide, he took refuge at the house of a fellow poet, Luis Rosales, whose brothers were prominent members of the rebel-supporting Falange party. Here, at 1 Calle de Ángulo, next to the Plaza de la Trinidad, it was hoped that Granada's most famous son would now be under the protection of a family with influence in the new regime.

It was not to be. Lorca's hiding place remained secret for only a week. The streets in the area around the house were cordoned off for the arrest, and notwithstanding the protests of the Rosales family, the poet was driven away for questioning at the civil government headquarters—today's Law Faculty—only a short distance away around the corner from his hiding place. He was locked in a room on the first floor whilst the Rosales family continued to plead for his release. The man they had to persuade was Valdés Guzmán, now installed as civil governor and considered a confidant of Seville's ruthless General Queipo. Valdés had no sympathy for the poet or his international reputation, and sometime in the middle of the night of 18 August, Lorca was driven to the road between the villages of Víznar and Alfacar in the hills to the north of the city. Whilst Granada had quickly come under Nationalist control, the majority of the surrounding region was still held by the Republicans, and Víznar was being used as a base by the Nationalists to prevent resistance in these hills. Like Granada's cemetery wall, Víznar was to become a notorious place of mass execution, and it was here that Granada's most acclaimed poet of the modern era was shot, a short walk away from the Fuente de Aynadamar, the eleventh-century reservoir so essential to the creation story of the city he loved.

Lorca was not alone among his friendship circle to be murdered during the Nationalist takeover of the city. His brother-in-law, the mayor, had been shot in the early days of the uprising along with most of the local left-wing officials. His friend and fellow Rinconcillista, the editor of *El Defensor de Granada* Constantino Ruiz Carnero, was also shot against the cemetery wall, as was Juan José Santa Cruz, the engineer who had designed the tram to the Sierra Nevada. Some intellectuals considered to be of the left, such as Torres Balbás, had the fortune to be away from the city when the rebellion broke out. As he was unable to return, this architect's visionary restorations at the Alhambra, with the outbreak of the war, would come to an end. Other key figures of Granada's artistic and intellectual scene would eventually go into exile, including Manuel de Falla, who left in 1939 to end his days in Argentina, and Lorca's former teacher Fernando de los Ríos, who spent the period of the Civil War as Spain's ambassador to the United States and would later settle there on a permanent basis.

But Spain's civil war was never a simple matter. Across the country, friends found themselves on different political sides, often according to the class into which they had been born. There was little possibility of taking a centre-ground position, and sides were often chosen based on perceptions of what would happen if the other side won. In Granada, some of Lorca's friends from the Rinconcillo chose to align themselves with the Nationalists. One of these was Antonio Gallego Burín, the art historian and organiser of the *auto sacramental* of 1927. Like many from upper-middle-class families, Gallego Burín had a deep suspicion of the left and had been profoundly impacted by the riots and church destructions that had been taking place for the past few years. Those on the centre right feared the potential for a workers' uprising similar to that which had taken place in Russia, bringing with it extreme violence against the wealthier classes. Gallego Burín's political conservatism and sympathies for the right meant that with the Nationalist uprising, he took the side of the rebels, soon, like all Nationalist supporters, becoming a member of the Falange.[13]

Gallego Burín was to play a part in the rebels' second stage of subduing the places they controlled: the propaganda war. As the fighting continued elsewhere in Spain, in Granada the early terror began to simmer down, as the authorities trusted that in large part the local populace had started to conform to the new system. This did not mean a complete end to the terror; the torture chambers at Las Palmas, an interrogation centre at the top of the Cuesta de los Molinos, remained in existence long after the war ended, and shootings at the cemetery wall continued for many years after the conflict. However, whilst the acts of terror had certainly not completely halted, militias such as the *Escuadra Negra* were taken in hand so as to bring about an end to the general fear of unexpected, summary execution.[14] Instead, the authorities concentrated on indoctrinating the people of the city in the ideology of their cause.

Gallego Burín's expertise in art and history was to aid greatly in this propaganda war. In January 1938, he organised an exhibition at the Lonja, the sixteenth-century mercantile exchange adjoining the Capilla Real, to demonstrate the damage done to Granada's heritage by 'the reds'. A report in *Ideal* described the exhibits as: 'Faces of Virgins wounded by the slash of knives, bullets, and blows from stones; clear demonstrations of the red barbarity stamped on sacred sculptures, paintings and religious treasures.'[15] Examples of damaged art and demonstrations of the church burnings of the Republican era were also used in another propaganda initiative of the Civil War era, *las rutas de Guerra* (war routes). These formed a part of Franco's early tourism policy, whereby foreign visitors could visit sites—even at the height of the Civil War—and see the Nationalist narrative on the situation in terms of the destruction of art caused by 'the reds'. Granada, as an occupied city, was naturally included as a destination in southern Spain.[16]

Gallego Burín's support for the Nationalists paved the way for him to achieve the political power that had eluded him at the ballot box. In June 1938, he was chosen to be mayor, and just under a year later and shortly after the Civil War officially ended in April 1939, he accompanied Franco himself around the city as part of the Caudillo's first tour as head of state. For Franco, a stop in Granada during his visit to Andalusia was ideal propaganda since the Nationalists had likened their fight against the left to the Reconquista against the Moors. Visiting the Capilla Real, therefore, allowed him to pay homage at the tombs of Isabella and Ferdinand. A wing of the Ayuntamiento had been converted into appropriate accommodation for his overnight stay, and as with earlier welcomes for heads of state, the city had set up triumphal arches in his honour; crowds lined the streets, cheering and waving flags and banners. Later, Franco's tour of the city took in both the German and Italian consulates as a courteous show of friendship to his allies, and he descended to the Cruz de los Caídos—the Cross of the Fallen—which had been erected at the bottom of the Carretera de la Sierra, to pay his respects to those who had died for the Nationalist cause.

The end of the Civil War brought about a drive on the part of the victors to eradicate any remaining support for 'the reds'. This, naturally, was a nationwide effort, but in Granada it had started early, in the initial days of the uprising, not only with the violence but also through planned physical changes to the cityscape.[17] Nowhere was this seen more than in the Albaicín, considered by the authorities as a hotbed of Marxism. To combat this, a process of 'Christianisation' was begun. The archbishop of Granada explained the idea behind this in an article in *Ideal*:

> We have to free the Albayzin from its Marxism without God ... which supplanted all the spirit of idealism and piety and [brought about] a total forgetting of the most elevated aspirations of the soul. We have to detoxicate it of the poison, digested over so many years, as the fruit of a crazy, stupid and destructive communism. We have to elevate it culturally, morally and religiously, and we have to do it ourselves.[18]

One aspect of this process involved the restoration of churches that had been destroyed or damaged during the pre-war years. Not only was this a chance for the winners to glorify Christianity, but it was also a way to punish the people of the district for supporting the wrong side.[19] Funding for the rebuilding was officially collected from local residents, who were already struggling greatly as a result of the post-war economic problems but who equally could not afford politically to be seen as unsupportive of the measures. Meanwhile, prisoners of war were drafted in to undertake the building work.

Another of the symbolic acts of Christianising the Albaicín was the re-erection of the crosses that had been taken down or destroyed during the pre-war years. These, such as the Cruz de la Rauda that was restored as early as September 1936, were supposed to bring back Christian faith and emotion to the *barrio* in place of the 'barbarianism' of life under 'the reds'.[20] And, in an effort to return to a time when these crosses were venerated, the annual 3 May festival of the *Día de la Cruz*, a traditional spring celebration with its carnival and suggestive pagan spirit, was given greater prominence, and prizes began to be awarded for the most attractive displays.[21] Other measures were taken to beautify the Albaicín in a way that fit with a stereotypical southern Spanish image: whitewashed houses adorned with the local *fajalauza* pottery. In years to come, this beautification would be taken further, as Franco enthused about the idea of creating an 'authentic' Andalusia as part of Spain's tourism policy.

Despite the superficial changes to the Albaicín, however, the end of the war was certainly not the end of the suffering. The post-war years were marked by severe hunger across the country, with long lines of people queuing for the meagre rations officially available to them. The alleys were filled with beggars and street urchins dressed in rags. In the struggle for families to adequately feed themselves with an inefficient ration system, the black market centred around the Plaza de Bibarrambla prospered. The suffering naturally fell more heavily on those who had opposed the regime and particularly those who had fought for the

Republicans during the war. Whilst Nationalist fighters had been welcomed back with honour to their homes in Granada, those on the other side returned to face incarceration or even death. Prisons filled up, as they had in July 1936, with returning Republican fighters, and buildings such as the bullring were turned into temporary prisons to cope with the overspill. However, amongst these returnees would be found some prepared to make a last stand against Spain's dictatorship, the most famous—or perhaps infamous—of these in Granada being the Hermanos Quero.[22]

Antonio, Pepe, Pedro, and Paco Quero were four brothers from the Albaicín who had escaped the city to fight for the Republicans during the Civil War. Like many on the losing side, upon their return to Granada they found themselves incarcerated in desperately poor conditions in the converted stables and barns known as the *Campana*, one of the centres set up to take in inmates for whom no room could be found in the Provincial Prison across the road. They were held for over a year, during which time they learned of bands of rebels continuing the fight against the regime around the province. Their escape in June 1940 was the first of their impressive careers, though perhaps the least spectacular given that converted barns do not make for the most secure prisons. Once outside, they fled to join up with the small bands of armed resistance remaining in the villages outside the city, before deciding to set themselves up in Granada itself, based initially in the caves of the Barranco del Abogado. The brothers were to become notorious amongst the city's authorities and were feared for their daring kidnappings of rich supporters of the regime. One of their first, in 1941, was that of Eduardo Entrala Ríos, a rich and retired colonel, near the Paseo del Salón. Capturing him in broad daylight and bundling him into a car, they drove him at full speed up the Carretera de la Sierra, where they kept their prisoner hostage for three days in a cave in a village nearby. They then demanded half a million pesetas from the colonel's son in exchange for his father's life. When this was duly paid, the hostage was released. Over the next few years, their audacious abductions of the wealthy and connected continued, the ransom money used to procure more firepower for the resistance effort. Legends abounded about these fearless brothers, who would appear on the streets of the city every so often, faces undisguised, demonstrating their generosity by leaving large tips in Granada's bars. They enjoyed popularity amongst some local people, who, despite generally living under a surface level of conformity with the governing regime, relished the stories of these heroic, Robin Hood–like figures outwitting the authorities.

The brothers' reputation was enhanced greatly by the sensational manner in which they were able to escape the security forces sent to capture them. Their escapes from shootouts around Granada became infamous, including occasions when their cave hideouts of the Sacromonte or the Llano de la Perdiz were completely surrounded, leaving them to fight their way out in a hail of bullets and escape across the hills. The authorities rued the underground passageways and both the caves of the Sabika hill and those of the Albaicín and Sacromonte for providing these fighters with their means of escape and places to hide. Nevertheless, these dramatic exchanges of gunfire did not only occur in the city's outlying districts. Some of the most notorious happened right in the centre of the city, such as the one that took place on the Paseo del Salón during the 3 May *Día de la Cruz* festivities in 1944, when the police had set up an ambush for the brothers amidst the crowds from which, as usual, they managed to escape in daring fashion.[23]

Swearing to commit suicide rather than be taken alive, each of the brothers would die remaining true to their cause, in shootouts and sieges across the city. The most eventful of these took place in July 1945 in the upper Albaicín, near to the brothers' family home.[24] Police had surrounded their hideout following a tip-off and began firing on the house. In the smoke and confusion, the two brothers inside—Paco and Pedro—made it onto the roof, only for Paco to be hit in the eye by a bullet. Unconscious for a number of minutes, Paco was defended by his brother as more and more police arrived. When Paco regained consciousness, blood pouring from his eye, Pedro persuaded him they had to leave the building, but as they jumped down off the roof, Pedro landed badly, breaking his leg. One brother could not walk; the other could barely see. Refusing to give up, Paco picked up his brother and carried him over his shoulder as Pedro pointed his pistol behind him to cover their escape.

Their intimate knowledge of the winding alleys of the Albaicín enabled them once again to evade their pursuers. With the assistance of a friend, Pedro made it to a shelter in a small cave inside the Sacromonte hill, whilst Paco, his eye still bleeding profusely, went to find more help. Paco lost his left eye in the assault, but worse was to come for Pedro. 'Another tip-off brought the police, who surrounded his cave hideout, and with Pedro unable to do more than crawl, this time there was to be no spectacular escape. Nevertheless, lying on the floor of his shelter, he continued to take pot shots at the police, preventing them from entering and arresting him. The siege went on and the police, determined to take Pedro alive, brought his sister-in-law to the scene to persuade him to hand himself in. She approached the cave and offered Pedro a cigarette. His would-be captors waited as their prey took his time smoking in the cave. Suddenly a shot rang out. Pedro had decided to put the gun to his own head rather than fall into the hands of the authorities whom he and his brothers had outwitted for so long.

The brothers had believed in the imminent collapse of Franco's dictatorship and that their guerrilla campaign would be as celebrated in a new democratic era as the French Resistance was, now that authoritarian regimes had fallen across the rest of Europe. Their popularity reached its height as the fascists were defeated in Germany and Italy in 1945. However, the Western powers seemed uninterested in bringing down Franco's regime, being more concerned about the potential communist threat from the East. The authorities in Granada grew confident, and efforts against the remaining Hermanos Quero increased. With the death of the last of the brothers, Antonio, in a siege on the Camino de Ronda, their legend fell into obscurity as the regime outlived its allies in Germany and Italy to remain in power for another three decades.

Resistance to the dictatorship in Granada diminished with the demise of the Hermanos Quero and people settled into the status quo. This allowed the city's leaders to return to the question that had plagued the Ayuntamiento for the previous two centuries: that of how to turn Granada into a place fit for the modern era. During the Second Republic, urban planners had already recognised that they needed a vision for the city as a whole rather than the ad hoc approach that had been followed in the past with what were widely considered to be poor results.[25] The thoughtless urban reform policies of Granada's leaders had long been a particular bugbear of Gallego Burín, now mayor of the city. This former Rinconcillista had been actively working both to preserve Granada's historic buildings and to improve its living conditions for decades prior to achieving his new role. For example, he had been a key figure in the transformation of the Casa de los Tiros into a museum and cultural centre, as well as a major figure working with musicians such as Falla in promoting Granada as a centre of music and artistic festivals. Now with political power, he was in a position to truly turn his passion for his city into action, something that required preserving Granada's history while also enabling it to function as a modern city, adapting to innovations such as the motor car.

Gallego Burín's name continues to be revered in the history of modern Granada, and he is often referred to as its greatest mayor.[26] His vision was one he believed would radically improve the living conditions of local residents. And, indeed, it is for this that he is most fondly remembered in the city. His projects included improving the state of the streets, many of which at the time remained unpaved, and beautifying Granada's squares, with an emphasis on care for ornamental details. He was determined to improve the condition of Granada's water sources, an aspect of the city that had long been a cause of concern. He also continued to be a passionate driver for Granada to become a centre for the arts. Some of the projects he brought into the city, such as the International Festival of Music and Dance, which continues to be held in the summer months, must have been inspired by his former debates and sharing of ideas with Manuel de Falla and Lorca as a Rinconcillista.

Yet, despite his claims to be a preserver of Granada's historic identity, Gallego Burín's vision was not without its critics.[27] Some quite momentous changes to large areas of the city were undertaken on his watch. One of the most famous was the destruction of the area that lay behind the Puerta Real, known as La Manigua.[28] This area had long been a cause of concern for the municipal authorities owing to its insalubrious and over-crowded streets located right in the centre of the city. Worse, for some, was that this was the city's red-light district, its narrow, winding streets home to taverns and brothels and frequented by those on the edge of society while avoided by the 'respectable classes'. It was a major embarrassment for the city, particularly in terms of the image it presented to tourists passing through. Its destruction was to form a major part of Gallego Burín's drive to clean up the city. In June 1940, *Ideal* printed a photo showing the mayor symbolically striking the first blows in the demolition of La Manigua with a pickaxe. Whilst Gallego

Burín is generally thought of as having been a man of vision for Granada, bringing many positive transformations, it can at first be difficult to understand the attraction of the new street that replaced much of La Manigua, as well as why Gallego Burín chose to name it after his hero, Ángel Ganivet—so vociferous a critic back in the nineteenth century of the destruction of small streets in favour of wide boulevards that seem so out of place in a city such as Granada.

Gallego Burín's vision for the future of Granada's urban layout was not to be as successful as he had hoped for a number of reasons. Firstly, he was unable to anticipate the population growth that began in the 1950s, or the ever-growing desire that people had for moving out of the historic centre and into areas more accommodating to the age of the motor car. Another reason is that urban transformation takes time, and thirteen years in power could only mean a start to the necessary reforms. Gallego Burín stood down as mayor in the early 1950s, moving to a prestigious role in the arts in Madrid, and it would be under his successors at the Ayuntamiento that the modern problems of urban transformation truly began, when far less consideration was given to Granada's heritage than had been under Gallego Burín. Whereas historic locations such as the cathedral and the Alhambra were tended with care, other areas of the city were considered less worthy, and just as with the transformations made to the city in the nineteenth century, many of the changes that took place mainly benefitted property speculators rather than local residents.[29]

This change to Gallego Burín's vision can be seen quite clearly on Calle Ángel Ganivet, which may at least have provided a dramatic approach to the Teatro Cervantes. Unfortunately, this nineteenth-century institution, opened during the time of the French occupation of the city, was pulled down in the 1960s and replaced with a residential building that is out of keeping with the original vision for the street. Another example of a major change that happened after Gallego Burín stood down was the urban sprawl that reached out to the Camino de Ronda. The original intention when this thoroughfare was built in the late 1930s was for it to act as a bypass that would enable traffic to circulate without destroying the historic structure of Granada. After Gallego Burín, however, this road was treated as just another space for meeting the increasing need for housing. Tall buildings were erected along the street, and for the first time in its thousand-year history, the city of Granada was separated from its Vega. Whereas once Lorca's summer home, the Huerta de San Vicente, had been in a semi-rural area, it was now in danger of being enveloped by the encroaching suburbs. Changes continued with the widening of Calle Recogidas as an arterial route into the centre; the convent where Mariana Pineda had spent her final weeks was knocked down in the process.

As with the criticisms that were made in the nineteenth century, it can be easy to condemn modernisation in favour of a romantic preservation of the past, but it must be recognised that Granada faced many serious problems in those post-war decades. However, the solutions to these often left a lot to be desired. The acute shortage of accommodation was a major issue in the growing city, particularly for the poor. As early as 1936, a plan for 'cheap housing' was conceived, but with empty municipal coffers, implementing this proved problematic.[30] Priority for the housing was given to the war-wounded and to large families. They were to be places for the 'ideal' Catholic family, which would be numerous, with the mother tending the home and the man out at work. New housing developments, therefore, were meant to promote this vision of the perfect Catholic family, and ultimately this policy led to the development of many of Granada's outlying districts and in the process massive urban sprawl. The most visible manifestation was the creation—and, for the next few decades, the uncontrolled expansion—of the Zaidín district, which encroached far into Granada's Vega.

Another example of drastic change in the 1950s, this time in the centre of the city, was the remodelling of Triunfo. New gardens were laid out on the site of the former Plaza de Toros de la Maestranza bullring, and the seventeenth-century statue of Mary of the Immaculate Conception was moved to its present location. However, the priority that the Ayuntamiento had in mind was not the gardens, but rather vehicle access to the city. What is today the Avenida de la Constitución was for most of the twentieth century an *alameda*—a tree-lined street where people could promenade of an evening—considered to be one of the most beautiful in Andalusia.[31] In the 1970s and 1980s this was turned into a busy boulevard, and the area around it—San Lázaro, a traditional area dating back to the time of the Reconquista—was transformed into a modern area popular with wealthier citizens who valued the luxury of garaging for their cars and easy access to the motorway. The development of this area also saw the expansion of Granada University with its Fuentenueva campus.

Over in the Sacromonte, on the other hand, it was the weather that prompted the authorities to bring about sweeping changes to what was one of the few remaining untouched areas of the historic city. For several days in February 1963, the wider region was inundated with torrential rain, and whilst the whole of Granada was affected by the subsequent flooding, the Sacromonte was hardest hit. Many of the caves became uninhabitable and thousands of Granada's *gitano* community had to be rehoused. For this purpose, makeshift dwellings were erected around the edges of the city, many built out of concrete with corrugated aluminium roofs. These acted like an oven in the summer and a refrigerator in the winter[32]—a far cry from the excellent conditions provided by cave living in Granada, which by contrast provides cool in the scorching summer months and warmth during the winter. Permanent housing for people living in these slum areas of the city was slow in coming; the makeshift shanties were not completely cleared until the early 1980s. Over time, however, those who had once been residents of the caves of the Sacromonte instead found themselves inhabitants of newly built suburbs such as Almanjáyar. And in moving the gypsies away from the Sacromonte and other cave communities around the city, little was done to enable the preservation of the extended family in the new areas, thereby breaking up important aspects of *gitano* culture.[33]

The Sacromonte, meanwhile, was left largely bereft of its traditional atmosphere. In the 1950s, around 4,000 caves in the area had been home to some 15,000 people,[34] but after the floods of 1963, the vast majority were removed to other parts of the city. Nonetheless, perversely, having transferred most of the inhabitants out, the city authorities began to exploit the district, building a series of museums and cultural centres dedicated to the *gitano* way of life, providing visitors with an official, acceptable version of gypsy history and traditions. In this way, as with the Albaicín before it, the Sacromonte began to be turned into an idealised and picturesque image of an idyllic past to present to visitors. However, it would be after the death of Franco in 1975 that the drive to capitalise on the tourism potential of this area, as well as of the rest of Granada's beauty, traditions, and history, would truly reach its zenith.

14

GRANADA TODAY

That Granada is a special place that draws people to it is nothing new. From Arab scholars to Christian pilgrims and from Romantic poets and artists to whistle-stop coach parties, there have long been tourists of one sort or another coming to Granada. That it is a city of change is also as true today as it was when mosques made way for churches, when a river disappeared from view, or indeed when Zawi ibn Ziri persuaded the people of Elvira to first move there in the eleventh century. People, including whole communities, have come and gone over the centuries, and Granada's leaders have variously either resisted or adapted to the challenges of each new era. Nowadays, however, tourism is a vast industry, and as do other small cities steeped in history around the world, Granada faces all the opportunities and threats it presents.

Tourism also has long been a major part of Granada's economy, and it was the visitors of the nineteenth century who spurred local leaders to take greater strides to protect the city's historic monuments, the most important being, of course, the Alhambra. Spain is consistently among the most visited countries in Europe, and the mediaeval complex one of its most popular attractions. The age of cheap flights and places to stay has brought significant revenues[1] and created many jobs in Granada, as well as providing added impetus to cultural events that take place throughout the year, such as the International Festival of Music and Dance, initiated under the watch of that passionate art historian and mayor of the city, Antonio Gallego Burín. Tourism encourages and funds local investment in infrastructure, restoration, and beautification that benefit resident and visitor alike.

However, it is not all good news. Jobs in tourism can be precarious and are not infrequently low-paid;[2] crowds of tourists can and do impact on the quality and cost of living for local residents, especially in traditional areas with narrow streets and picturesque architecture; diversity of businesses and employment is reduced as greengrocers' become restaurants and barbers' are turned into souvenir shops. Places such as Venice, Barcelona, and Dubrovnik have all felt the effects of their historic centres becoming impossibly crowded photo opportunities and daily life morphing into a surreal pastiche of the local culture. The location of the Alhambra on top of the Sabika hill, largely away from the centre of the city, has meant that Granada's city centre has not, perhaps, suffered to the same extent, but as the demands of tourism have changed, the impact has started to be felt more in what were once primarily residential districts.

Whereas once backpackers stayed a few days in hostels and package tours bussed holidaymakers around and provided custom for larger hotels, modern tourism is of a much more unruly character. This raises new questions for both Granada's local residents and those making strategic decisions about the city. Balancing being a place that is wonderful to visit and at the same time to live in is not easy, and relying on tourism for the local economy comes with considerable risk. Since 2020, the Covid-19 pandemic has demonstrated clearly how many people depend on the presence of tourists for their livelihoods, with hospitality and retail affected to a much greater extent than if their income had come primarily from local sources. At the same time, the absence of tourism has also provided locals with the opportunity to witness something not seen for decades: a city largely devoid of visitors, with the joy that could be found in quieter and less frenetic visits to the city's most popular monument—the Alhambra. And here the issue of tourism is another one for decision makers to focus on: how to protect the fragile monument? After all, a few hundred of Napoleon's soldiers living in the compound had a devastating impact on Granada's treasured but delicate landmark 200 years ago; the footfall at the Alhambra and Generalife in recent times has been approaching three million people each year.[3] As a UNESCO World Heritage Site, the Alhambra in the modern era has far more legal protection than in the past, and numbers of visitors to the palaces are strictly limited; however, questions about the preservation of the Nasrids' most precious legacy continue.

Meanwhile, elsewhere in the city, there are other major questions that face modern-day Granada, often surrounding the legacy of its long and fascinating history. The defensive nature of its location, perfect for mediaeval times, does not, for example, transfer well to the era of the car, and traffic has long been a major headache for the Ayuntamiento. Narrow, winding streets leading to areas such as the Albaicín and the Realejo were laid out centuries before vehicular access or parking were even thought of. Another, more fundamental, feature of Granada is the mountainous terrain that surrounds it. Although this may not be immediately obvious, Granada suffers the second-worst congestion problems in Spain after Barcelona.[4] A major source of frustration for those commuting in from surrounding towns and villages is rush-hour traffic jams due in large part to the fact that the city's 'ring' road cannot fully encircle it. This is because the hills behind Granada rise up towards the Sierra Nevada, and the Sabika hill is now a protected site. The mountainous topography has the effect of trapping polluted air, and as a result, Granada consistently ranks poorly among Spanish cities in terms of air quality.[5]

If Zawi's choice of geographical location back in the eleventh century throws up many issues for Granada today, so too, to a certain extent, do many other questions related to the city's history prior to 1492. Gone are the days when anyone in the city wants to overlook its Muslim heritage in favour of an ancient Christian past, as had been the case during the time of Juan de Flores; nevertheless, many issues remain unaddressed, including the fate of the city's inhabitants of so many centuries: the Moors. Various legal remedies have been enacted over the years to provide redress to the descendants of the Sephardi Jews expelled from Spain in 1492, which include the right of return and to take Spanish citizenship; those who can trace their ancestry back to the Moriscos expelled just over a century later have so far not been granted this.[6] There is also debate over how to remember Granada's Moorish inhabitants. Some statues have been erected in places around the city, including one of Boabdil outside the Alcázar Genil. However, each year on 2 January, the anniversary of the fall of Granada to the Catholic Monarchs, there is a controversial celebration known as the *Día de la Toma*, which sees local people dress up as Moors and Christians of the time to re-enact the capitulation. These festivities have in recent years increasingly become accompanied by vocal protests arguing that the event glorifies a great tragedy and can be considered offensive to both modern-day Muslims and those who wish to honour the great history of the Moors of al-Andalus.

Yet changes have occurred that seek to address Granada's Muslim past. In 2003, Granada's first officially recognised mosque since the fifteenth century was inaugurated, although this was also not without controversy in terms of the decisions about its location and appearance.[7] Situated adjacent to the Mirador de San Nicolás, this beautiful new mosque and its tranquil gardens sit facing the Alhambra across the valley. Meanwhile, Moroccan immigration to the city and the opening of shops selling clothes and ornaments from across the strait mean that there has almost certainly been an unconscious form of return for descendants of some of the tens of thousands of Moriscos expelled in the 1560s. But nothing has been done to address the descendants of those expulsions on an official level.

But it is not just the city's Moorish past where issues remain unaddressed. Some of Granada's post-Reconquista journey is also, at times, in danger of being forgotten. On the one hand, there is the University of Granada, founded by Charles V in the sixteenth century, which continues to be a major part of the modern city and frequently polls top of the list of most popular destinations for Erasmus students—unsurprising, perhaps, given that Granada is famous for its complimentary tapas with every drink. The university has spread far out from its original nucleus around the cathedral and, later, the Plaza de la Universidad, with campuses at La Cartuja and the more central Fuentenueva. However, other institutions also founded in the sixteenth century—Granada's many convent buildings—are in danger of closure. In the nineteenth century, the *desamortización* led to the destruction of many of Granada's most important Christian buildings, and the issue has resurfaced over the past few decades as many of the city's remaining convents have started to empty, with the decline in women wishing to enter the religious life. Solutions for what to do with such huge buildings are not easy to find, but losing them would be a blow to the city, since they preserve so much Christian art and form a major part of the legacy of an important era, when Granada attracted a wide range of remarkable characters, like San Juan de Dios or San Juan de la Cruz.

And Granada's more recent history also raises fresh problems. In common with the rest of Spain, debate continues over how to address what happened in the city during the Civil War. Recent decades have seen memorials erected to those who died in those terrible times, including one to the victims of the conflict that was erected over the mass graves at the municipal cemetery. Meanwhile, there have been attempts to locate the remains of Lorca, Granada's most internationally famous casualty of the war. He lies buried somewhere close to the Fuente de Aynadamar, where a park has been created in his memory. Another reminder of the trauma of those times has come, as it has elsewhere in Spain, in terms of renaming streets and taking down monuments erected during the Nationalist era. One symbol of the great divisions between right and left during the 1930s remains particularly prominent in Granada: an inscription on the façade of the Church of El Sagrario honouring the Falange Española founder José Antonio Primo de Rivera. Calls have been made for this to be removed, which provoked debate at the Ayuntamiento between those in favour of such a move and those who argue that this only digs up the painful divisions of the past.[8] In a gesture recalling these divisions, red paint is from time to time thrown over the inscription by those who oppose its continued presence.

Finally, the authorities also continue to be challenged by the consequences of Granada's twentieth-century expansion. The areas where so many thousands of people were rehoused after the floods of the 1960s continue to experience difficulties, particularly in terms of the poor and inadequate nature of the accommodation provided for families at that time. And, just as in the nineteenth century, when the then working-class Albaicín district was overlooked in favour of the commercial heart of the city, accusations continue to be made against Granada's politicians that today's poorer areas on the outskirts are similarly neglected in comparison to wealthier districts. Meanwhile, over in the Sacromonte, an area fundamentally changed when large parts of its population were moved out in the 1960s, there is some evidence of how threads from the past are hard to eliminate. Cave living outside the conventional continues both here and in other areas in the surrounding hills, with people seeking an alternative lifestyle off the grid moving into existing caves or excavating their own. The Ayuntamiento is keen to evict them, ostensibly on the grounds that the structures are illegal and unsafe, and also that the residents pay no taxes—though neither do they enjoy any local amenities. For now, at least, these alternative communities remain, and those who live there demonstrate a different way of life and serve as a reminder that the Sacromonte has always been home to people who did not quite fit in with the way the society of the rest of Granada around them was organised.

Nowhere can truly escape the legacy of the past, and much of Granada's history continues to affect the city today. This is also true for the residents of the city themselves. Despite genetic mapping showing low levels of North African DNA from the Arab conquests of the eighth century in the blood of today's residents,[9] it is hard to believe that the blood of the Moors was so eradicated from the city with the expulsion as this study suggests. Every so often, signs emerge that seem to link the residents of today with those of centuries gone by. Granadinos, for example, frequently say that their most distinctive characteristic is that of *malafollá*—a state of surliness or bad mood that it is argued characterises people born in the city.[10] Much has been said about the origins of *malafollá*; some suggest it dates from the time of New Christians moving into the city in the sixteenth century. Perhaps, though, it goes right back to those first inhabitants of the eleventh-century city. So antisocial were the Elvirans—the fourth Zirid ruler, Abdullah, tells us—that they built individual baths and mosques next to their houses in order to avoid contact with their neighbours. A touch of grumpiness, then, might seem to be a tiny vestige of the spirit of the initial settlers of the city that lives on today.

Another possible link back to the mentality of Granada in that glorious eleventh century can perhaps also be seen in its relationship with nearby Seville, which has always been one characterised by the contrast between two cities of such difference. In those days, the bigger and more domineering Seville was an ever-present threat for the Zirid kings, who fought for their new city's independence against the larger taifa state. Under the Almohads, Seville saw the construction of its famous Giralda—now, along with the Alhambra, one of the unmissable sights of Andalusia. In modern times, the differing atmospheres of the two cities have often been highlighted. Lorca made frequent allusions to this in poems, such as *Baladilla de los tres ríos* (Little Ballad of the Three Rivers), in which he uses geographical features to comment on the mentality of each city's residents, contrasting the flamboyant Sevillanos with the much more insular Granadinos. But even if the traditionally more conservative Granada is less showy than its bigger neighbour, this does nothing to dim the great pride Granadinos have for their hometown, which leads them to fully understand its draw to the millions of visitors who pass through each year.

In the sixteenth century, at the start of Seville's golden age as the port of embarkation for the New World, a famous painting of the city was emblazoned with the words, 'He who has not seen Seville, has not seen a wonder.' Today's Granadinos, however, would happily counter with their own local motto: 'He who has not seen Granada, has not seen a thing.'

GLOSSARY OF ARABIC AND SPANISH TERMS

Acequia	Type of canal channelling water into the city
Alcazaba	Citadel in cities of al-Andalus, from the Arabic *al-qasaba*
Alcázar	Moorish palace, from the Arabic *al-qasr*
Aljibe	Cistern
Ayuntamiento	Town council
Capilla Real	Royal Chapel
Carmen	Traditional Granada house based on houses of the Islamic era
Cofradía	Lay religious brotherhood; these organise the annual Semana Santa processions
Conversos	Christians of Jewish origin who had converted, often out of fear, to Christianity
Elche	Christian convert to Islam
Fajalauza	Style of local pottery
Fuente	Fountain or spring
Gitano	Gypsy
Junta	Name given to local administrations set up to build defences against French troops during the Napoleonic wars

GLOSSARY OF ARABIC AND SPANISH TERMS

Mashrabiya	Wooden latticework cover for a window, common in many countries in the Islamic world as a means of maintaining privacy
Mirador	Viewing place
Morabito	Type of hermitage where a holy man would live in seclusion
Morisco	Muslim converted to Christianity after the Reconquista
Mozarab	Christian living under Muslim rule
Mudéjar	Muslim who remained in al-Andalus after the Reconquista but who did not convert to Christianity; also a school of architecture heavily influenced by Moorish styles
Muwallad	Christian convert to Islam
Parias	Tribute paid to a more powerful Monarch for 'protection'
Puente	Bridge
Puerta	Gate
Real Chancillería	Royal Appellate Court; moved to Granada in the sixteenth century, it had the whole of the south of Castile under its jurisdiction
Rinconcillo	Group of artists and intellectuals who met regularly in the corner of a bar in Granada in the early twentieth century
Rinconcillista	Member of the Rinconcillo
Taifa	Arabic for faction; the term given to the small, self-governing states that made up al-Andalus during the eleventh century and at other times when parts of al-Andalus were ruled by local strongmen in place of an overarching dynasty
Torre	Tower

LIST OF ILLUSTRATIONS

1. The Fuente de Aynadamar (Fuente Grande) at Alfacar—this is the reservoir that fed Granada, enabling it to develop into one of the major cities of al-Andalus. (Source: Javier Martin, 2007, Wikimedia Commons, CC BY 3.0)
2. An example of an *aljibe*, one of a network of cisterns to store water when it reached Granada from the Fuente de Aynadamar. (Authors' photograph, 2021)
3. The remains of the Bab al-Difaf, a Zirid-era sluice gate enabling the flow of the river Darro to be controlled. (Authors' photograph, 2021)
4. The bell tower of San José Church, a converted Zirid-era minaret. (Authors' photograph, 2021)
5. The eleventh-century Zirid/Almoravid walls of the old Alcazaba. (Authors' photograph, 2021)
6. The fourteenth-century Nasrid walls, built to protect the enlarged city that housed refugees fleeing areas of al-Andalus conquered by the Christians. (Source: rheins, 2013, Wikimedia Commons, CC BY 3.0)
7. The Alhambra—since its foundations in the thirteenth century, the complex has continuously evolved. This view shows how Charles V's palace deliberately dominates over the more delicate Nasrid Palaces. (Source: Dimitry B, Unsplash, 2019)

LIST OF ILLUSTRATIONS

NOTES

1. INTRODUCTION AND EARLY HISTORY

1. For detailed information about Flores and his excavations, see Sotomayor Muro and Orfila Pons (2006), and Orfila Pons et al. (2012).
2. For estimates of the number of expulsions, see Elliott (2002), pp. 305–7, and Adams (2008).
3. This aspect to the continual evolution of the Alhambra is beautifully captured in Irwin (2005).
4. For a study into the many different theories about pre-Islamic Granada, see García Granados (1996).
5. For more in-depth studies of Granada prior to the Romans, see Ouriachen (2011).
6. For articles about Roman Granada, see many written by Orfila Pons, including Orfila Pons and Sánchez López (2011) and Orfila Pons (2013).
7. Orfila Pons et al. (2012).
8. Orihuela (2013).
9. Gozalbes Cravioto (1992).
10. Buluggīn (1986), p. 56.
11. Ibn Idhari (2013), Vol. 2, p. 58.
12. Kennedy (2014), p. 26.
13. Much of the information about the archaeological evidence from Elvira comes from the authors' visit to the site.

2. THE ZIRID DYNASTY

1. Buluggīn (1986), p. 46. Republished with permission of Brill Publishers, from *The Tibyān: Memoirs of 'Abd Allāh B. Buluggīn, Last Zīrid Amīr of Granada* by Amin T. Tibi (1986); permission conveyed through Copyright Clearance Center, Inc.

2. Buluggīn (1986), p. 48.

3. For perspectives on the fall of Cordoba that differ from Buluggīn's naturally pro-Zirid account, see Wasserstein (1985) and Kennedy (2014).

4. For a comprehensive account of Zirid Granada, see Sarr (2011).

5. Sarr (2011).

6. For a more detailed description of the life of Samuel ibn Naghrila, see Schirmann (1951).

7. Quoted in Schirmann (1951), p. 126.

8. Quoted in Schirmann (1951), p. 126.

9. From *The Monarch's Favors in A Jewish Prince in Moslem Spain* by Samuel Ibn Negrela, translated by Leon Weinberger. Copyright © 1973 by the University of Alabama Press. Reprinted by permission.

10. Schirmann (1951), p. 125.

11. Buluggīn (1986), p. 210 (translator's notes).

12. Kennedy (2014), p. 145.

13. For in-depth studies of the layout of early Granada, see Malpica Cuello (1994) and Sarr (2011).

14. For details of the *muwashshah*, including its incorporation into Hebrew literature, see Rosen (2000).

15. Marcos-Marín (1998).

16. From *Take this Book in A Jewish Prince in Moslem Spain* by Samuel Ibn Negrela, translated by Leon Weinberger. Copyright © 1973 by the University of Alabama Press. Reprinted by permission.

17. Buluggīn (1986), p. 88.

18. Buluggīn (1986), p. 91.

19. Buluggīn (1986), p. 92.

20. Buluggīn (1986), p. 124.

21. Buluggīn (1986), p. 129.

22. Buluggīn (1986), p. 134.

23. Buluggīn (1986), p. 149.

24. Buluggīn (1986), p. 151.
25. Buluggīn (1986), p. 155.
26. Buluggīn (1986), pp. 145–6.

3. THE ALMORAVIDS AND THE ALMOHADS

1. For a highly readable account of the Almoravids starting with their early tribal origins, see Messier (2010). Other sources used on the Almoravids: Wasserstein (1985), Messier (2001), and Kennedy (2014).
2. Messier (2010).
3. Buluggīn (1986), p. 164.
4. Quoted in Brody (1934), p. 313.
5. From *The Dream of the Poem: Hebrew Poetry from Muslim and Christian Spain, 950–1492*, translated, edited, and introduced by Peter Cole. Copyright © 2007 by Princeton University Press. Reprinted by permission.
6. Visit to the site of Medinat Elvira (2018).
7. Sarr (2011).
8. For the way in which the Almoravids controlled al-Andalus, see Kennedy (2014), pp. 174–9.
9. Messier (2011), p. 78.
10. This story is told in an anonymous Arabic text from the Nasrid era: *al-Hulal al-mawshiyya fi dhikr al-Marrakushiya* (1979), p. 91, authors' translation.
11. *al-Hulal* (1979), p. 91, authors' translation.
12. Kennedy (2014), p. 186.
13. For more on the Almohads in Granada, see Kennedy (2014) and Malpica Cuello (2002).
14. Schippers (1993), pp. 148–50.
15. For a full translastion of this poem, see Hafsa, 'Exchange' in Arberry (1953), pp. 94–5.
16. Ibn Sahib al-Sala (1987).
17. Ibn Sahib al-Sala (1987), p. 125, authors' translation.
18. Ibn Sahib al-Sala (1987), p. 133, authors' translation.
19. Ibn Sahib al-Sala (1987), p. 134, authors' translation.

20. For a study of the changes to the city around this time, see Malpica Cuello (2002) and Orihuela (2013).
21. For a description of Granada's main mosque, see Fernández-Puertas (2004).
22. Malpica Cuello (1994), p. 201.
23. Jiménez-Torrecillas et al. (2014).
24. Galán (1987).
25. For an Arab history of the rise of Ibn al-Ahmar and his battles against Ibn Hud written close to the time, see Ibn Idhari (2013), Vol. 3. For a modern in-depth study of Ibn al-Ahmar, see Boloix Gallardo (2017).
26. Ibn Idhari (2013), Vol. 3, p. 471.

4. THE NASRIDS: FOUNDATION OF A DYNASTY

1. Ibn al-Khatib (2009), p. 68.
2. Ibn Idhari (2013), Vol. 3, provides descriptions of Ibn al-Ahmar's reign based on sources from the time. For a modern study of this first Nasrid king, see Boloix Gallardo (2017).
3. For a detailed study of the construction of the Alhambra throughout the Nasrid period, see Puerta Vílchez (2007).
4. Ibn Idhari (2013), Vol. 3, p. 480, authors' translation.
5. Buluggīn (1986), p. 136.
6. Puerta Vílchez (2007), p. 190.
7. Ibn al-Khatib (2009), p. 46, authors' translation.
8. Puerta Vílchez (2007), p. 190.
9. Hagen and Cruz Márquez (2010).
10. Alfonso X of Castile (1906), p. 746, authors' translation.
11. For a detailed account of the Nasrids and why they survived so long, see Harvey (1990).
12. For a biography of Alfonso X, see Doubleday (2015).
13. Ibn Idhari (2013), Vol. 3, p. 542.
14. Ibn Idhari (2013), Vol. 3, p. 568.
15. For an analysis of the Revolt of the Mudéjars, see O'Callaghan (2011).
16. For details of the Volunteers of the Faith, see Kennedy (2014).
17. The best description of the lives of the kings of Nasrid Granada down to and including Muhammad V is Ibn al-Khatib (2009).

18. Vílchez Vílchez (2011).
19. Mármol Carvajal (1991), p. 37.
20. Harvey (1990), p. 7.
21. Ibn al-Khatib (1973–77), Vol. 2.
22. Ibn al-Khatib (1973–77), Vol. 2.
23. Ibn al-Khatib (2009), p. 96.
24. Rubiera Mata (1996), pp. 183–9.
25. Ibn al Khatib (2009), p. 109.
26. For a detailed study of the monarchs who reigned at the height of the Nasrid dynasty, see Fernández-Puertas (1997).
27. Translation by Jon Trout in Puerta Vílchez (2011), p. 340.

5. THE NASRIDS: SPLENDOUR AND DECLINE

1. Ibn al-Khatib (2009), p. 127, authors' translation.
2. For a detailed study of the poetry on the walls of the Alhambra, see Puerta Vílchez (2011).
3. For a modern biography of Ibn al-Khatib, see Molina López (2001).
4. Ibn al-Khatib (1973–77), Vol. 1, pp. 508–9, authors' translation.
5. For hypothetical sketches of the gate in Nasrid times, see Almagro Gorbea, Orihuela Uzal, and Vílchez Vílchez (1992).
6. For an analysis of Ibn al-Khatib's writing about the Black Death, see Ober and Aloush (1982).
7. For an account of Ibn Battuta's visit to Granada, see Gibb (1929), p. 315.
8. Gibb (1929), p. 315.
9. See Ibn al-Khatib (2009), Parts 2 and 4, for both physical descriptions of Granada at the time and descriptions of the people and their customs.
10. Enan (1941), p. 31.
11. This story can be read in the Chronicle of Peter I's reign. See López de Ayala (1779), pp. 343–9.
12. For an in-depth look at Ibn al-Khatib's life as vizier and his later trial, see Calero Secall (2001).
13. For a Spanish translation of Ibn al-Khatib's description of Muhammad V's newly constructed Mexuar, see López-López and Orihuela Uzal (1990).
14. Quoted in Molina López (2001), p. 122, authors' translation.

15. Enan (1941), p. 35.
16. For a recent biography of Ibn Khaldun, see Irwin (2018).
17. Gibb (1929).
18. Calero Secall (2001).
19. al-Maqqari (1968), p. 112, authors' translation.
20. For a study of the sources related to the Palacio de los Alijares, see Higuera Rodríguez and Morales Delgado (1999).
21. For a detailed study of Granada's economy under the Nasrids, see Domínguez Rojas (2006).
22. For a study of Granada's silk industry, see Fábregas García (2004).
23. For studies of the commercial district of Granada during Nasrid times, including the spice market and the traders' inns, see Torres Balbás 1946 and 1949.
24. For a study of the Genoese trade in Granada, including the ceramics industry, see García Porras and Fábregas García (2010).
25. Much of the information here presented about the later Nasrids comes from Harvey (1990).
26. For research into these kingmakers, see Fosalba Vela (2002).
27. There is a useful website which allows a close inspection of the painting: www.alcaiceria.com/alcaiceria/pags/Grabados/000_grabados/pags_grabados/001.htm (last accessed 12 April 2021).
28. Information about the earthquakes and their effects can be found at University of Granada, Instituto Andaluz de Geofísica (2021): http://iagpds.ugr.es/pages/informacion_divulgacion/terremotos_julio_1431?theme=pdf (last accessed 12 April 2021).
29. For Baeza's account of events at the fall of the Nasrid kingdom, see Baeza (1868).
30. For an analysis of Baeza's text, see Delgado Pérez 2017a and 2017b.
31. Fosalba (2002), p. 318.
32. This account has been published in the original Arabic alongside its Spanish translation. See *Kitab nubdhat al-'asr fi akhbar Bani Nasr* (1940).

6. THE RECONQUISTA

1. For detailed studies of the events leading up to the Reconquista, see Harvey (1990), O'Callaghan (2014), and Drayson (2018).

2. Pulgar (1780), p. 133, authors' translation.
3. Byron (1986), p. 103.
4. For an eyewitness account of Granada just after the fall of the city, see Münzer (2014).
5. *Kitab nubdhat* (1940), p. 5.
6. Along with the *Kitab nubdhat*, see Baeza (1868).
7. For a study of the various legends regarding the Abencerrajes, see Fosalba (2002).
8. Some sources refer to Boabdil as Muhammad XI; for evidence of an earlier Muhammad XI, see Fosalba (2002).
9. *Kitab nubdhat* (1940), p. 12.
10. Baeza (1868), pp. 32–3, authors' translation.
11. Harvey (1990), p. 291.
12. Mármol Carvajal (1991), p. 50.
13. For a strong defence of Boabdil's character, see Drayson (2018).
14. Baeza (1868), p. 37.
15. Irving (2007), p. 86.
16. Irving (2007), p. 88.
17. For the events at the camp of Santa Fe, see Bernáldez (1870), pp. 298–9.
18. The best source for the struggles inside the city in those final Nasrid years comes from the anonymous Arabic source *Kitab nubdhat* (1940).
19. Columbus (2010), p. 15.
20. Mármol Carvajal (1991), p. 57, authors' translation.

7. MUDÉJARS

1. Interview with Federico García Lorca, *El Sol*, Madrid, 10 June 1936, authors' translation.
2. Surrender Treaty of the Kingdom of Granada (1491), in Cowans (2003), p. 16.
3. *Kitab nubdhat* (1940).
4. For an account of how Isabella and Ferdinand reacted to the fall of Granada, see Tremlett (2017).
5. Quoted in O'Callaghan (2014), p. 190.
6. Surrender Treaty of the Kingdom of Granada (1491), in Cowans (2003), p. 18.

7. For a study of the Mendoza family and their impact on Granada, see Jiménez Estrella (2005).

8. Coleman (2003), p. 76.

9. For details about Granada's first post-Reconquista town council, see Harvey (1990), p. 326, and Coleman (2003), p. 41.

10. Decree of Expulsion of the Jews (1492), in Cowans (2003), pp. 21–2.

11. Ibn al-Khatib (2009), p. 110.

12. Fábregas García (2004).

13. Ladero Quesada (2007).

14. For more on the debates surrounding the location of Granada's Jewish community, see Spivakovsky (1976).

15. Chapters 26 and 27 of Tremlett (2017) give accounts of the terrible experiences of the Jews as they left Spain.

16. Münzer (2014).

17. Münzer (2014), p. 61.

18. Münzer (2014), p. 61.

19. Mármol Carvajal (1991), p. 58, authors' translation.

20. Coleman (2003), p. 28.

21. Hurtado de Mendoza (1982), p. 169.

22. Coleman (2003), pp. 58–60.

23. For a description of the life and beliefs of Talavera, see Ladero Quesada (2008).

24. Münzer (2014), p. 71.

25. For a study of Talavera's methods in comparison to later Christian leaders of the city, see Edwards (1987).

26. Núñez Muley (2007).

27. Rummel (1999), p. 33.

28. Vallejo (1913), p. 35.

29. Mármol Carvajal (1991), p. 60, authors' translation.

30. Surrender Treaty of the Kingdom of Granada (1491), in Cowans (2003), p. 18.

31. Mármol Carvajal (1991), p. 60.

32. Edwards (1987).

33. Vallejo (1913), p. 35, authors' translation.

34. For a detailed account of the rebellions by the Moors against the Christian conquerors, see Harvey (2005) and Carr (2017).

35. Vallejo (1913), p. 38, authors' translation.
36. Carr (2017), p. 83.

8. MORISCOS

1. For a readable history of the Moriscos, see Carr (2017).
2. For an analysis of the letters sent to both the Ottoman and the Mamluk courts, see Van Koningsveld et al. (1999).
3. Mármol Carvajal (1991), p. 63, authors' translation.
4. Vallejo (1913).
5. For more on the relations between the Moriscos and the New Christian immigrants, see Coleman (2003).
6. Núñez Muley (2007).
7. Quoted from original letter in Brothers (1994), p. 81.
8. Quoted from original letter in Brothers (1994), p. 83.
9. Coleman (2003), pp. 122–3.
10. For a detailed study of Charles V's policies towards the Moriscos, see Benítez Sánchez-Blanco (2001).
11. An analysis of Charles V's decision to build his palace in the Alhambra is contained in Brothers (1994).
12. Núñez Muley (2007).
13. Carr (2017), p. 95.
14. For a more detailed consideration of Moriscos integrating into Christian Granada, see Coleman (2003), p. 32.
15. Coleman (2003), p. 178.
16. For a study into the perceived Morisco threat to Spain, see Hess (1968).
17. Coleman (2003), p. 15.
18. Edwards (1987).
19. Carr (2017), p. 160.
20. For a more detailed account of the problems faced by the Mendozas, see Jiménez Estrella (2005).
21. Carr (2017), p. 166.
22. Jiménez Estrella (2005).
23. Núñez Muley (2007), p. 70.
24. Núñez Muley (2007), p. 92.
25. Núñez Muley (2007), p. 84.

26. Hurtado de Mendoza (1982), p. 39.
27. Hurtado de Mendoza (1982), p. 53.
28. Hurtado de Mendoza (1982), p. 59.
29. Hurtado de Mendoza (1982), p. 43.
30. Coleman (2003), p. 157.
31. For an in-depth study of this war, see Carr (2017).
32. Hess (1968).
33. Hurtado de Mendoza (1982), p. 65.
34. For an account of the prison slaughter, see Mármol Carvajal (1991), p. 158.
35. Mármol Carvajal (1991), p. 163.
36. Mármol Carvajal (1991), p. 184, authors' translation.
37. For studies of the reception of Granada's Moriscos in other parts of Spain, see Dadson (2011) and García Ruipérez (2014).
38. Mármol Carvajal (1991), p. 184.
39. Coleman (2003), p. 184.
40. Soria Mesa (1992).
41. Elliott (2002), p. 307.
42. Elliott (2002), pp. 305–7, and Adams et al. (2008).
43. Soria Mesa (2012).
44. Adams et al. (2008).

9. A VERY CHRISTIAN CITY

1. For a study of the parchment of the Torre Turpiana, see Van Koningsveld et al. (2003).
2. For detailed research into the lead books of the Sacromonte, see Harris 1999 and 2002.
3. For an entertaining and detailed description of Bermúdez de Pedraza's work, see Harris (1999).
4. Barrios Aguilera (2011).
5. For a very readable book about the transformation of Granada into a Christian city, see Coleman (2003).
6. For a detailed study of Granada Cathedral, see Rosenthal (1961).
7. Collado Ruiz (2013).
8. Montero Priego (2017).

9. López Guzmán et al. (2017).

10. For more detail on the religious reformers who came to the city, including the Jesuits, see Coleman (2003).

11. Coleman (2003), p. 159.

12. Castro (1995), Chapter 5.

13. Castro (1995), pp. 17–18, authors' translation.

14. Castro (1995), pp. 21–2, authors' translation.

15. Castro (1995), p. 33, authors' translation.

16. Juan de la Cruz (1994), p. 34, authors' translation.

17. Coleman (2003), p. 15.

18. Carr (2017), p. 201.

19. Kugel (2001).

20. For more on the origin of these religious festivals in Granada, see Coleman (2003).

21. For a study of the early *cofradías* in Granada, see López Muñoz (1995) and Coleman (2003).

22. Coleman (2003), p. 188.

23. López Muñoz (1995).

24. For a comprehensive account of Flores and his excavations, see Orfila Pons et al. (2012).

25. Orfila Pons et al. (2012), p. 55.

10. HORACE I, KING OF GRANADA

1. For a detailed study of Granada under Napoleon's troops, see Barrios Rozúa (2013).

2. For an in-depth study of Napoleon's invasion of Spain, see Esdaile (2003).

3. For more details about the formation of the Juntas, see Esdaile (1988).

4. Barrios Rozúa (2013), p. 52.

5. Semple (1812), p. 195.

6. Semple (1812), p. 192.

7. Barrios Rozúa (2013), p. 71.

8. *Gazeta del Gobierno de Granada*, 6 February 1810.

9. For this lengthy description of Sebastiani's alleged character flaws, see Bouillé (1911), pp. 412–19.

10. Blayney (1814).
11. *Gazeta de Madrid*, 30 January 1810.
12. Bouillé (1911), p. 415.
13. For a detailed analysis of how different social groups reacted to the French occupation, see Barrios Rozúa (2013), p. 111.
14. Blayney (1814), p. 74.
15. Blayney (1814), p. 77.
16. For details about the king's visit to Granada, see Díaz Torrejón (2010).
17. *Gazeta del Gobierno de Granada*, 9 March 1810.
18. *Gazeta de Madrid*, 25 March 1810, authors' translation.
19. *Gazeta de Madrid*, 4 April 1810.
20. *Gazeta de Madrid*, 12 April 1810.
21. Barrios Rozúa (2013), p. 130.
22. Bouillé (1911), p. 389, authors' translation.
23. Barrios Rozúa (2013), p. 14.
24. Irving (2007), p. 34.
25. Blayney (1814), p. 84.
26. For more about the decline of the Mendozas' power in Granada, see Jiménez Estrella (2005).
27. Bermúdez Pareja and Angustias Moreno (1966).
28. Laguna Reche (2015).
29. Gay Armenteros (2010).
30. Barrios Rozúa (2013), p. 153.
31. Blayney (1814), p. 103.
32. Barrios Rozúa (2013), p. 205.
33. *Gazeta de Madrid*, 24 March 1810.
34. For more on the Puerta de Elvira and its original structure, see Almagro Gorbea et al. (1992).
35. Barrios Rozúa (2013), p. 182.
36. Bouillé (1911), p. 413, authors' translation.
37. Barrios Rozúa (2013), p. 259.
38. *ABC España*, 13 February 2015.

11. DREAMS OF THE PAST, VISIONS FOR THE FUTURE

1. Ford (1855), p. 294.

2. Ford (1855), p. 291.
3. For more on the after-effects of the French withdrawal, see the final chapters of Barrios Rozúa (2013).
4. Quoted in Gibson (1989), p. 131.
5. García Lorca (1962), p. 19.
6. For a more detailed study of Mariana Pineda's life, see Rodrigo (2008).
7. Quoted in Rodrigo (2008), p. 53, authors' translation.
8. Chateaubriand (1903), p. 13, authors' translation.
9. Chateaubriand (1903), p. 28, authors' translation.
10. Fernández Manzano (2017).
11. Quoted in Fernández Manzano (2017), pp. 184–5.
12. González Pérez (2017).
13. Barrios Rozúa (2013), p. 275.
14. Barrios Rozúa (2013), p. 276.
15. Barrios Rozúa (2013), p. 280.
16. For details about the Alhambra during this period, in particular the restoration projects of Rafael Contreras, see González Pérez (2017).
17. Quoted in González Pérez (2017), p. 34.
18. González Pérez (2017), p. 35.
19. Quoted in González Pérez (2017), pp. 35–6.
20. For a detailed study of the way Granada was transformed in the nineteenth century, see Barrios Rozúa (2000).
21. For a contemporary's criticisms of the changes made to the city, see Ganivet (1896).
22. Ford (1855), p. 316.
23. Barrios Rozúa (2000), p. 155.
24. Barrios Rozúa (2016).
25. Ganivet (1896).
26. For more on the growth of the sugar beet industry, see Marrón Gaite (2011).
27. For criticisms of the creation of the Gran Vía de Colón, see Barrios Rozúa (2000), p. 156.

12. CREATION AND DESTRUCTION

1. Mendizabal et al. (2012).

2. Borrow (1914).
3. Borrow (1914), p. 99.
4. Hernández López (2016).
5. For details on Manuel de Falla and how flamenco was perceived at the turn of the twentieth century, see Christoforidis (2007).
6. For a very detailed and readable account of Lorca's life, see Gibson (1989).
7. For more on the Rinconcillo, see Gibson (1989), pp. 52–61.
8. Gibson (1989).
9. Serrera Contreras (2010), p. 392, authors' translation.
10. Ford (1855), p. 323.
11. Barrios Rozúa (2003), p. 71.
12. Quoted in Gibson (1989), p. 135.
13. Serrera Contreras (2010).
14. Serrera Contreras (2010).
15. For more about Gallego Burín's *auto sacramental*, see González Ramírez (2009).
16. López Muñoz (1995), p. 8.
17. Quoted in López Muñoz (1995), p. 6, authors' translation.
18. Quoted in Díaz Gómez (2017), p. 103, authors' translation.
19. For the Junta de Andalucía's population statistics for Granada since the eighteenth century, see www.juntadeandalucia.es/institutodeestadisti-caycartografia/ehpa/ehpaTablas.htm
20. López Osuna and Robles Egea (2015).
21. Canes Garrido (1999).
22. Quoted in Canes Garrido (1999), p. 151, authors' translation.
23. López Osuna and Robles Egea (2015).
24. For details about the life and works of Torres Balbás, see Muñoz Cosme (2005).
25. Muñoz Cosme (2005), pp. 121–2.
26. *El Defensor de Granada*, 15 April 1931, authors' translation.
27. Brenan (2014).
28. *El Defensor de Granada*, 13 May 1931.
29. *El Defensor de Granada*, 13 May 1931.
30. *El Defensor de Granada*, 12 & 13 August 1932.

31. Barrios Rozúa (2003), pp. 83–4.
32. Barrios Rozúa (2003), p. 86.
33. Brenan (2014).
34. For a detailed account of the events running up to the military uprisings in Granada, see Gibson (1987).
35. Brenan (2014), pp. 97–8.

13. CIVIL WAR AND DICTATORSHIP

1. Marco (2010), pp. 55–7.
2. For a detailed study of Granada just before and at the start of the Civil War, see Gibson (1987).
3. Ponce Alberca et al. (2008).
4. *Ideal*, 21 July 1936, authors' translation.
5. *Ideal*, 21 July 1936, authors' translation.
6. For a detailed study into the Nationalist tactics to control Granada, see Moya Hidalgo (2015).
7. Moya Hidalgo (2015).
8. Marco (2010), p. 85.
9. For this foreigner's eyewitness account of the uprising in Granada, see Nicholson (1937).
10. For a detailed study of the killings at the cemetery wall, see Barrera Maturana (2011).
11. For greater details about the final days of Lorca, see Gibson 1987 and 1989.
12. Interview with Federico García Lorca in *El Sol*, Madrid, 10 June 1936, authors' translation.
13. For a more detailed account of Gallego Burín's political journey, see Hernández Burgos (2011).
14. Moya Hidalgo (2015).
15. *Ideal*, 19 January 1938, authors' translation.
16. López (2014).
17. For a detailed study of the post-war drive to Christianise Granada, see Barrios Rozúa (2010).
18. *Ideal*, 16 April 1937, authors' translation.
19. Barrios Rozúa (2010), p. 170.

20. *Ideal*, 20 September 1936.
21. Barrios Rozúa (2010), p. 172.
22. For an in-depth study of the Hermanos Quero, see Marco (2010).
23. Marco (2010), pp. 245–50.
24. Marco (2010), pp. 360–8.
25. For one study into the changes made to Granada following the Civil War, see Segarra Lagunes (2018).
26. *Granada Hoy*, 29 July 2013.
27. For example, see Malpica Cuello (1994), p. 196, and Barrios Rozúa (2010).
28. For a history of the destruction of La Manigua, see Contreras García (2019).
29. Bosque Maurel (1992), p. 193.
30. For more on Granada's post-war housing projects, see Barrios Rozúa (2010), pp. 174–8.
31. Bosque Maurel (1992), p. 195.
32. *Ideal*, 1 April 2017.
33. For a study of the *gitanos* and cave living, see Pérez Casas (1982).
34. Bosque Maurel (1992), p. 198.

14. GRANADA TODAY

1. *Granada Hoy*, 23 January 2020.
2. *Granada Hoy*, 11 February 2020.
3. The Junta de Andalusia's tourism statistics can be accessed here: Junta de Andalucía (2018), https://www.juntadeandalucia.es/export/drupaljda/estadisticas/13/03/EspaciosCulturales18_3.pdf (last accessed 12 April 2021).
4. *Ideal*, 30 January 2020.
5. *Ideal*, 22 July 2020.
6. *Ideal*, 14 February 2002.
7. For a study of the controversy of the building of the mosque, see Bush (2015).
8. *Granada Hoy*, 29 July 2017.
9. Adams et al. (2008).
10. *Ideal*, 18 February 2012.

BIBLIOGRAPHY

Adams, Susan M., Elena Bosch, Patricia L. Balaresque, et al., 'The Genetic Legacy of Religious Diversity and Intolerance: Paternal Lineages of Christians, Jews, and Muslims in the Iberian Peninsula,' *The American Journal of Human Genetics, 83* (2008), pp. 725–36.

Alfonso X of Castile, *Primera crónica general: Estoria de España*, Ramón Menéndez Pidal (Ed.), Madrid: Bailly-Bailliére é Hijos, 1906.

Almagro Gorbea, Antonio, Antonio Orihuela Uzal, and Carlos Vílchez Vílchez, 'La puerta de Elvira en Granada y su reciente restauración,' *Al-qantara, 13* (1992), pp. 505–36.

Arberry, Arthur J., *Moorish Poetry: A Translation of the Pennants, An Anthology Compiled in 1243 by the Andalusian Ibn Sa'id*, Cambridge: Cambridge University Press, 1953.

Baeza, Hernando de, *Relaciones de algunos sucesos de los últimos tiempos del reino de Granada*, Emilio Lafuente y Alcántara (Ed.), Madrid: Rivadeneyra, 1868.

Barrera Maturana, José Ignacio, 'Grafitos y memoria histórica: la tapia del cementerio de Granada,' in *Actes du XVIIe Colloque International de Glyptographie de Cracovie*, Braine-le-Château: Centre International de Recherches Glyptographiques, 2011, pp. 47–69.

Barrios Aguilera, Manuel, 'Los moriscos Alonso del Castillo y Miguel de Luna: ¿Autores de los libros plúmbeos de Granada?' *Andalucía en la Historia, 34* (2011), pp. 44–8.

BIBLIOGRAPHY

Barrios Rozúa, Juan Manuel, 'Las élites granadinas frente al patrimonio histórico durante el siglo XIX,' *Demófilo, 35* (2000), pp. 149–66.

————, 'Iconoclastia y resacralización del espacio urbano en el Albaicín,' in Juan Manuel Barrios Rozúa (Ed.), *El Albaicín, paraíso cerrado, conflicto urbano*, Granada: Centro de Investigaciones Etnológicas Angel Ganivet, 2003, pp. 71–94.

————, 'La ciudad de Dios: urbanismo y arquitectura en Granada durante la Guerra Civil,' in Anne-Marie Arnal Gely and José Antonio González Alcantud (Eds), *La ciudad mediterránea: sedimentos y reflejos de la memoria*, Granada: Editorial Universidad de Granada, 2010, pp. 167–83.

————, *Granada napoleónica: ciudad, arquitectura y patrimonio*, Granada: Editorial Universidad de Granada, 2013.

————, 'El ocaso de la plaza de bibarrambla como teatro,' in Juan Calatrava, Francisco García Pérez, and David Arredondo Garrido, *La cultura y la ciudad*, Granada: Editorial Universidad de Granada, 2016, pp. 887–96.

Benítez Sánchez-Blanco, Rafael, *La política de Carlos V hacia los moriscos granadinos*, Madrid: Sociedad Estatal para la Conmemoración de los Centenarios de Felipe II y Carlos V, 2001, pp. 415–46.

Bermúdez Pareja, Jesús, and María Angustias Moreno, 'Documentos de una catastrofe en la Alhambra,' *Cuadernos de la Alhambra, 2* (1966), pp. 77–87.

Bernáldez, Andrés, *Historia de los reyes católicos D. Fernando y Doña Isabel*, Seville: José María Geofrin, 1870.

Blayney, Andrew T., *Narrative of a Forced Journey through Spain and France, as a Prisoner of War, in the Years 1810 to 1814*, London: E. Kerby, 1814.

Boloix Gallardo, Bárbara, *Ibn al-Ahmar: Vida y reinado del primer Sultán de Granada (1195–1273)*, Granada: Editorial Universidad de Granada, 2017.

Borrow, George, *The Zincali: An Account of the Gypsies of Spain*, London: J.M. Dent & Sons, 1914.

Bosque Maurel, Joaquín, 'Crecimiento y remodelación en la ciudad de Granada (1960–1990),' *Anales de Geografía de la Universidad Complutense, 2* (1992), pp. 191–203.

BIBLIOGRAPHY

Bouillé, Louis de, *Souvenirs et fragments pour servir aux mémoires de ma vie et de mon temps, Vol. III*, Paris: La Société d'Histoire Contemporaine, 1911.

Brenan, Gerald, *The Spanish Labyrinth: An Account of the Social and Political Background of the Spanish Civil War*, Cambridge: Cambridge University Press, 2014.

Brody, Heinrich, 'Moses ibn Ezra: Incidents in His Life,' *The Jewish Quarterly Review, 24* (1934), pp. 309–20.

Brothers, Cammy, 'The Renaissance Reception of the Alhambra: The Letters of Andrea Navagero and the Palace of Charles V,' in Gülru Necipoglu (Ed.), *Muqarnas XI: An Annual on Islamic Art and Architecture*, Leiden: Brill, 1994, pp. 79–102.

Buluggīn, 'Abd Allāh B., *The Tibyān: Memoirs of 'Abd Allāh B. Buluggīn, Last Zīrid Amīr of Granada*, Amin T. Tibi (Trans.), Leiden: Brill, 1986.

Bush, Olga, 'Entangled Gazes: The Polysemy of the New Great Mosque of Granada,' *Muqarnas, 32* (2015), pp. 97–133.

Byron, George G., *The Complete Poetical Works* (Vol. 4), Jerome J. McGann (Ed.), Oxford: Oxford University Press, 1986.

Calero Secall, María Isabel, 'El proceso de Ibn al-Jatib,' *Al-Qantara, 2* (2001), pp. 421–61.

Canes Garrido, Francisco, 'Las escuelas del Ave María: Una institución renovadora de finales del siglo XIX en España,' *Revista Complutense de Educación, 10* (1999), pp. 149–66.

Carr, Matthew, *Blood and Faith: The Purging of Muslim Spain, 1492–1614*, London: Hurst & Co., 2017.

Castro, Francisco de, *Historia de la vida y santas obras de San Juan de Dios y de la institución de su orden y principios de su hospital*, Córdoba: Publicaciones Obra Cultural Cajasur, 1995.

Chateaubriand, François-René, *Les Aventures du dernier Abencerage*, New York: American Book Company, 1903.

Christoforidis, Michael, 'Manuel de Falla, Flamenco and Spanish Identity,' in Julie Brown (Ed.), *Western Music and Race*, Cambridge and New York: Cambridge University Press, 2007, pp. 230–43.

Cole, Peter, *The Dream of the Poem: Hebrew Poetry from Muslim and Christian Spain, 950–1492*, Princeton: Princeton University Press, 2007.

BIBLIOGRAPHY

Coleman, David, *Creating Christian Granada*, Ithaca and London: Cornell University Press, 2003.

Collado Ruiz, María José, 'El Sagrario de Granada. Antiguo espacio de enterramiento,' *Laboratorio de Arte, 25* (2013), pp. 133–42.

Columbus, Christopher, 'Journal of the First Voyage of Columbus,' in Clements Markham (Ed.), *Journal of Christopher Columbus (During his First Voyage, 1492–93): And Documents Relating the Voyages of John Cabot and Gaspar Corte Real*, Cambridge: Cambridge University Press, 2010.

Contreras García, Javier, 'La Manigua: los proyectos de reforma interior de principios del siglo XX,' *Cuadernos de Arte de la Universidad de Granada, 50* (2019), pp. 131–52.

Cowans, Jon (Ed.), *Early Modern Spain: A Documentary History*, Philadelphia: University of Pennsylvania Press, 2003.

Dadson, Trevor J., 'The Assimilation of Spain's Moriscos: Fiction or Reality?' *Journal of Levantine Studies, 1* (2011), pp. 11–30.

Delgado Pérez, María Mercedes, 'A Newly Discovered Manuscript of the Historia de los Reyes Moros de Granada by Hernando de Baeza,' *Manuscript Studies, 2* (2017a), pp. 540–94.

————, 'La historia de los reyes moros de Granada de Hernando de Baeza. Una crónica entre el romance de frontera, la autobiografía y la leyenda,' *Philologia Hispalensis, 31* (2017b), pp. 15–36.

Díaz Gómez, José Antonio, 'Entre la devoción y el entretenimiento burgués: el papel del Centro Artístico y Literario en la revitalización de la Semana Santa de Granada,' in María del Amor Rodríguez Miranda, Isaac Palomino Ruiz, José Antonio Díaz Gómez (Eds), *Compendio de estudios histórico-artísticos sobre Semana Santa: ritos, tradiciones y devociones*, Córdoba: Asociación Hurtado Izquierdo, (2017), pp. 80–105.

Díaz Torrejón, Francisco Luis, 'En olor de multitudes: La visita regia de José Bonaparte a Granada,' *Boletín Centro Pedro Suárez, 23* (2010), pp. 37–58.

Domínguez Rojas, Salud María, 'La economía del reino nazarí a través de las fetuas recogidas en el Miyār de Al-Wanšarīsī,' *Anaquel de Estudios Árabes, 17* (2006), pp. 77–107.

Doubleday, Simon R., *The Wise King: A Christian Prince, Muslim Spain, and the Birth of the Renaissance*, New York: Basic Books, 2015.

BIBLIOGRAPHY

Drayson, Elizabeth, *The Moor's Last Stand*, London: Profile Books, 2018.

Edwards, John, 'Christian mission in the kingdom of Granada, 1492–1568,' *Culture, Theory and Critique, 31* (1987), pp. 20–33.

Elliott, J.H., *Imperial Spain 1469–1716*, London: Penguin, 2002.

Enan, Mohammad Abdullah, *Ibn Khaldun: His Life and Works*, Lahore: Ashraf Press, 1941.

Esdaile, Charles, 'War and Politics in Spain: 1808–1814,' *The Historical Journal, 31* (1988), pp. 295–317.

———, *The Peninsular War*, London: Penguin, 2003.

Fábregas García, Adela, 'Aprovisionamiento de la seda en el reino nazarí de Granada. Vías de intervención directa practicadas por la comunidad mercantil genovesa,' *En la España Medieval, 27* (2004), pp. 53–75.

Fernández Manzano, Reynaldo, 'Two Glances at the Fandango: The Fandango in Classical Music, and an Example of Popular Andalusian Fandangos—el Trovo de la Alpujarra,' in K. Meira Goldberg and Antoni Pizà (Eds), *The Global Reach of the Fandango in Music, Song and Dance: Spaniards, Indians and Gypsies*, Cambridge: Cambridge Scholars Publishing (2016), pp. 182–90.

Fernández-Puertas, Antonio, 'La mezquita aljama de Granada,' *Miscelanea de Estudios Arabes y Hebraicos, 53* (2004), pp. 39–76.

———, 'The Three Great Sultans of al-Dawla al-Ismā'īliyya al-Naṣriyya Who Built the Fourteenth-Century Alhambra: Ismā'īl I, Yūsuf I, Muḥammad V (713–793/1314–1391),' *Journal of the Royal Asiatic Society, 7* (1997), pp. 1–25.

Ford, Richard, *A Handbook for Travellers in Spain*, London: John Murray, 1855.

Fosalba Vela, Eugenia, 'Sobre la verdad de los Abencerrajes,' *Boletín de la Real Academia de Buenas Letras de Barcelona, 48* (2002), pp. 313–34.

Galán, Juan Eslava, 'La campaña de 1225 y el primer cerco de Jaén por Fernando III,' *Boletín del Instituto de Estudios Giennenses* (1987), pp. 23–38.

Ganivet, Ángel, *Granada la Bella*, Helsinki: J. C. Frenckell & Son, 1896.

García Granados, Juan Antonio, 'La primera cerca medieval en Granada: Análisis historiográfico,' *Arqueología y Territorio Medieval, 3* (1996), pp. 91–148.

BIBLIOGRAPHY

García Lorca, Federico, 'Mariana Pineda: "A Popular Ballad in Three Prints,"' James Graham-Luján (Trans.), *The Tulane Drama Review, 7* (1962), pp. 18–75.

García Porras, Alberto, and Adela Fábregas García, 'Genoese Trade Networks in the Southern Iberian Peninsula: Trade, Transmission of Technical Knowledge and Economic Interactions,' *Mediterranean Historical Review, 25* (2010), pp. 35–51.

García Ruipérez, Mariano, 'La expulsión de los Moriscos del Reino de Granada en los documentos municipales. Estudio Archivístico,' *Documenta & Instrumenta, 12* (2014), pp. 61–93.

Gay Armenteros, Juan Cristóbal, 'La guerra de la independencia en Granada,' *Boletín Centro de Estudios, 23* (2010), pp. 15–36.

Gibb, H.A.R., *Ibn Battuta: Travels in Asia and Africa 1325–1354*, London: Routledge, 1929.

Gibson, Ian, *El asesinato de García Lorca*, Barcelona: Plaza & Janés, 1987.

———, *Federico García Lorca*, London: Faber, 1989.

González Pérez, Asun, 'Reconstructing the Alhambra: Rafael Contreras and Architectural Models of the Alhambra in the Nineteenth Century,' *Art in Translation, 9* (2017), pp. 29–49.

González Ramírez, David, 'La escenificación de "El gran teatro del mundo" (Granada, 1927): Conclusiones sobre la "vuelta a Calderón,"' *Boletín Millares Carlo, 28* (2009), pp. 305–34.

Gozalbes Cravioto, Enrique, 'Establecimiento de barrios judíos en las ciudades de al-Andalus: El caso de Granada,' *Revista del Centro de Estudios Históricos de Granada y su Reino, 6* (1992), pp. 11–32.

Hagen, Katrin, and Rafael de la Cruz Márquez, 'El agua en los bosques de la Alhambra,' in J.R. Guzmán Álvarez and R.M. Navarro Cerrillo (Eds), *El agua domesticada: Los paisajes de los regadíos de montaña en Andalucía*, Seville: Agencia Andaluza del Agua, Consejería de Medio Ambiente, Junta de Andalucía, 2010, pp. 132–7.

Harris, A. Katie, 'Forging History: The Plomos of the Sacromonte of Granada in Francisco Bermudez de Pedraza's Historia Eclesiastica,' *Sixteenth Century Journal, 30* (1999), pp. 945–66.

———, 'The Sacromonte and the Geography of the Sacred in Early Modern Granada,' *Al-Qantara, 23* (2002), pp. 517–43.

BIBLIOGRAPHY

Harvey, Leonard P., *Islamic Spain, 1250–1500*, Chicago and London: University of Chicago Press, 1990.

———, *Muslims in Spain: 1500 to 1614*, Chicago: University of Chicago Press, 2005.

Hernández Burgos, Claudio, 'El largo camino hacia el franquismo: Antonio Gallego Burín (1915–1939),' *Revista del CEHGR, 23* (2011), pp. 193–206.

Hernández López, María Encarnación, 'La Alhambra, la primera regularización de la visita pública,' *Revista del Centro de Estudios Históricos de Granada y su Reino, 28* (2016), pp. 287–307.

Hess, Andrew C., 'The Moriscos: An Ottoman Fifth Column in Sixteenth-Century Spain,' *The American Historical Review, 74* (1968), pp. 1–25.

Higuera Rodríguez, Alicia de la, and Antonio Morales Delgado, 'La almunia de los Alijares según dos autores: Ibn 'Asim e Ibn Zamrak,' *Cuadernos de La Alhambra, 35* (1999), pp. 31–48.

al-Hulal al-mawshiyya fi dhikr al-Marrakushiya, Suhail Zakar and Abd al-Qadir Zamama (Eds), Casablanca: Dar al-Rashad al-Haditha, 1979 [Author unknown].

Hurtado de Mendoza, Diego, *The War in Granada*, Martin Shuttleworth (Trans.), London: The Folio Society, 1982.

Ibn al-Khatib, Abu 'Abd Allah Muhammad 'Lisan al-Din,' *Al-lamha al-badriya fi-al-daulat al-nasriya*, Muhammad Masoud Jibran (Ed.), Beirut: Dar al-madar al-Islami, 2009.

———, *Al-Ihata fi akhbar Gharnata*, Muhammad Inan (Ed.), Cairo: Maktabat al-Khanji, 1973–77.

Ibn Idhari, Abu al-Abbas, *Al-bayan al-mughrib fi ikhtisar akhbar al-Andalus wa-al-Maghrib*, Tunis: Dar al-Gharb al-Islami, 2013.

Ibn Sahib al-Sala, 'Abd al-Malik b. Muhammad, *Al-Mann bi l-Imama: Ta'rikh bilad al-Maghrib wa l-Andalus fi 'ahd al-Muwahhidin*, 'Abd al-Hadi al-Tazi (Ed.), Beirut: Dar al-Garbi al-Islam, 1987.

Irving, Washington, *Tales of the Alhambra*, Granada: Ediciones Miguel Sanchez, 2007.

Irwin, Robert, *Ibn Khaldun: An Intellectual Biography*, Princeton: Princeton University Press, 2018.

———, *The Alhambra*, London: Profile Books, 2005.

BIBLIOGRAPHY

Jiménez Estrella, Antonio, 'El Conde de Tendilla y su estirpe: El poder político y militar de una familia nobiliaria,' in Antonio Luis Cortés Peña, Miguel Luis López-Guadalupe Muñoz and Francisco Sánchez-Montes González (Eds), *Estudios en homenaje al profesor José Szmolka Clares*, Granada: Editorial Universidad de Granada, 2005, pp. 345–58.

Jiménez-Torrecillas, Antonio, Ricardo Hernández-Soriano, L.M. Ruiz, et al., 'Integración de restos arqueológicos almohades en el metropolitano de Granada: La investigación multidisciplinar para el proyecto y desarrollo de infraestructuras contemporáneas en los centros históricos,' *Informes de la Construcción, 66* (2014), pp. 1–11.

Juan de la Cruz, San, *Poesia completa*, Jorge Garza Castillo (Ed.), Barcelona: Edicomunicación, 1994.

Kennedy, Hugh, *Muslim Spain and Portugal: A Political History of al-Andalus*, Abingdon: Routledge, 2014.

Kitab nubdhat al-'asr fi akhbar Bani Nasr (with Spanish translation: *Fragmento de la epoca sobre noticias de los Reyes Nazaritas o capitulacion de Granada y emigracion de los andaluces a Marruecos*), Alfredo Bustani and Carlos Quiros (Eds), Morocco: Larache, 1940 [Author unknown].

Kugel, Chistiane E., 'Los cármenes de Granada,' *Narria, 93–96* (2001), pp. 10–15.

Ladero Quesada, Miguel-Ángel, 'De nuevo sobre los judíos granadinos al tiempo de su expulsión,' *En La España Medieval, 30* (2007), pp. 281–315.

———, 'Fray Hernando de Talavera en 1492: De la corte a la misión,' *Chronica nova, 34* (2008), pp. 249–75.

Laguna Reche, Jesús Daniel, 'Los festejos taurinos de la Alhambra (Siglos XVI-XIX),' *Revista de Estudios Taurinos, 36* (2015), pp. 91–118.

López, Eva Concejal, 'Las Rutas de Guerra del Servicio Nacional de Turismo (1938–1939),' in *Visite España: La memoria rescatada*, País: Ministerio de Cultura, Subdirección General de Publicaciones, Información y Documentación, 2014, pp. 258–73.

López de Ayala, Pedro, *Cronicas de los Reyes de Castilla Don Pedro, Don Enrique II, Don Juan I, Don Enrique III*, Madrid: Antonio de Sancha, 1779.

López Guzmán, Rafael Jesús, and María Elena Díez Jorge, 'Aynadamar en

BIBLIOGRAPHY

la edad moderna: El monasterio de Cartuja y su entorno,' in Margarita Orfila Pons and María Luisa Bellido Gant (Eds), *Crónica de un paisaje: Descubriendo el Campus de Cartuja*, Granada: Editorial Universidad de Granada (2017), pp. 35–58.

López Muñoz, Miguel Luis, 'Las cofradías de penitencia de Granada en la Edad Moderna,' *Gazeta de Antropología, 11* (1995), pp. 1–10.

López Osuna, Alvaro, and Antonio Robles Egea, 'La protesta contra el caciquismo y la contienda política en Granada, 1919,' *Historia Social, 83* (2015), pp. 133–56.

López-López, Ángel C., and Antonio Orihuela Uzal, 'Una nueva interpretación del texto de Ibn al-Jatib sobre la Alhambra en 1362,' *Cuadernos de la Alhambra, 26* (1990), pp. 121–44.

Lorca—see García Lorca.

Malpica Cuello, Antonio, 'Granada, ciudad islámica: centro histórico y periferia urbana,' *Arqueología y Territorio Medieval, 1* (1994), pp. 195–208.

————, 'La expansión de la ciudad de Granada en época Almohade: Ensayo de reconstrucción de su configuración,' *Miscelánea Medieval Murciana, 25–26* (2002), pp. 67–116.

al-Maqqari, Ahmad ibn Muhammad, *Nafh al-tib min ghusn al-Andalus al-ratib*, (Vol. 5), Ihsan 'Abbas (Ed.), Beirut: Dar Sadir, 1968.

Marco, Jorge, *Hijos de una guerra: Los hermanos Quero y la resistencia antifranquista*, Granada: Comares, 2010.

Marcos-Marín, Francisco, 'Romance andalusí y mozárabe: dos términos no sinónimos,' *Estudios de Lingüística y Filología Españolas: Homenaje a Germán Colón*, Madrid: Gredos, 1998, pp. 335–41.

Mármol Carvajal, Luis del, *Historia de la rebelión y castigo de los moriscos del Reino de Granada*, Málaga: Editorial Arguval, 1991.

Marrón Gaite, María Jesús, 'La adopción de una innovación agraria en España: los orígenes del cultivo de la remolacha azucarera: Experiencias pioneras y su repercusión económica y territorial,' *Estudios Geográficos, 72* (2011), pp. 103–34.

Mendizabal, Isabel, Oscar Lao, Urko M. Marigota, et al., 'Reconstructing the population history of European Romani from genome-wide data,' *Current Biology, 22* (2012), pp. 2342–9.

BIBLIOGRAPHY

Messier, Ronald A., *The Almoravids and the Meaning of Jihad*, Santa Barbara: Praeger, 2010.

———, 'Re-thinking the Almoravids, re-thinking Ibn Khaldun,' *The Journal of North African Studies, 6* (2001), pp. 59–80.

Molina López, Emilio, *Ibn al-Jatib*, Granada: Editorial Comares, 2001.

Montero Priego, Andrea, 'La transformación urbana en Granada del Medievo a la modernidad,' *Arqueología y Territorio, 14* (2017), pp. 159–74.

Moya Hidalgo, Alberto, 'La represión nacionalista en la ciudad de Granada durante la guerra civil, 1936–1939,' *Revista del CEHGR* 27, (2015), pp. 109–21.

Muñoz Cosme, Alfonso, *La vida y la obra de Leopoldo Torres Balbás*, Sevilla: Junta de Andalucía, Consejería de Cultura, 2005.

Münzer, Hieronymous, *Doctor Hieronymus Münzer's Itinerary (1494 and 1495) and Discovery of Guinea*, James Firth (Trans.), London: Firth, 2014.

Nicholson, Helen, *Death in the Morning*, London: Lovat Dickson, 1937.

Núñez Muley, Francisco, *A memorandum for the President of the Royal Audiencia and Chancery Court of the City and Kingdom of Granada*, Vincent Barletta (Trans.), Chicago: University of Chicago Press, 2007.

Ober, William B., and Nabil Aloush, 'The plague at Granada, 1348–1349: Ibn Al-Khatib and ideas of contagion,' *Bulletin of the New York Academy of Medicine, 58* (1982), pp. 418–24.

O'Callaghan, Joseph F., *The Gibraltar Crusade: Castile and the Battle for the Strait*, Philadelphia: University of Pennsylvania Press, 2011.

———, *The Last Crusade in the West: Castile and the Conquest of Granada*, Philadelphia: University of Pennsylvania Press, 2014.

Orfila Pons, Margarita, 'Granada en época romana: los restos arqueológicos, una visión global,' *Revista del CEHGR, 25* (2013), pp. 15–28.

Orfila Pons, Margarita, and Elena Sánchez López, 'La ciudad de los "Valerii Vegetii,"' *Itálica: revista de arqueología clásica de Andalucía, 1* (2011), pp. 105–20.

Orfila Pons, Margarita, Manuel Sotomayor, Elena Sánchez, and Purificación Marín, *La Granada 'falsificada:' el pícaro Juan de Flores*, Catálogo Exposición: Diputación de Granada, 2012.

BIBLIOGRAPHY

Orihuela, Antonio, *Granada, between the Zirids and the Nasrids*, Granada: Patronato de la Alhambra y Generalife, 2013.

Ouriachen, El Housin Helal, 'Antes, durante y después de la Granada tardoantigua,' *Revista de Clases historia, 218* (2011).

Pérez Casas, Ángel, 'Los gitanos y las cuevas, en Granada,' *Gazeta de Antropología, 1* (1982), pp. 1–20.

Ponce Alberca, Julio, Jesús García Bonilla, and Diego Ramos Sánchez, *Guerra, Franquismo y Transición: Los gobernadores civiles en Andalucía (1936–1979)*, Seville: Fundación Centro de Estudios Andaluces, 2008.

Puerta Vílchez, José Miguel, 'La Alhambra y el Generalife de Granada,' *Artigrama, 22* (2007), pp. 187–232.

———, *Reading the Alhambra: A Visual Guide to the Alhambra Through Its Inscriptions*, Granada: The Alhambra and Generalife Trust, 2011.

Pulgar, Hernando del, *Crónica de los Señores Reyes Católicos Don Fernando y Doña Isabel de Castilla y de Aragón*, Valencia: Benito Monfort, 1780.

Rodrigo, Antonina, *Mariana Pineda: Memoria viva*, Granada: Caja Granada, 2008.

Rosen, Tova, 'The muwashshah,' in María Rosa Menocal, Raymond P. Scheindlin, and Michael Sells (Eds), *The Literature of Al-Andalus (The Cambridge History of Arabic Literature)*, Cambridge: Cambridge University Press, 2000, pp. 163–89.

Rosenthal, Earl E., *The Cathedral of Granada*, Princeton: Princeton University Press, 1961.

Rubiera Mata, María Jesús, 'La Princesa Fátima Bint al-Ahmar: La "María De Molina" de la Dinastía Nazarí de Granada,' *Medievalismo, 6* (1996), pp. 183–9.

Rummel, Erika, *Jiménez de Cisneros: On the Threshold of Spain's Golden Age*, Arizona Center for Medieval and Renaissance Studies: Arizona, 1999.

Sarr, Bilal, *La Granada Zirí (1013–1090)*, Granada: Alhulia, 2011.

Schippers, Arie, 'The role of women in medieval Andalusian Arabic storytelling,' in F. de Jong (Ed.), *Verse and the Fair Sex: Studies in Arabic Poetry and in the Representation of Women in Arabic Literature*, Utrecht: M. Th. Houtsma Stichting, 1993, pp. 139–52.

Schirmann, Jefim, 'Samuel Hannagid, the Man, the Soldier, the Politician,' *Jewish Social Studies, 13* (1951), pp. 99–126.

BIBLIOGRAPHY

Segarra Lagunes, Silvia, 'Los espacios públicos y el mobiliario urbano en la Granada de la posguerra,' *II Simposio de la FHD, Diseño y franquismo* (2018).

Semple, Robert, *A Second Journey in Spain, in the Spring of 1809*, London: Robert Baldwin, 1812.

Serrera Contreras, Ramón María, 'Falla, Lorca y Fernando de los Ríos: Tres personajes claves en el concurso de cante jondo de Granada de 1922,' *Boletín de la Real academia Sevillana de Buenas Letras: Minervae Baeticae, 38* (2010), pp. 371–406.

Soria Mesa, Enrique, 'Los moriscos que se quedaron: La permanencia de la población de origen islámico en la España Moderna (Reino de Granada, siglos XVII-XVIII),' *Vínculos de Historia, 1* (2012), pp. 205–30.

———, 'De la conquista a la asimilación: la integración de la aristocracia nazarí en la oligarquía granadina, siglos XV-XVII,' *Revista internacional de ciencias sociales, 14* (1992), pp. 49–64.

Sotomayor Muro, Manuel, and Margarita Orfila Pons, 'D. Juan de Flores y el "Carmen de la muralla" en el Albaicín,' *Florentia Iliberritana, 17* (2006), pp. 411–31.

Spivakovsky, Erika, 'The Jewish presence in Granada,' *Journal of Medieval History, 2* (1976), pp. 215–37.

Torres Balbás, Leopoldo, 'Las alhóndigas hispanomusulmanas y el Corral del Carbón de Granada,' *Al-Andalus, 11* (1946), pp. 219–66.

———, 'Alcaicerías,' *Al-Andalus, 14* (1949), pp. 431–41.

Tremlett, Giles, *Isabella of Castile: Europe's First Great Queen*, London: Bloomsbury, 2017.

Vallejo, Juan de, *Memorial de la vida de fray Francisco Jiménez de Cisneros*, Madrid: Bailly-Bailliere, 1913.

Van Koningsveld, Peter Sjoerd, and Gerard A. Wiegers, 'An Appeal of the Moriscos to the Mamluk Sultan and Its Counterpart to the Ottoman Court: Textual Analysis, Context, and Wider Historical Background,' *Al-Qantara, 20* (1999), pp. 161–89.

———, 'The Parchment of the "Torre Turpiana": The Original Document and its Early Interpreters,' *Al-Qantara, 24* (2003), pp. 327–58.

Vílchez Vílchez, Carlos, *El castillo de Bibataubín, 1238–1752*, Granada: Universidad de Granada, 2011.

BIBLIOGRAPHY

Wasserstein, David, *The Rise and Fall of the Party-Kings: Politics and Society in Islamic Spain 1002–1086*, Princeton: Princeton University Press, 1985.

Weinberger, Leon J., *Jewish Prince in Moslem Spain: Selected Poems of Samuel ibn Nagrela*, Tuscaloosa and London: University of Alabama Press, 1973.

INDEX

INDEX

INDEX

INDEX

INDEX

INDEX

INDEX

INDEX

INDEX

INDEX

INDEX

INDEX